Interactive Storytelling

Taking a cross-media approach to the ever-changing field of digital storytelling, this book offers an essential introduction to producing and editing interactive storytelling content, and to the platforms that host it.

Merging algorithmic and AI approaches with basic writing technique, the authors begin by providing a brief history of the field before moving on to practical step-by-step guides on techniques, models and software architectures. Examples and exercises are drawn from free-to-access, purpose-built software created by the authors as well as exemplary interactive storytelling work. Assuming the perspective of the storyteller and focusing on elements shared across different fields of professional communication, the book is designed to be a primer for digital communicators, irrespective of the medium they are working with. As such, the methods provided will be applicable across the spectrum of TV, film, videogames, web and mobile storytelling.

Interactive Storytelling is recommended reading for professionals as well as advanced undergraduate and postgraduate students of interactive entertainment, multimedia design and production, and digital journalism.

Antonio Pizzo is Associate Professor of Theatre and Multimedia at the University of Turin, Italy.

Vincenzo Lombardo is Full Professor of Informatics at the University of Turin, Italy.

Rossana Damiano is Associate Professor of Computer Science at the University of Turin, Italy.

Interactive Storytelling

A Cross-Media Approach to Writing, Producing and Editing with AI

Antonio Pizzo, Vincenzo Lombardo and Rossana Damiano

NEW YORK AND LONDON

Designed cover image: © Getty Images

First published 2024
by Routledge
605 Third Avenue, New York, NY 10158

and by Routledge
4 Park Square, Milton Park, Abingdon, Oxon OX14 4RN

Routledge is an imprint of the Taylor & Francis Group, an informa business

© 2024 Antonio Pizzo, Vincenzo Lombardo and Rossana Damiano

The right of Antonio Pizzo, Vincenzo Lombardo and Rossana Damiano to be identified as authors of this work has been asserted in accordance with sections 77 and 78 of the Copyright, Designs and Patents Act 1988.

All rights reserved. No part of this book may be reprinted or reproduced or utilised in any form or by any electronic, mechanical, or other means, now known or hereafter invented, including photocopying and recording, or in any information storage or retrieval system, without permission in writing from the publishers.

Trademark notice: Product or corporate names may be trademarks or registered trademarks, and are used only for identification and explanation without intent to infringe.

English edition based on a translation of the Italian title, Interactive Storytelling (ISBN: 9788875274788), published with permission by Dino Audino S.r.l., Rome, Italy.

Library of Congress Cataloging-in-Publication Data
Names: Pizzo, Antonio, author. | Lombardo, Vincenzo, author. | Damiano, Rossana, author.
Title: Interactive storytelling : a cross-media approach to writing, producing and editing with AI / Antonio Pizzo, Vincenzo Lombardo and Rossana Damiano.
Other titles: Interactive storytelling. English
Description: New York, NY : Routledge, 2024. | "English edition based on a translation of the Italian title 'Interactive Storytelling (ISBN 9788875274788) published with permission by Dino Audino, Rome, Italy" --T.p. verso | Includes bibliographical references and index. | In English, translated from the original Italian.
Identifiers: LCCN 2023012655 (print) | LCCN 2023012656 (ebook) | ISBN 9781032371634 (hardback) | ISBN 9781032371641 (paperback) | ISBN 9781003335627 (ebook)
Subjects: LCSH: Storytelling in mass media. | Digital storytelling. | Authorship--Data processing. | Interactive multimedia | Artificial intelligence.
Classification: LCC P96.S78 P59 2024 (print) | LCC P96.S78 (ebook) | DDC 808.5/430285--dc23/eng/20230705
LC record available at https://lccn.loc.gov/2023012655
LC ebook record available at https://lccn.loc.gov/2023012656

ISBN: 978-1-032-37163-4 (hbk)
ISBN: 978-1-032-37164-1 (pbk)
ISBN: 978-1-003-33562-7 (ebk)

DOI: 10.4324/9781003335627

Typeset in Galliard
by Taylor & Francis Books

Contents

List of illustrations x
Preface xii
Acknowledgements xvi

1 Introduction 1

   1.1 Preliminary definitions 1
      1.1.1 The fascination with interactivity 1
      1.1.2 Digital, virtual, interactive 2
      1.1.3 Interacting, participating, collaborating 3
   1.2 Telling stories through actions 6
      1.2.1 Dramatic media 6
      1.2.2 Actions and events 7
      1.2.3 Dramatic action 8
      1.2.4 Narrative action 9
      1.2.5 Sequence of actions 10
      1.2.6 Generating events 13
   1.3 General issues 15
      1.3.1 Author, authorship, control 15
      1.3.2 Characters or stories 16
      1.3.3 The field of investigation 18
      1.3.4 Database, narrative and video contents 19
      1.3.5 Delimiting the field 20
   1.4 A general model of analysis 21

2 Dynamic elements: The units 25

   2.1 What are units? 25
   2.2 The logical relationship between the units 27
   2.3 Organising the multilinear project 28
   2.4 What separates the units 31

    2.5 *Tagging the units: the metadata 33*
    2.6 *Exercises 38*
        2.6.1 The flow chart of dynamic elements 39
        2.6.2 The user actions 40

3   Dynamic elements: The agents   42

    3.1 *Agent and audience 42*
    3.2 *Intelligent agents 44*
        3.2.1 Planning as improvisation 47
        3.2.2 Planning as directing 49
        3.2.3 Scripting as planning 50
    3.3 *Emotions and agents 51*
        3.3.1 The (mental) reality of emotions 52
        3.3.2 The social component of emotions 53
        3.3.3 Emotions as a behavioural driver 53
    3.4 *Exercises 54*
        3.4.1 Describing the state of the world 55
        3.4.2 Writing the actions 55
        3.4.3 Writing preconditions and effects 55
        3.4.4 Simulating the execution 56
        3.4.5 Starting from the goal state 57
        3.4.6 Reusing the plan 57

4   Display: Audience, system, emotions   59

    4.1 *Participation 59*
        4.1.1 Narratology vs ludology 59
        4.1.2 Interaction vs narration 60
        4.1.3 Balancing the agency 61
        4.1.4 Intensity of the process 62
        4.1.5 User's action 63
        4.1.6 Intelligible actions 66
    4.2 *Writing the interaction through the units 67*
        4.2.1 Interaction by navigating the map 68
        4.2.2 Interaction by dialogues and behaviours 69
        4.2.3 Interaction by physical actions 70
    4.3 *Emotions in computational systems 70*
        4.3.1 Coding characters' emotions 72
        4.3.2 The emotions of the audience 73
    4.4 *Cross-media contents' communication 75*
    4.5. *Exercises 77*

5 Engines and systems: Supporting creativity and dramatic tension   80

    5.1 Systems and automation 80
    5.2 System classification 81
    5.3 Fully manual authorship 83
    5.4 Manually authored database and automation for plot generation 86
        5.4.1 Plot grammars 87
        5.4.2 Constraints on plot generation 92
        5.4.3 Planning for plot generation 94
        5.4.4 Plot generation based on dramatic tension 100
    5.5 Database and automation 107
    5.6 Emergent narratives: joint automation of plot and database 108
        5.6.1 Constraints on the plot and modifications of database elements 108
        5.6.2 Plot and database modelled with constraints 110
        5.6.3 Full plot automation and database simulation 112
    5.7 General considerations regarding storytelling systems 119
    5.8 Exercises 120
        5.8.1 The form of the story, or the application of a template 120
        5.8.2 The constrained plot generation: preconditions and effects annotation 122
        5.8.3 The dramatic tension of the story 124

6 Examples of interactive storytelling: Description and analysis   130

    6.1 1966: Eliza *130*
        Description 130
        Analysis 131
        Further details 132
    6.2 1976: Adventure *133*
        Description 133
        Analysis 134
        Further details 135
    6.3 1978: Aspen Movie Map *135*
        Description 135
        Analysis 136
        Further details 137
    6.4 1987: Afternoon, a Story *137*
        Description 137
        Analysis 138

Further details 139
6.5 1987: City in Transition: New Orleans, 1983–86 *139*
    Description 139
    Analysis 139
    Further details 140
6.6 1991: Angels *140*
    Description 140
    Analysis 141
    Further details 143
6.7 1993: Myst *143*
    Description 143
    Analysis 144
    Further details 145
6.8 1996: Pokémon *145*
    Description 145
    Analysis 146
    Further details 148
6.9 1999: Desert Rain *148*
    Description 148
    Analysis 149
    Further details 151
6.10 2001: Can You See Me Now? *151*
    Description 151
    Analysis 152
    Further details 153
6.11 2003: Façade *154*
    Description 154
    Analysis 155
    Further details 156
6.12 2005: FearNot! *156*
    Description 156
    Analysis 157
    Further details 159
6.13 2006: DramaTour *159*
    Description 159
    Analysis 160
    Further details 161
6.14 2012: The Walking Dead *161*
    Description 161
    Analysis 162
    Further details 163

6.15 2013: Nothing for Dinner *163*
    Description 163
    Analysis 164
    Further details 165
6.16 2018: Black Mirror: Bandersnatch *165*
    Description 165
    Analysis 166
    Further details 167
6.17 2019: The Invisible Guardian *167*
    Description 167
    Analysis 168
    Further details 169
6.18 2020: Down the Rabbit Hole *169*
    Description 169
    Analysis 170
    Further details 172

Index   175

Illustrations

Figures

1.1	Example of storytelling as linear sequence	10
1.2	Example of storytelling as multilinear sequence	11
1.3	Example of multilinear single ending storytelling	12
1.4	Example of hypertextual storytelling	12
1.5	Schema of generative model of storytelling	14
1.6	General scheme of analysis for interactive storytelling	21
2.1	Example of tagging the hypertext	29
2.2	The division into parts	29
2.3	Grouping the different hypertext's units	30
2.4	Grouping different hypertext's units and avoiding branching proliferation	31
2.5	The partition of the units according to topics	32
2.6	The partition of the units according to character's intention	33
2.7	Tagging the units	36
2.8	The ideal visit model for the interactive visit in DramaTour	37
2.9	Example of graph with one beginning and two endings	39
3.1	Sequencing the units by the interaction with an agent	43
3.2	Sequencing the units by the interaction with multiple agents in Façade	44
4.1	Local and global agency in a videogame structure with cutscenes	62
4.2	Schema of cross-media distribution of an interactive storytelling work	76
5.1	Lakoff's state diagram to represent Propp's structure	89
5.2	The syntax of Lakoff's grammar is represented in the form of a hierarchy	89
5.3	Two variants of *Merchant of Venice* interactive	99
5.4	Typical example of a dramatic arc divided into three acts	101
5.5	Dramatic arc of the *Façade* example execution	105
5.6	A sample UNIVERSE character	114

Tables

1.1	Role of author vs procedural author	16

		List of illustrations xi
1.2	Character-centred modelling vs. plot-centred modelling	17
4.1	The four ways of representing the actions in the interactive *The Merchant of Venice*, depending on the POVs	97

Boxes

1.1	The most relevant scientific conferences	3
1.2	A definition of interactivity	4
1.3	Examples of the difference between chronicle, plot and drama	10
1.4	Definitions of graph, nodes and tree	14
2.1	The definition of lexia	26
3.1	The BDI paradigm of intelligent agents	45
4.1	Agency	61
6.1	Example of a chat with *Eliza*. U = User; E = *Eliza*.	132

Preface

Where to start?

In one of the very first attempts to describe and understand the features and possibilities of interactive narrative, in 1984, Niesz and Holland (scholars in Drama and Literature, respectively) compared the various new possibilities offered by computers (and emerging network technology) for storytelling. Interactive narrative had only emerged a few years earlier, but the technology already seemed to be making huge strides, and the two scholars were rightly amazed by "the incredibly fast video arcade games of today, like 'Pac-Man' or 'Asteroids 2' (Niesz and Holland 1984, p. 114). Besides the early computers that took up an entire room, the so-called mainframes, which were only available to large companies and their employees because of their high cost, the first microcomputers were already becoming available, and these small machines were the precursors of personal computers. Everything that happened pointed to rich growth. They wrote:

> We think it likely that within the next decade, interactive fiction, which as of 1984 can boast only a dozen texts that go beyond the adventure game, will become as popular a medium of entertainment as television is today. It could well become a competitor to other forms of light fiction, indeed, an improvement over the usual spy, detective, or romantic stories in being more open, less passive, more challenging to a reader's mind. Should major writers turn to writing "compufiction," we imagine it could become a major innovation, a genre for intense creative activity, like the early novels.
>
> (ibid., p. 126)

Almost 40 years later, we have seen that things have turned out somewhat differently: there has been no confirmation of "compufiction" as a new literary genre, and interactivity has taken hold mainly in the games sector and in the design of consumer goods. Nevertheless, it is also true that the element of storytelling seems to thrive among the different types of interactive entertainment, and today experts are trying to come up with more stable definitions.

IDN (interactive digital narrative) can now be defined as an expressive narrative form in digital media implemented as a computational system containing potential narratives and experienced through a participatory process that results in products representing instantiated narratives (Koenitz 2015, p. 98).

Our aim in this volume is not to provide a conceptualisation of interactive storytelling. We believe that there are already many of them, and the reader can easily find them, for example, in the Wikipedia entry for "interactive storytelling".

The aim of this volume is to build on existing practices to abstract the elements that emerge as a common feature in different production practices. The work flow, the essential steps in production, the audience experience, all of these can be conceptualised with different schemes or metaphors. However, it does not seem that the different theoretical descriptions have had any real impact on the production methods. It is possible, of course, that the creation of a list of definitions of basic cinematographic techniques (such as dissolves, pans, close-ups), as distilled by some pioneers of interactive fiction, can be useful in thinking about the logic of presenting a virtual environment and its interactivity (Smith and Bates 1989). But the effectiveness of this list remains unclear when it comes to defining the production standards for interactive storytelling. This volume turns to a perspective inspired by an applied approach and practical questions. It therefore avoids listing rules and norms, preferring to name elements that have become established in practice over the decades. In other words – to use a linguistic metaphor – we rely on the analysis of the language of interactive storytelling works to identify the emerging syntactic forms, the common communicative elements, or the rhetorical forms that have proved more intriguing. In short, the various theories, although they seem to be rapidly becoming obsolete as guidelines for the creation of works of interactive storytelling, have been conceived on a framework of elements that remain quite stable and, we believe, are summarised in this volume. While we resort to some abstraction here, the overarching aim will always be to draw out the common elements. Moreover, we will not propose abstractions that relate to user experience, but only those that cover the factors implicit in production.

The emphasis is clearly on production. We assume that our readers are students and generally people approaching the world of interactive entertainment. We know that people working in this field already have their methods, their work flows and their idiosyncrasies and may not agree with what we write here. Nevertheless, years of experience in this field have led us to believe that this might be an effective way to approach the task. The book is moderately prescriptive and able to highlight the basic elements that any reader who is or will be involved in interactive storytelling can later incorporate into their professional and creative practice. The roles involved in creating interactive entertainment products are many and varied, as is the case with most digital creative production.

Szilas has distilled three different processes and just as many products in the field of interactive storytelling (2015, p. 140):

- the design conceived by coders and engineers and that produces the computational systems (that may include both the engine that activates the narrative and the tools for the content creation);

- the creation of the contents by the author who is in charge of the final product;
- the playing session by the end users that produces the interactive experience of the narrative.

This volume focuses on the first two processes with particular attention to content creation and the tasks of authors. It is clear that the three processes described by Szilas cannot be understood as completely independent of each other. Just as a writer should have his or her own tastes in novels and literature, the creator of interactive content should have his or her own tastes and preferences in participatory experiences. Just as a screenwriter should have some knowledge of film techniques, the creator of interactive stories should have a general understanding of the computer system being used.

Last but not least, this volume is an example of permeability between worlds that too often do not communicate with each other. Szilas has said that research on interactive storytelling is almost incompatible with the academic environment, which is rigorously divided into disciplines, sectors and fields. This volume is the result of more than ten years of collaboration between three scholars from different educational backgrounds and disciplines. The volume is based on a continuous dialogue and comparison of research methods and results. In all these years, we have not only looked at the same object (the interactive narrative) from different scientific perspectives, but rather we have shared our knowledge and methods in order to develop common competences on the subject. There were moments when it was not possible to distinguish between the approaches of computer science, linguistics and dramaturgy. We believe that this is more or less the same situation that authors will find themselves in when working on the production of narrative content for interactive devices.

This may seem like a daunting leap into the unknown, for example, for the humanities scholar who has to help create an algorithm, or for the computer scientist who has to decide on the personality of the character. Our final piece of advice, however, is not to be afraid: for us, this has been one of the most stimulating opportunities for new knowledge, and we believe it will be one of the most stimulating fields of innovation in the next decades.

The structure of the book

The various chapters of this volume follow the general model of analysis that we define in Chapter 1, Section 1.4. Thus, the volume begins with Chapter 1, a detailed introduction in which we provide some cultural coordinates as a guide to navigate the issues raised by the debate on interactive storytelling. Here we begin by introducing some basic concepts, such as the difference between hierarchical and hypertextual graphs that model the sequence of narrative units, or the generative approach to creating narratives. We also introduce some more specific definitions, such as procedural authorship, the notion of character and its importance as a central element of storytelling, or the different ways of conceptualising plot. Chapter 1 ends with the definition of the general model of analysis.

Chapter 2 ("Dynamic elements: the units") explores what we consider to be the basic elements in constructing a narrative in which the user can actively participate. In particular, we provide guidelines for segmenting, sequencing and tagging of narrative units.

Then, in Chapter 3, the focus shifts to the agents ("Dynamic elements: the agents"), who are thought of as the elements that carry out the actions within the units and establish the relationship with the audience. We describe a practical model of an intelligent agent that gives space both to the description of deliberative behaviours and to the representation of emotions as mental states. We also consider the cases where the agents performing actions are guided or embodied by the participants in the interactive narrative.

Chapter 4 ("Display: audience, system, emotions") deals in detail with the way the narrative is conveyed to the audience. Instead of discussing the different ways in which a narrative is presented, we focus on the relationship that the narrative needs to establish with the audience, the way in which the computer system creates or manages interactivity, and the importance of the emotional engagement of the whole arrangement.

Since interactive storytelling starts from a narrative that unfolds thanks to a system in which the computer allows the audience's intervention, Chapter 5 ("Engines and systems: supporting creativity and dramatic tension") describes, in general terms, the different algorithms and computer procedures that have been used to design/generate narratives. Here we propose a classification of the different systems (called engines) responsible for activating the dynamic elements and tasked with keeping audience participation alive by means of narrative consistency and dramatic tension along the sequence of events. This volume also provides a companion IDN editor, "Storygraphia", for testing the use of the dynamic elements and the engine components.

The volume also contains a number of examples of interactive storytelling works in Chapter 6 ("Examples of interactive storytelling: description and analysis") which we consider seminal, and which have been selected with the aim of supporting the arguments of the previous chapters. Each example is briefly described and analysed both in terms of its historical relevance and according to our general model of analysis.

References

Koenitz, Hartmut. 2015. "Towards a Specific Theory of Interactive Digital Narrative". In Hartmut Koenitz, Gabriele Ferri, Mads Haahr, Diğdem Sezen, and Tonguç İbrahim Sezen (eds), *Interactive Digital Narrative*. New York: Routledge, pp. 91–105.

Niesz, Anthony J., and Norman N. Holland. 1984. "Interactive Fiction". *Critical Inquiry* 11 (1): 110–129.

Smith, Sean, and Joseph Bates. 1989. *Toward a Theory of Narrative for Interactive Fiction*. Pittsburgh, PA: Carnegie Mellon University. doi:10.1184/R1/6611009.v1.

Szilas, Nicolas. 2015. "Reconsidering the Role of AI in Interactive Digital Narrative". In Hartmut Koenitz, Gabriele Ferri, Mads Haahr, Diğdem Sezen, and Tonguç İbrahim Sezen (eds), *Interactive Digital Narrative*. New York: Routledge, pp. 136–149.

Acknowledgements

The authors would like to thank: Dino Audino for having suggested and supported the first Italian version of this volume; Susan Broadhurst for encouraging the idea of an English edition; Naoko Matsumoto and Hiroto Yotsuda for sharing their knowledge about RPG and historical games in Japan; Michael Mateas and the EIS group of the University of California at Santa Cruz, for pointing out some contributions of relevance for interactive storytelling systems.

The authors would also like to thank Federico Favole for the re-enactment of *DramaTour* application, the Information System Division of the University of Turin and the Department of Informatics for hosting the repositories of CIRMA and Storygraphia software.

The entire contents of this volume were conceived, shared and revised by the three authors. The writing was distributed as follows:

- *Antonio Pizzo*: Chapter 1, pp. 1–20, Chapter 2, pp. 25–33, 38–40, Chapter 3, pp. 42–44, Chapter 4, pp. 59–70, 75–77, Chapter 6, pp. 130–140, 143–145, 148–156, 159–169.
- *Vincenzo Lombardo*: Chapter 1, pp. 21–23, Chapter 2, pp. 34–38, Chapter 5, pp. 80–125, Chapter 6, pp. 140–143, 145–148.
- *Rossana Damiano*: Chapter 3, pp. 44–57, Chapter 4, pp. 70–75, Chapter 6, pp. 156–159, 170–172.

1 Introduction

1.1 Preliminary definitions

1.1.1 The fascination with interactivity

In the dystopian world described in Aldous Huxley's *Brave New World* of 1932, there is a new kind of movie theatre, the "feelies", in which viewers can feel the emotions depicted on the screen by grasping a pair of knobs on the armrests of their seat (Frost 2006). In *Fahrenheit 451* by Ray Bradbury ([1953] 2003), the protagonist's wife is sitting in her living room waiting for a fiction to be broadcast on her three walls (TV). She is very excited because she can take part in the action with just a few lines to say when the protagonist asks her questions from the screen:

> They write the script with one part missing. It's a new idea. The homemaker, that's me, is the missing part. When it comes times for the missing lines, they all look at me out of the three walls and I say the lines.
>
> (ibid., p. 50)

A few years after the advent of the grand cinema narrative – in the first case – and then almost at the dawn of television – in the second case – science fiction already tended to anticipate a kind of more intense spectator participation, both by assuming greater sensory engagement and by predicting intervention in the fictional plot. Either way, participation was made possible by a fictional impressive new technology.

Not long after, these fantasies began to take shape in the real world. In 1967, Radúz Činčera, a Czech screenwriter and director, in the Czechoslovakian pavilion at the Expo in Montreal, presented his *Kinoautomat*. This innovative system allowed events narrated in a film on a screen to take different turns depending on the audience's reaction. "It involved live actors performing in tandem with a projected nonlinear film entitled *One Man and His House* in a custom-built 123-seat cinema with a red and green push button box attached to every seat" (Hales 2015, p. 38). Each member of the audience in the cinema could press the button at a particular moment in the narrative to choose between two options: the decision of the majority affected the course of the narrative accordingly.

DOI: 10.4324/9781003335627-1

The quest for a kind of technology that enabled a non-passive attitude on the part of the audience gained ground when it could be supported by computer software. In 1966, Joseph Weizenbaum at MIT invented the first simulation of an artificial agent, *Eliza* (see Chapter 6, Section 6.1), that impersonated a therapist with whom users could engage in dialogue. In 1976, *Adventure* (see Chapter 6, Section 6.2) was the first text-based adventure that could be played on a computer: since then, a new horizon of possibilities has opened up in the world of entertainment, creating a range of new opportunities and giving rise to the fascination of interactivity (Koenitz et al. 2015).

1.1.2 Digital, virtual, interactive

In the last 20 years, the possibilities for a narrative in which users can participate through technological tools have grown by leaps and bounds, expanding to a wide range of products, from entertainment to communication. There is no clear limit to the scope of interactive storytelling, as it ranges from novels, role-playing games and museum guides to film, television, theatre, performance and – of course – video games. In this time, scholars and artists working in this field have questioned the nature of this new narrative and art form.

There is not a single and common vocabulary for the field of interactive storytelling (Koenitz and Palosaari Eladhar 2019). The term has been identified and defined differently over the years. For example, the term applies to gamebooks, where the narrative structure branches out along different paths (defined by different sections or pages) and allows the reader to participate in the story by making choices. The use of computers has given rise to the term compufiction for interactive novels. But there are other definitions: interactive fiction, interactive narrative and also interactive drama. As technology allowed experimentation beyond the text-based interface, other definitions, such as interactive cinema and interactive TV, came along. The proliferation of mobile devices that allow interaction beyond the keyboard or screen has led to the emergence of terms such as interactive performance or, more recently, pervasive gaming. The world of games, even if it has shared terminology with other forms of entertainment, has grown and reached such a scale that it requires its own and autonomous classification of genres (Egenfeldt-Nielsen, Smith and Tosca 2008). There is no list that does justice to the plethora of definitions, but it is important to recall at least three of them that have played a role in the field covered by this book.

For some years now, the term "Digital Storytelling" has included all more or less interactive works that make use of digital technology to tell stories. Today, the term encompasses any more or less sequential communication practice based mainly on language (text or speech) and involving different media. It is mainly used to define the new practice of people using digital tools to tell their own stories. Therefore, the definition also includes social media and other tools for producing and sharing digital content. Sometimes the term is also used broadly to refer to the production of videos or media campaigns in advertising, both for commercial and non-commercial purposes. Given the enormous proliferation of videos (especially thanks to smartphones), the production of audio and video content in social media has increased exponentially. Digital Storytelling thus encompasses all content that can easily be produced and shared, thanks to the convergence of various mobile devices with the Internet. Media can include any combination of text, images, video, audio, social media elements (such as tweets) or interactive elements (such as maps). Digital Storytelling has found numerous applications, from the social world (where influencers' stories have millions of followers) to education (where teachers use it in the classroom and in group work).

At the end of the 1990s, a new term entered the debate: "Virtual Storytelling". The definition aimed to shift the focus from the media to the computer system. The latter is capable of processing and executing a narrative or even just providing a formal representation of the basic elements of the narrative.

A short time later, this field was called "Interactive Storytelling". The term refers primarily to products created using digital devices, but it refers specifically to the computational component and the ability to automatically control the user's interaction. This development is particularly evident when we look at some academic conferences (Box 1.1) (which have also been attended by practitioners who have a mixed profile between programmer and artist). Recently, more specific terms have become accepted among the genre's aficionados: interactive digital narrative, intelligent narrative technologies, or narrative game.

> **Box 1.1 The most relevant scientific conferences**
>
> - Hypertext: ACM conference on hypertext and hypermedia from 1990 (active).
> - ICVS (International Conference on Virtual Storytelling): since 2001, and then TIDSE (Technologies for Interactive Digital Storytelling and Entertainment) since 2003. In 2008, it converged in ICIDS (active).
> - ICIDS Interactive Storytelling (International Conference on Interactive Digital Storytelling) (active).
> - INT (Intelligent Narrative Technologies) from 2007 to 2017.
> - AIIDE (Artificial Intelligence and Interactive Digital Entertainment): since 2005 (active), part of the AAAI (American Association for Artificial Intelligence).
> - Workshop on Computational Models of Narrative: from 2009 to 2017.

1.1.3 Interacting, participating, collaborating

These various names and designations are the reason for the ongoing practical and intellectual work aimed at finding a definition for this elusive field. This book, whose title was chosen for brevity and effectiveness, is not about providing specific definitions. Behind the rush to find a definition there is always (more or less hidden) the dangerous tendency to lay down a theory that should determine the practice of interactive storytelling, or, in other words, to have an abstract model of interactive storytelling to which actual practice must conform in order to be recognised as such. This does not usually work in the field of creativity (at least not in the last century), and theoretical efforts, instead of focusing on the historical understanding of the field, end up following the practice, which in turn will always follow its own unpredictable path.

Therefore, in this volume, we will not attempt to define the qualities that a work should possess or the necessary and sufficient conditions in order to be considered interactive storytelling. Nor will we enumerate the technologies that may or may not belong to this field. And we will definitely not prescribe the ways in which readers, visitors, users and players can participate in an interactive work. Instead, we have selected the elements that have proven to be common and recurring in practice, and we try to include a wide range of typologies and examples.

The *Oxford English Dictionary* defines interaction as "reciprocal action; action or influence of persons or things on each other" or "the action between atomic and subatomic particles". Chris Crawford, a video game developer and researcher, believes that interactivity is "a cyclic process between two or more active agents in which each agent alternately listens, thinks, and speaks" (2013, p. 28). Wikipedia describes interactivity as a process between users and computers and other machines in which two or more elements (agents of systems) interact. Essential to interactivity is the notion of bidirectionality, which is the main difference from the notion of cause-effect.

Since we want to avoid rigid theoretical definitions, we start from a broader notion of interactivity (see Box 1.2), taking into account that it is always the result of a particular arrangement in real practice and not a prescribed norm. In other words: if someone wonders what the term means in the fields of creativity and entertainment, we can only answer that the meaning cannot be absolute, but rather relative, since the relationship to the user is specific to each individual work.

Box 1.2 A definition of interactivity

Paolo Rosa (founder of Studio Azzurro) and Andrea Balzola (experts in multimedia dramaturgy) have stated, in a volume on art and digital creativity, that interactivity is exclusively technological and therefore able to capture the traces left by users and interpret them as behaviours. According to Rosa and Balzola, this is the feature that distinguishes interactivity from interaction (the latter is common to all relational activities) (2010, pp. 19, 92–93).

On the other hand, if the question refers to the notion of storytelling, we should simply understand it as the act of telling a narrative content, in any modality and with any kind of media. Moreover, the term "storytelling" expresses a sense of action, an actionality that we believe has a particular affinity with the notion of interactivity. So the focus is on the kind of action that takes place and that the user experiences. Storytelling is not about the stories that someone tells, but about our (cognitive, emotional and physical) involvement in what is happening. Moreover, in today's cultural framework, it is quite common to define almost any media communication as storytelling.

We also skip the old diatribe about whether interactive narrative is a novelty or not and whether a narrative requires some reader participation or not. Already intuitively, audience participation in the various practices we are confronted with today is not only to be understood as a cognitive act, but as a process to be carried out either in the real or in the virtual world. This participation has also been understood as collaboration: hence the idea that "the reader does not merely passively accept or receive a given literary work, but through the act of reading participates along with the author in the creation of the fictional world evoked by the heretofore lifeless text" (Niesz and Holland 1984, p. 123). We always prefer the more practical approach when considering participation, relying on the notion that there is a certain kind of literature where "nontrivial effort is required to allow the reader to traverse the text" (Aarseth 1997, p. 1). In the age of Virtual Reality (VR), Augmented Reality (AR) and Extended Reality (XR), we consider that participation is not just a cognitive act. Participation is not limited to turning the pages, but is an actional, immersive and physical experience.

This book provides a comprehensive overview of the different types of participation in storytelling. The only distinguishing feature – which is almost implicit in the current historical period – is the inclusion of some kind of technology to manage interactivity.

The (implicit but constant) debate about the term to describe who experiences an interactive narrative work seems endless. Early studies took narratology as their starting point and thus also used the term "reader" to describe interactive stories. With the advent of video and computer graphics, the term became obsolete. Since then, there have been various definitions, but the term "user" has prevailed – perhaps because of its generality – and seems to cover the widest possible meaning. Sometimes the term "interactor" is also used to emphasise the participatory behaviour in the narrative. In the broad field of video games, the term "player" has become accepted, regardless of genre or technology. One of the earlier descriptions of this new participant is still valid, as someone who explicitly interacts with the fictional works explicitly by means of queries or answers, taking an active role in the story, and deliberately changes the development of the plot, characters, setting or language together with the author (Niesz and Holland 1984, p. 111).

This is the idea that runs through this volume, even though we prefer the term "user". We tend to be deliberately generic when referring to the person participating in the narrative, and we avoid choosing between singular or plural, because the descriptions we give in this volume are intended for a wide range of interactive narratives available to individual users or group audiences.

For the rest, it does not matter whether it is an entertainment product that you watch on a computer screen or experience with a VR headset, or whether it is an installation that you can visit or a performance that you attend. In Chapter 6, we will discuss many very different typologies of interactive storytelling.

1.2 Telling stories through actions

1.2.1 Dramatic media

The more engaging forms of interactive storytelling use dramatic elements. Of course, there are mainstream examples such as *Bandersnatch* from the *Black Mirror* film series (see Chapter 6, Section 6.16) or the video game *The Walking Dead* (see Chapter 6, Section 6.14) that rely on a form of dramatic writing; but there are also more experimental projects, such as *Façade* (see Chapter 6, Section 6.11) that rely on interaction with agents in a situation where conflict escalates as the plot unfolds. As early as 1991, Brenda Laurel, referring to the multimedia computer in general terms at the time, had pointed out that digital media have a dramatic character because their content is usually manifested through some type of agents (Laurel 1991). The participatory nature of various forms of interactivity suggests a proximity to dramatic media. While it is true that we are increasingly consuming narrative fiction, informational and educational content, it is also true that we often do so through formats of storytelling that have dramatic qualities. According to Martin Esslin, dramatic media are defined by "the mimetic actions, in the sense of the re-enactment of 'real' or fictional events, involving the actions and interaction of human beings, real or simulated, before an audience as though they were happening at that very moment" (1987, p. 28). Although this definition was conceived for theatre, film and television, we believe it also fits the broad field of digital entertainment.

Even in the early experiments with interactive storytelling, where the form was more directly derived from traditional fiction (the novel), there seemed to be a specific dramatic component. As early as 1984, Niesz and Holland believed that interactive fiction lent itself "to doing and to themes involving action, conflict and adventure" (1984, p. 123). In the early 1990s, the OZ group at Carnegie Mellon University, which helped to establish the notion of interactive storytelling, argued that dramatic tension is one of the three main lines to follow in creating interactive works (the other two being autonomous agents and visualisation systems) (Bates 1992). According to Michael Mateas, who was part of this group, there is an "affinity between drama's focus on action and the action-based, real-time, responsive behaviour of interactive computer systems" (Mateas and Sengers 2003, p. 13).

This means that the affinity with dramatic media is based on interaction, which is conceived as a real-time event. The actional factor of interactive narrative implies (more or less obviously) the user's perception of time as present when participating in the event, the presence of operable elements or of functions that record the user's actions (even unintentional ones), and – last but not least – the participation of some kind of agent (human or artificial) that gives meaning and effect to these actions in the course of the story. The participatory component implies the coexistence of the character, the user or the audience in the here and now, in this specific sequence of events, in this very moment, but – even more – it implies the focus of the participants on a specific sequence of actions.

1.2.2 Actions and events

A dramatic story develops thanks to the participation of some agent who performs actions, and in its interactive version these are also produced by the person who experiences the narrative and plays a role in it. Therefore, actions are crucial in the discussion of interactive storytelling, as they are the fundamental element of its structure. By the term "action", we mean a process that takes place in the time and space of the narrative. However, it is useful to distinguish between two types of processes:

- *Actions*: the enactment of some agent's deliberations (including the user's actions). In narratives, we consider as actions all activities performed by characters (humans, animals or imaginary creatures) as a consequence of their will. These are causal processes.
- *Events*: the processes that are not the result of a specific intention but occur due to other causes, i.e., the person experiencing the narrative cannot relate them to some agent's intention. These are random events, such as the outbreak of a storm, the eruption of a volcano or a bolt of lightning. As events, we consider what happens to the characters without their will, like slipping on a banana peel, falling into a ravine… These are aleatory processes.

The logic of a narrative is based on the possibility of acknowledging the causality of processes in order to give meaning to a certain sequence of happenings. Although events can play an important role within the story, it should be noted that their aleatory character compromises the logical chain of the narrative sequence (see Chapter 2, Section 2.2) and thus weakens the user's interest in the story.

In the context of interactivity, events can have greater utility as an incentive for the user's actions. An example of this is the arcade games of the 1990s, where a series of random events (e.g., cars racing a road that must be crossed, falling geometric pieces that must be arranged into horizontal rows of blocks) required constant intervention by the player. However, these were forms of interactive entertainment with a low degree of narrativity. In fact, many of these games, where random events determined the course of the action, have been enriched over the years with more and more narrative clues, thanks to artificial agents that convey the meaning of intentional actions to which the user must react (like the gorilla in *Super Mario*). In short, events take place in the world of interactive storytelling when they help drive the actions of the agent (be it the user's avatar or some automatic elements of the system). Consequently, writing an interactive narrative in most cases means designing actions.

However, the design of actions in interactive storytelling involves three different elements:

1. *Dramatic action*: the action performed by one agent that has an impact on other agents in the story.

2   *Narrative action*: the action generated by the story itself, which sets its own narrative direction and has an effect on the audience.
3   *The action of the audience*: both the cognitive process and the actual intervention in the system.

In what follows we will describe the first two, while the third will be dealt with in Chapter 4, Section 4.1.5. Note that while these categories are clearly separate in theory, in practice, they do not have sharp boundaries and may sometimes overlap.

1.2.3 Dramatic action

The long tradition of dramatic writing studies has often raised the question of which qualities make an action dramatic, believable and engaging, and so have modern scriptwriting manuals. Of course, there have been different points of view over the centuries, and it is the wealth of opinions, ideas and solutions in the various publications on the subject that allows us to digest a list of basic and common features about the dramatic action:

- It is the fundamental element of narrative movement in a dramatic work.
- It is structured according to a logic of cause and effect, giving the impression that one action motivates the next.
- It is motivated by a character's goal (and the reasoning that results from it), which must be obvious and understandable to the audience.
- It is part of a character's behaviour with a certain degree of unity and wholeness, so that a character's various actions can be traced back to its basic characteristics.
- It defines the character's function in the plot; thus, characters show themselves only through their own actions and nothing else: characters are what they do.
- It is a scalable concept. The whole drama is an action that can be broken down into smaller and smaller parts. All the above characteristics can apply to both larger (time extended) actions (e.g., revenge for the murder of a father) and smaller (punctual) actions (the killing of the murderer).

Although narratives are not always based on the dialogic interaction of characters, although they may be more epic and less dramatic, it is unlikely that they will not present some entity whose intentions motivate the course of events. Therefore, the authors of an interactive narrative must be able to devise meaningful actions. There are many manuals on theatre, film and television where you can learn how to design actions that are meaningful and engaging to the audience.

However, here is some general advice. Designing meaningful actions requires a clear idea of who is acting. We do not refer to the complex treatment of the so-called character bible, i.e., the various characteristics (physical, psychological, social) as used in film or television productions. We are simply emphasising that the story should be based on and focus on agents who are capable of carrying out the actions that the author has come up with. In other words: if the author decides (for whatever reason) that the meaningful action is John entering the restaurant, then the passing friend (who greets him on the street), the taxi driver (who takes him there) and the dog (who sleeps on the sidewalk) do not exist as agents unless they are needed to make John's entry into the restaurant more dramatic.

To design units that contain actions that are effective for the purposes of interactive storytelling, the author must focus on the goals of the agent performing the actions in the world of the story, avoiding any descriptive, stylistic, or rhetorical bells and whistles (these can always be added after). Also, the author must have a clear idea of the goals the action will pursue in the course of the narrative (e.g., it is important that John enters the restaurant because there is where he will meet the waiter with whom he will have a passionate romance). So if the author has decided that one character – John – is the main agent in this plot, then it would be better if the user's eventual intervention had an effect on him. This seems quite intuitive when we think of a first-person immersive VR adventure like *Wanderer* (2021, by Mighty Eyes), where the player explores different environments and can take actions throughout the game. However, not all of these are relevant to the character. Indeed, the *Wanderer* works best when the character reaches a flat that serves as an escape room and also as a hub for many other areas with a similar structure: the many available actions and manipulable objects have a direct impact on the character and on the unfolding of the story.

1.2.4 Narrative action

The designer and creator of content for an interactive story must control (more or less strictly) the relationship between user activity and the narrative. Therefore, when the authors design the story, the actions and the events, it is important to have an idea of the narratological role, and this goes beyond the narrative content. Is it a beginning where we have to give some information about the place and the situation? Is it part of the increasing complications the character faces? Is it necessary to elicit a certain behaviour? Does it have to lead to the end of the story? So, each part of the story, then, not only reflects the actions that take place in the fictional world, but also pursues a goal itself, with a narrative action that determines the sequence of events. The first scenes of *Tokyo Chronos* (2019, by MyDearest) are clearly set up as a beginning. They introduce the protagonist, the antagonist and the setting, and even hint at the mystery to be solved.

It is important to have a description of the action that shapes the narrative. This can be achieved, for example, by marking the narrative and dramatic features in the units (see Chapter 2, Section 2.5), as this indicates the narrative action of that particular unit. The unit is, for example, the introduction, or one of the obstacles to be overcome, or a finale. Even in works based on an epic narrative model, where events do not arise through real-time interactions between different agents (the dramatic actions), the narrative actions remain important in shaping the story. And this contributes to the effective creation of dramatic tension (see Chapter 5, Section 5.8.3).

1.2.5 Sequence of actions

A sequence of actions attracts our attention if it represents some kind of relationship that holds the actions together in a meaningful order, usually a causal relationship. There is a classic example that describes the difference between enumerating facts and telling a story. E.M. Forster, the famous English novelist, explained in 1927 that the story is a "narrative of events arranged in their time-sequence" and that the plot is also a narrative of events but "the emphasis falling on causality" (1985, p. 86). The former is conceived as a kind of chronicle or factual account (see Box 1.3), the latter is defined by the causal relationship between actions. This causality is often motivated by a feeling, a value, an emotion in the character living the story. Therefore, the chronicle becomes a plot because the narrative makes sense to the audience, thanks to a series of implications created by the way the facts are strung together. The plot shows how the implications affect the characters, and it can be more or less dramatic depending on how these facts are presented. The facts can be rendered as a narrative in which the plot starts from the manifestation of causality, but they can also be developed in a drama when they are represented by actions.

> **Box 1.3 Examples of the difference between chronicle, plot and drama**
>
> E.M. Forster has described the difference between a chronicle and a story. Here are the two famous examples he created and a third we have devised for dramatisation:
>
> > The king died and then the queen died = chronicle (facts)
> > The king died, and then the queen died of grief = plot (implications)
> > A SERVANT (*Enters the room, panting*) My Lady …. (*pause*) The King has died. THE QUEEN (*turning pale*) No! no! (*She is short of breath and presses her hands to her heart*) Argh! (*She falls to the ground, lifeless*) = drama (actions)

We usually tell and experience stories that follow a monolinear and unidirectional path (Figure 1.1), regardless of the organisation of the genre as a whole part (like the novel or the classic film) or as fragmented parts (as in a TV series). Even in narrative

Figure 1.1 Example of storytelling as linear sequence

forms traditionally divided into chapters or episodes, the plot progresses linearly; sometimes it follows the fates of a main character, sometimes it follows the progress of parallel storylines, but the narrative content is arranged according to a predefined order that the author deems dramatic and effective.

It is easy to imagine that one and the same beginning can trigger several sequences of events, so that the plot has different endings (Figure 1.2).

In this case, the storylines may be as different as the path we take, but progress goes in only one direction. Within the whole sequence we can see consistent stages of narrative (five, in the example in Figure 1.2) organised hierarchically in levels: the first level precedes the second, and so on. In this model, it is not possible for a unit belonging to a lower level to lead to a unit of a higher level. In other words, the sequence is multilinear and unidirectional (in Figure 1.2, from left to right). A multilinear structure can also be laid out in such a way that it runs towards a single end (Figure 1.3).

If the sequence of actions is not organised hierarchically, the story can follow several paths, as in a hypertextual scheme (Figure 1.4): the sequence of events cannot be described as a sequence of levels, its order is not hierarchical, and it can also be other than unidirectional.

The last two models describe – very briefly – the possible approaches to interactive storytelling. Regardless of whether the model is based on branching choices (hierarchical) or on exploring different paths towards some closure (labyrinthine) (Galyean 1995), these models have two basic elements in common:

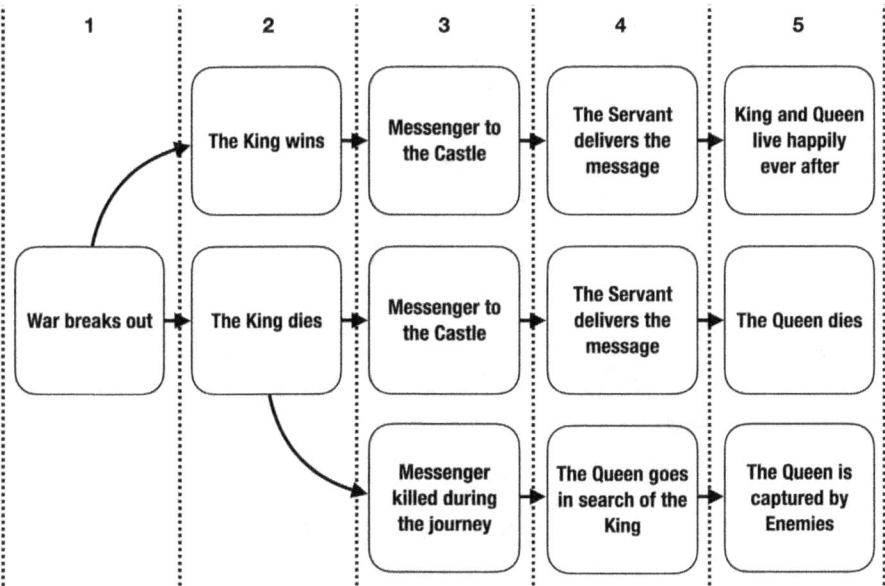

Figure 1.2 Example of storytelling as multilinear sequence

12   *Introduction*

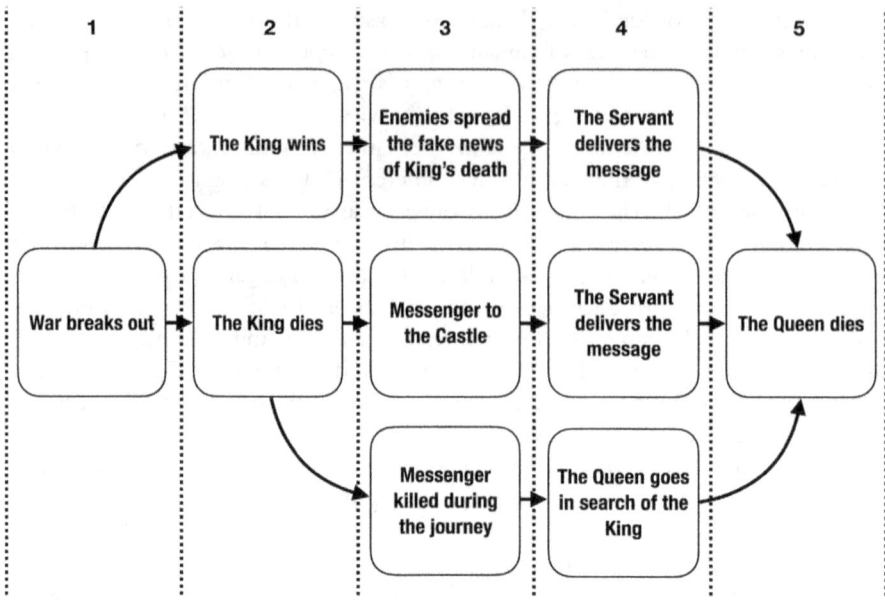

Figure 1.3 Example of multilinear single ending storytelling

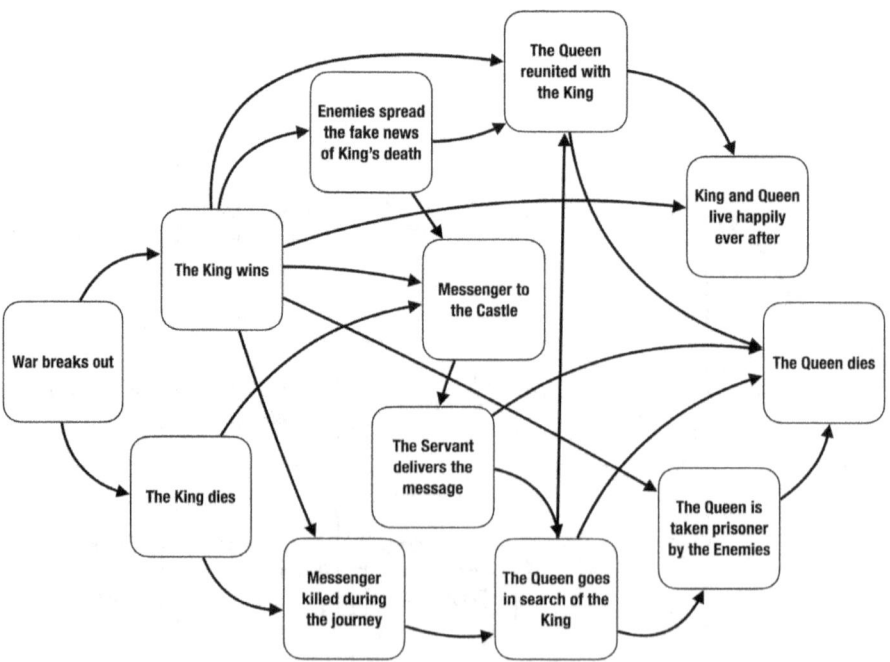

Figure 1.4 Example of hypertextual storytelling

1   The story segmentation: episodes, phases, events (in Chapter 2, Section 2.1, we will provide a more detailed definition of these segments as narrative units).
2   A system to represent the various possible paths (in Chapter 2, Section 2.2, it will be described as ordering).

These are the cases where computation can play a key role because it can select an available sequence of units that match the user's actions. Whether the user clicks on a link on the screen or rotates a VR headset, the system's job (which is more or less complicated depending on the configuration) is to deliver the part of the story that is activated by those specific actions and fits a believable plot.

1.2.6 Generating events

The actions in the storyline can be implemented according to a model different from those described so far, and in which there are no pre-existing events that can be combined. This model is not represented by a graph (whose nodes represent the events around the king or queen, as in the previous examples) (Box 1.4). Rather, we should imagine a set of characters (the king, the queen, the servant) with some kind of standard description (what they desire, what they know, what they can do). Then we add a description of the world they live in (which time period, which laws, what relationships between the characters). At this point, we could describe an initial event that matches the given description (the king goes to battle and the queen waits in the castle) and maybe even the desired ending (they live happily ever after). So we would have a starting point, an ending point and some rules that determine the characters' attributes and the story world features. If these elements were written in a machine-readable, formal language and were therefore controlled by an algorithm, the computer system could ensure that the necessary events occurred to get from the starting point to the end point. This is – in short – what we mean by a generative system (Figure 1.5) and is perhaps reminiscent of a dramatic improvisation in which a group of actors perform a scenario based on given instructions about the characters and the situation. If one transposes this configuration into a computer system, the task of the algorithm would not only be to sequence events, but also to generate them. This would be an autonomous narrative generation system that could take as input an ending to the story (the dramatic goal) where, for example, the queen falls in love with the enemy prince, to generate the events necessary to achieve that goal. Of course, the system should take into account the given descriptions as rules to be followed (the queen is always well dressed, she has servants) and set the condition that the enemy prince and the queen meet. In addition, the system should include some basic rules to generate events that are believable, logical and captivating (there must be a reason why the queen falls in love with the enemy prince: he is terribly handsome). In other words, the algorithm should include some rules on how to tell a story (this is covered in detail in Chapter 5).

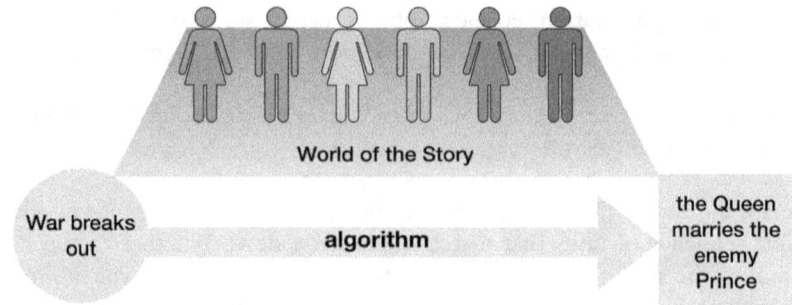

Figure 1.5 Schema of generative model of storytelling

Box 1.4 Definitions of graph, nodes and tree

- *Graph*: in mathematics, a structure amounting to a set of points (vertices or nodes) and lines (edge) that connect the pairs of points; on formal level, the graph describes some specific relation between points (as, in the case we have seen, the causal logic in the narrative).
- *Node*: vertices or nodes are the basic element of graphs and are intended as indivisible objects. They do not need to be provided with a formal description (they can be treated as featureless); yet they may have additional structure depending on the application from which the graph arises (e.g., one or more nodes in one or more story graphs can be labelled as "beginning" or as "endings").
- *Tree* (or *hierarchy*) is a data structure in graph theory that uses the notions of tree and root. A tree consists of two types of basic substructures: the node (which usually contains the information) and the edge (which defines the hierarchical connection between two nodes). The terminology used for this structure refers to the parent (higher level) for the node having an edge to a child (lower level). The tree structure represents a directed graph, i.e., the edges have an orientation. In this structure, a child node can only be linked to one parent node (i.e., the node has a single inbound edge); multiple edges can originate from a parent node (i.e., the node has more outbound edges). The tree structure must contain a single node with no inbound edge (the root node) and at least one node with no outbound edges (the leaf node). A node can also be both a parent (if it has an outbound edge) and a child (if it has an inbound edge). The height or depth of the tree is defined by the length of the longer path from the root to the leaves.

A system of this kind is called generative because it does not control the browsing along already existing parts of the story, but produces the events and strings them together. This can be done either by providing the computer with a set of rules for writing the story (i.e., describing grammars or constraints as in Chapter 5, Sections 5.4.1 and 5.4.2) or by providing instructions for handling goals that motivate the characters' plans and actions (i.e., planning as described in Chapter 3, Section 3.2.1). This line of research was richer in the 1990s and most experiments had as a result a short text that looks like a well-formed narrative (Sharpies 1997). In these cases, the graph model based on nodes and edges (typical of hypertexts, either hierarchical or labyrinthine) is not applicable. The better metaphor to describe the generative model is that of the boat on the river, as proposed by Tinsley A. Galyean. The boat represents the user's experience and the river represents the story. The user can decide how to steer the story (slower, faster, steady, with interruptions), but the events flow in a certain direction. There may be moments when the story branches (like a river) into two different continuations. Then the continuation may not depend on the action the user takes at those moments, but on the actions the user has taken up to that point. In the river metaphor, the boat will take one of the two streams, depending on where it is when the river branches: the choice between the possible continuations depends on how the previous choices have influenced the course of the story at that particular moment (Galyean 1995).

This model still represents one of the most advanced goals in interactive storytelling today, even though it is already half a century old. We can trace its origins back to the 1960s, when the first experiments with computer-generated stories in natural language took place (Ryan 2017).

1.3 General issues

1.3.1 Author, authorship, control

In 1997, Janet Murray was one of the first to describe the new possibilities offered by the computer for narratives in digital interactive environments. She also highlighted the new role of the procedural author, who uses procedures to create multiform narratives. This "cyberbard" would structure "a coherent story not as a single sequence of events but as a multiform plot open to the collaborative participation of the interactor" and would exploit "the formulaic nature of storytelling" (Murray 2001, pp. 185–187).

The tasks of the new author include determining the events that can happen, setting the rules for the narrative, and defining the nature of participation. In addition, this new author must select some standard features of the narrative (such as style, genre) which, once in play, will shape the communicative pact with the users. This pact not only allows the user to experience the story with sufficient ease and freedom, but at the same time gives the author a sufficient degree of control over the progress of the story (see Table 1.1).

Murray's conception of narrative alters not only the tasks traditionally ascribed to the author who writes stories, but also the very notion of authorship. The creative deeds that inform the kind of storytelling described in this volume are

Table 1.1 Role of author vs procedural author

Author	Procedural author
Writes the sequence of events	Writes the events and the sequencing rules
Writes the characters' actions	Describes the characters' features and library of actions
Determines the lines to be delivered	Describes the type of lines that may be delivered
Describes the fictional world	Writes the logic that rules the fictional world
The narrative is linear	The narrative is multilinear, hypertextual, generative

sometimes different from those associated with the traditional image of the author sitting alone in front of the blank page. The procedural author is someone who is fully involved in collaborative projects, working out graphs and setting rules. However, this should not be completely unfamiliar. Even traditional novelists often create preparatory materials that contribute to the final elaboration of the story. For example, Gustave Flaubert used several detailed sketches, even describing the characters' emotions, when writing his famous *Madame Bovary* (Flaubert 1995). The major entertainment media (film, TV, Internet) have proven that the mainstream products of creativity and art can no longer be considered the result of a single creative will controlled by a single author. Most films, TV series and video games are the result of a very complex collaboration, and the final attribution to a single artist usually has a symbolic or commercial value. Eventually, even the public has become accustomed to this collective creativity; we often give credit to some films because they were produced by Pixar, or to some video games because they were developed by Electronic Arts (EA), even if we do not know the director or designer. The authoring model for interactive storytelling is always very collaborative, as we will see in the examples.

We cannot clearly delineate the role of the one who writes the story from the role of the one who programmes the system for interaction, just as we cannot define a sharp distinction between the one who is responsible for the interface and the one who programmes the instruments of control. Anyone approaching this area of creativity must be prepared to develop a strong interdisciplinary mindset and even deal with problems they would not traditionally face in their profession. A writer will have to participate in designing the algorithm that strings scenes together; a programmer will have to write the algorithm that better represents the rules of a particular narrative genre; a designer will have to figure out which interface is better for a particular narrative or character.

1.3.2 Characters or stories

In the most advanced forms of interactive storytelling, the author's tasks are not only distributed among different people, but also specifically parcelled out for each part that will make up the final interactive work. In a so-called intelligent narrative, the author must use a kind of machine-processable language when creating the content to describe the individual elements involved in the narrative (i.e., the characters, the setting, the nature of the events, a possible ending).

The idea that each individual element can be treated and created separately has revived a rather old diatribe in both academic research and artistic production. In his *Poetics* (fourth century BC), Aristotle said that the most important element of tragedy is the plot (the arrangement of events) (Aristotle 1998, 1450a). In the golden age of French theatre (the seventeenth century), the two playwrights Racine and Corneille each took a different approach to the composition of tragedy: while the former "constructed complex characters and a simple plot", the latter preferred "simple characters and complex plots" (Brockett 2007, p. 189). In modern writing manuals, authors are divided between those who believe that a good story comes from careful character creation and those who believe that the key is a good plot and a well-crafted sequence of events (Egri 1960; Lavandier 1994; Ryngaert 1996; Field 2005).

In short, it is a question of which of the two elements is more important: the character or the plot. If we think of the traditional work of an author, the question may seem purely speculative (or two sides of the same coin), and it may seem impossible to separate the moments when Tolstoy wrote the character Anna Karenina from those when he wrote her story. However, in the field of interactive storytelling, this question has acquired a particular relevance and importance, as the two processes are indeed conceptually and practically separable. In developing a computer system for interactive storytelling, it is indeed possible to model a finite number of agents (and even add a component that simulates emotions) capable of producing meaningful, reasoned, rational and believable actions to achieve a certain dramatic quality. However, it is also possible to take a different path and thus determine the types of actions allowed, the relationships and consequences, a main direction towards which to move, so that the sum of all actions creates the illusion of a character (see Table 1.2).

Table 1.2 Character-centred modelling vs. plot-centred modelling

Character-centred modelling	*Plot-centred modelling*
Automatic generation of behaviours that give the impression of an autonomous and believable agent (both in terms of intentions and emotions) that can appropriately respond to user input	Structuring a scalable and modular plot that builds a dramatic arc of tension, where the user interacts with given characters
Intelligent characters are agents with a specific personality who participate in a scenario that contains only a few rough instructions that they must follow. A planning system dictates the actions required, so that events are generated accordingly and the plot unfolds differently each time the interactive story is run.	The interactive narrative consists of actions and events that follow one another according to a certain grammar or set of constraints. The narrative can be represented as a diagram that defines each possible action.

18 *Introduction*

However, this is not a dilemma where we have to take sides. Rather, it is a matter of various aspects of design to which authors must pay attention. Especially when the interactive storytelling work involves narrative intelligence, automatic content generation and artificial agent design, it is important to be aware of the possibilities associated with these two design models and hopefully be able to draw insights and practical solutions from both.

1.3.3 The field of investigation

In a recent curated book on interactive storytelling, the editors write:

> The hybrid nature of interactive digital narratives—as narratives and procedural digital entities on software executed on computers—poses considerable challenges for analysis and categorisation. A further complication lies in the rapid evolvement of the underlying technologies for creation and dissemination as computing technology has developed dramatically in a very short time compared to the technologies fundamental for other forms of expression.
>
> (Koenitz et al. 2015, p. 69)

We agree with the complications given and therefore minimise any attempt to further categorise. However, we reserve the right to propose categories or taxonomies only in cases where this is necessary to clarify a practical or design issue.

We have seen that it is possible to divide the design of narrative content for interactive storytelling into two general families:

- *Navigation*: the systems have the task of managing already existing content, either created ad hoc for the system or obtained from external sources where it was created for other purposes.
- *Generation*: the system aims to generate the content that makes up the story. These can be either systems capable of writing short stories in natural language or simulation games where the world is created and developed on-the-fly according to the player's decisions.

Of course, there are also approaches to interactive storytelling that lead to hybrid outcomes, where computation plays a role both in sequencing and in generating and organising content, where the algorithm contributes in real time to the user's participation or to the execution of a live event together with performers and other human operators (see Chapter 5). The greater the emphasis on the autonomy of the algorithm in generating the story, the greater the attempt to distil and encode the narrative elements. It is precisely the computerised nature of the works that enables the automation of the processes involved. This automation, in turn, makes it possible to respond consistently to the variability of the events narrated. The possible variations include, of course, the actions of the users, i.e., the person who reads, listens, watches or enacts the narrative, depending on the modes of participation available. In other words, the more the algorithm implements the storytelling, the greater the potential participation.

Although the field of enquiry would include the participatory experience, it is true that this experience is the result of a complex set of creative choices and technological solutions that are combined. Therefore, it is difficult to consider user experience as a prescriptive starting point for design. It is better to treat it as part of different objectives of our interactive project, balanced by the constraints (economic, political, technological) that need to be considered. In Chapter 4, we will discuss the experience of the user in relation to the narrative computer system, but we will not delve into cognitive, sociological or psychological issues. Here we simply say that this experience will always be specific, local and transient. A historical perspective may suggest more and new categorisations for user participation in retrospect, but we believe that categorisation will always be the result of analysis based on existing practices, and that it is less effective when viewed as prescriptive norms guiding future productions. We only recommend being aware of the sheer complexity of the field of enquiry and going beyond the boundaries of what is traditionally considered narrative, as well as taking a very broad approach to what the user's participation in the story can be.

1.3.4 Database, narrative and video contents

In this area we can include a variety of systems that are able to independently process already existing content (text, graphics, multimedia), the results of which have been listed under the definition of database narrative. These are systems in which the narrative results neither from a predefined sequence of possible sequences (as in hypertext) nor from the autonomous generation of actions and events, but is built on some query rules, as in databases, and is usually defined as emergent. Nevertheless, the database narrative does not represent a third of the two general models presented earlier (hypertextual and generative) but is rather orthogonal to them. Theoretically, a hypertext could be created by a specific query in a database, or the database could contain behaviours of agents that generate a narrative when triggered by the right query.

The foundations of database narrative can be found in Glorianna Davenport's Interactive Cinema Group at the Media Lab, Lev Manovich's *Soft Cinema* and Florian Thalhofer's *Korsakow*. Davenport's work aimed to create interactive documentaries whose video content could be assembled according to the choices of the viewer, as in the case of the software ConTour and the documentary *Boston: Renewed Vistas*, produced in 1995 (Davenport and Murtaugh 1997). Lev Manovich's theoretical proposals and technical solutions also belong to this field of experimentation. We owe to Manovich the definition of database cinema, which took practical shape in the installation *Soft Cinema*. This is less about the multimedia nature of the content and more about the interfaces that allow access to this content (Manovich and Kratky 2005). Manovich's project aims to use a huge database of video clips to produce a potentially larger number of short films. In addition to the theoretical implications behind the *Korsakow* software, credit must be given to Florian Thalhofer for providing an important working tool for users willing to experiment in the field of interactive and hypertextual video. *Korsakow* is an interactive film editor and makes it possible to define rules for linking the various video clips without committing the author to a fixed order; on the contrary, the video clips are arranged spontaneously according to the decisions of the viewer.[1] Autonomous organisation of content has been used primarily in video archives, as it allows for the creation of works in which most (or even all) editing is done autonomously by the computer according to the (explicit or implicit) requests of the viewer.

The ability to navigate through different content has also found application outside the data processing paradigm. One of the first examples of interactive video narration dates back to 1991, when Oliver Hirshbiegel created *Mörderische Entscheidung* [Murderous Decision], a thriller that aired simultaneously on two television channels and showed the same story from the perspective of two different characters. While zapping from one channel to the other, viewers could switch between two perspectives on the same plot.

In 2000, Danish TV channel produced a similar experiment, *D-Dag* (by Krag-Jacobsen, Levring, Vinterberg and von Trier), in which the story of a bank robbery on New Year's Eve was broadcast on four different channels. Between December 2006 and January 2007, the Finnish TV channel YLE continued to push viewer interaction. While in the previous examples the only option was to switch between the differently edited video tracks of the identical story, in *Accidental Lovers* viewers could influence the development of the story via text messages. Leena Saarinen (writer) and Mika Tuomola (director) created a TV musical comedy with a number of characters involved in the traditional love story, but some events in the plot were triggered by keywords. Thus, the final plot depended on the keywords found in the texts sent by the viewers during the programme (Saarinen 2007, p. 147). In recent years, the best-known interactive fiction from TV is undoubtedly the episode *Bandersnatch* (2018) of the Netflix-produced series *Black Mirror* (see Chapter 6, Section 6.16). Here, at the end of some scenes, viewers can choose between two or more possible actions using the remote control. Each choice leads to a different development of the plot and ultimately to a different ending.

1.3.5 Delimiting the field

Today, it is quite difficult to distinguish between the specific features that separate the database narrative from interactive TV. For several decades, first with CD and DVD and now with streaming on the Internet, viewers have been able to interact with fiction in various ways, jumping from one scene to another, accessing additional information or even changing the content. "In fact, there is no longer any simple definition of what constitutes an interactive film, as audiences may be active in other ways than selecting from premade content ... interactivity itself has changed" (Hales 2015, p. 45).

The field is still vast and confusing; it includes various works and formats. In this volume, we will try to offer as broad a perspective as possible by pointing out some mainstream terms and selecting relevant case studies. However, we are aware that our perspective will always be partial, as we will not be able to consider works that are either niche or eccentric in comparison to the content of interactive storytelling. For example, we will give very little space to the use of the web as an environment for the design and presentation of interactive narratives, and we will exclude works of contemporary art.

1.4 A general model of analysis

We present a general analysis model for interactive storytelling that is intended to be an ideal reference for component-based analysis of interactive storytelling systems. Each system can focus on certain components and leave others implicit or exclude them from the conceptualisation.

With a broad definition of interactive storytelling in mind, three main components can be identified as recurring in most applications:

- *Sequence management*: the creation and navigation of narrative sequences and their compositional units, either automatically or manually.
- *Actions and agents*: the representation of the agents who act in the story and the actions they can perform; in some cases, actions – rather than agents – are the basic component, with agents assigned to them as participants.
- *Engagement and interactivity*: the modalities through which the audience can experience and engage with the story.

The interaction between the components described above is illustrated in Figure 1.6, which gives an overview of the objects and roles involved in the production of interactive stories.

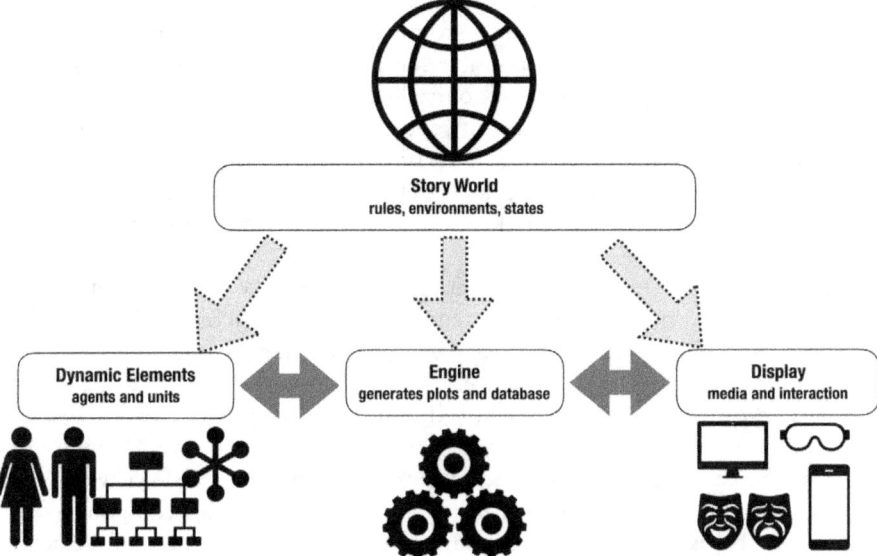

Figure 1.6 General scheme of analysis for interactive storytelling

- *Story world*: With some degree of approximation, we assume that every interactive storytelling project presupposes an explicit or implicit description of the world. Typically, the story world is described in terms of the objects it contains and their meaningful attributes, behaviours, make-up and individual attitudes. However, this list does not include most of the knowledge and conventions that characterise the specific culture and society relevant to each project. For instance, an online role-playing game must specify the rules that constrain the movements in the navigable areas; similarly, a video game must define the solids and surfaces which are (or not) penetrating surfaces, for example, one can dive into a surface of water but cannot walk through a wall. But at the same time, a mediaeval knightly character evokes a set of characteristics, usually based on shared cultural knowledge, that need not be formally described in the system. Or an interactive guide to a historical building or museum implicitly assumes a map of the location where the event takes place, and it needs not specify that the user cannot be teleported from one room to another. In general, what we call the story world comprises the set of genre conventions (historical drama, fantasy, thriller, etc.) and intertextual references (to particular characters, styles, etc.) that are relevant to the narrative but can be taken for granted (a kind of shared knowledge base) or, in other words, do not need to be encoded in a particular algorithm.
- *Dynamic elements*: The system needs a list or repository of all dynamic elements that contribute to the story and of the relationships between them. These are elements that need to be explicitly coded in a formal language. These include not only the characters and their behaviour, but also the narrative units and their groupings. For example, a drama system for interactive improvisation must list the possible actions that can be performed by the agents. Or a hypertextual narrative must list the narrative units (chapters, scenes, episodes) that can be arranged into a sequence depending on the navigation.
- *Engine*: In order to create a story from the elements listed, a narrative engine is needed. The engine is responsible for selecting and arranging the available elements (events, actions, behaviours) in a coherent whole according to the rules of the story world, the narrative logic and the interactions with the user. In other words, this component must be in charge of sequencing the elements described above according to a definition of permissible sequences (i.e., a grammar, a set of constraints) in order to create a believable and engaging narrative.
- *Display*: The design of the interactive story must take into account the language in which the story is presented. To do this, it must determine the device through which the narrative will manifest itself to the audience, i.e., a device that is suitable for the presentation of the narrative and allows the audience to participate in the narrative individually or as a group. By the term "display", we do not mean the device used to manifest the narrative. Of course, the narrative can be tailored to a specific device (a PC monitor, a 3D viewer, a theatre stage), yet we use the term to address the whole set of components that qualify the user's experience in terms of narrative engagement and interaction.

Therefore, it encompasses the notion of interface, interaction design and, more generally, the way the system deals with the audience's (not least emotional) involvement.

In order to define a set of agents, actions and narrative units, a story world is needed. The engine, then, must account for the specific characteristics of the elements it arranges into a sequence, and must follow rules that are consistent with the story world and the dynamic elements stored in the database of the system. Since the engine must be designed so as to be compliant with the other components, its design should run in parallel with them, although they will be employed later. Similarly, the display system must enable the interaction of the audience with the characteristics of the contents it will receive as input from the engine. The experience of an interactive digital narrative is the result of the well-orchestrated interplay of these four elements, each of which may acquire greater or lesser importance case by case. In the following, we will describe and discuss each component in more detail.

Note

1 A description of the system is available at https://vimeo.com/37364528. The software is available (free for small personal use and small productions) at http://www.korsakow.com.

References

Aarseth, Espen. 1997. *Cybertext: Perspectives on Ergodic Literature*. Baltimore, MD: Johns Hopkins University Press.
Aristotle. 1998. *Poetics*. Edited by Stephen Halliwell. Chicago: University of Chicago Press.
Bates, J. 1992. "Virtual Reality, Art, and Entertainment". *Presence: Teleoperators and Virtual Environments* 1 (1): 133–138.
Bradbury, Ray. 2003. *Fahrenheit* 451. New York: Simon & Schuster. doi:10.4324/9781003235750-14.
Brockett, Oscar Gross. 2007. *History of the Theatre*. Boston, MA: Allyn and Bacon.
Crawford, Chris. 2013. *Chris Crawford on Interactive Storytelling*. Berkeley, CA: New Riders. doi:10.1007/978-3-642-25289-1.
Davenport, Glorianna, and Michael Luke Murtaugh. 1997. "Automatist Storyteller Systems and the Shifting Sands of Story". *IBM Systems Journal* 36 (3): 446–456. doi:10.1147/sj.363.0446.
Egenfeldt-Nielsen, Simon, Jonas Heide Smith, and Susana Pajares Tosca. 2008. *Understanding Video Games: The Essential Introduction*. New York: Routledge. doi:10.1017/CBO9781107415324.004.
Egri, Lajos. 1960. *The Art of Dramatic Writing*. New York: Simon & Schuster.
Esslin, Martin. 1987. *The Field of Drama*. London: Methuen.
Field, Syd. 2005. *Screenplay*. New York: Delta.
Flaubert, Gustave. 1995. *Plans et Scénarios de Madame Bovary*. Edited by Yvan Leclerc. Paris: CNRS Editions.
Forster, E.M. 1985. *Aspects of the Novel*. New York: Harcourt Brace.
Frost, Laura. 2006. "Huxley's Feelies: The Cinema of Sensation in 'Brave New World'". *Twentieth Century Literature* 52 (4): 443–473. doi:10.1215/0041462X-2006-1001.

Galyean, Tinsley Azariah. 1995. "Narrative Guidance". In *AAAI Spring Symposium on Interactive Story Systems: Plot and Character*. Stanford, CA: AAAI.

Hales, Chris. 2015. "Interactive Cinema in the Digital Age". In Hartmut Koenitz, Gabriele Ferri, Mads Haahr, Diğdem Sezen, and Tonguç İbrahim Sezen (eds), *Interactive Digital Narrative*. New York: Routledge, pp. 36–50.

Koenitz, Hartmut, Gabriele Ferri, Mads Haahr, Diğdem Sezen, and Tonguç İbrahim Sezen (eds) 2015. *Interactive Digital Narrative*. New York: Routledge. doi:10.4324/9781315769189.

Koenitz, Hartmut, and Mirjam Palosaari Eladhar. 2019. "Challenges of IDN Research and Teaching". In Rogelio E. Cardona-Rivera, Anne Sullivan, and R. Michael Young (eds), *ICIDS 2019*, vol. 1. Cham: Springer International Publishing, pp. 26–39. doi:10.1007/978-3-030-33894-7.

Laurel, Brenda. 1991. *Computer as Theatre*. Boston, MA: Addison-Wesley.

Lavandier, Yves. 1994. *La Dramaturgie*. Paris: Le Clown et l'Enfant.

Manovich, Lev, and Andreas Kratky. 2005. *Soft Cinema: Navigating the Database*. Cambridge, MA: MIT Press.

Mateas, Michael, and Phoebe Sengers. 2003. "Narrative Intelligence". In Michael Mateas and Phoebe Sengers (eds), *Narrative Intelligence*. Amsterdam: John Benjamins, pp. 1–25. doi:10.1075/aicr.46.

Murray, Janet H. 2001. *Hamlet on the Holodeck: The Future of Narrative in Cyberspace*. Cambridge, MA: MIT Press.

Niesz, Anthony J., and Norman N. Holland. 1984. "Interactive Fiction". *Critical Inquiry* 11 (1): 110–129.

Rosa, Paolo, and Andrea Balzola. 2010. *L'arte Fuori di Sé*. Milan: Feltrinelli.

Ryan, James. 2017. "Grimes' Fairy Tales: A 1960s Story Generator". In *10th International Conference on Interactive Digital Storytelling*, 10690. Berlin: Springer Verlag. doi:10.1007/978-3-319-71027-3.

Ryngaert, Jean-Pierre. 1996. *Introduction à l'analyse du théâtre*. Paris: Dunod.

Saarinen, Leena. 2007. "Comedy Machine: Interactive Comedy as Rule-Based Genre". *Digital Creativity* 18 (3): 143–150. doi:10.1080/14626260701531969.

Sharpies, Mike. 1997. "Storytelling by Computer". *Digital Creativity* 8 (1): 20–29. doi:10.1080/09579139708567070.

2 Dynamic elements
The units

2.1 What are units?

In Chapter 1, Section 1.2.5 we saw that the narrative is the product of a certain sequence of actions, and we have used the word "actions" – until now – to informally describe the segments (episodes, scenes, sequences) of the story. From now on, we will refer to these segments as units in order to avoid confusion with the discussion in Chapter 1, Section 1.2.2.

By unit, we mean the element that results from a logical partition of the story, regardless of the way it is described. In Chapter 1, Figure 1.2, for example, the segment in which the message is delivered to the castle can be represented with the text "the messenger entered the main courtyard of the castle on horseback before the guards could stop him" (in the text-based story) or with a subjective film sequence of the messenger on horseback riding quickly under the entrance arch of the castle (in a video clip). In the text-based *Adventure* (see Chapter 6, Section 6.2), each description of the different places the player visits is intended as a unit, and the same is true for the CG renderings in *Myst* (see Chapter 6, Section 6.7) or for the immersive VR in *Down the Rabbit Hole* (see Chapter 6, Section 6.18); in *DramaTour* (see Chapter 6, Section 6.13), each unit is intended as a specific, very short video clip delivered by the mobile device, and the same is true for the on-screen cinematic sequences for *Bandersnatch* (see Chapter 6, Section 6.16).

If we trace the history of the rules that have been developed since classical oratory to govern a good narrative in a linear sense, we can see that the creation of a story requires a proper arrangement of the content; that is, the sequence of units that make up the story must be organised in some order. We have seen that in the age of computer the units can be sequenced by an algorithm. Therefore, a narrative computer system must depend on some partition of the story into units before it is able to elaborate an ordered sequence. This almost always requires that authors must know how to segment the narrative content they want to make interactive.

Aristotle believed that tragedy consisted of at least three basic parts (beginning, middle and end) (Aristotle 1998); Horace was the first to propose segmenting the drama into the famous five-act outline (13 BC) (Horace 1989, ll. 189–192), which

DOI: 10.4324/9781003335627-2

was maintained until the eighteenth century. In the textbooks and manuals of the nineteenth century, the parts of the dramatic action were no longer described in terms of entrances and exits of characters or changes in scenography, but in terms of phases of action. Gustav Freytag (1863) proposed five sequences of varying length (introduction, evolution, climax, fall and catastrophe) and was so influential that only some years ago Robert McKee (1997) suggested in one of the best-selling writing manuals that every story could be divided into five parts for all practical purposes (inciting incident, complication, crisis, climax, and resolution). In recent years, others, such as Syd Field (2005), have claimed that a good screenplay should instead be divided into three acts.

In the twentieth century, hypotheses about the partition of the story spread in many directions, based on various models: some success was achieved, for example, by the 12 parts defined by Vogler (1998), who adapted Campbell's (2008) hero's journey (that dates back to 1949) for cinema.

However, in the countless technical proposals for the composition of dramatic stories, the idea that there is some form of partition that allows the story to be segmented into units does not change. Moreover, it is common practice to assume that the smaller units can be grouped together in a fractal pattern to form larger units with the same properties (Lavandier 1994). Basically, a scene, a sequence and an act have the same structure (a similar organisation of actions) but different scales.

In the specific field of interactive storytelling, the evolution of practices shows that the notion of the narrative segment has been fundamental since the first experiments with electronic texts through which the reader could navigate, and which became known as hypertextual fiction (Box 2.1).

Box 2.1 The definition of lexia

Hypertext Fiction (HF) is based on the principles of segmentation and connection, where authors create screen-sized segments called lexia and connect them with various kinds of links. Those who read these screens browse the story by selecting links and uncovering new lexia or returning to those they have already visited (Koenitz et al. 2015).

The idea of combining segments continued to be fundamental, both in the creation of diversified multimedia content (video clips, graphics) and in the definition of atomic behaviours of individual agents. *Afternoon, a Story* (see Chapter, 6, Section 6.4) was composed by fragmenting the protagonist's stream of consciousness into small units that were assembled with an almost a-logical linkage; in *Façade* (see Chapter 6, Section 6.11), the story of a kind of chamber play is segmented into 27 scenes activated by the interaction between two synthetic agents and the player. Finally, it is clear that the entire video game industry has developed its own narrative modes based on editing practices first developed in cinema (Fassone 2017).

The notion of a story as a partition and organisation of elements that acquire a specific meaning precisely through their sequence is therefore almost ubiquitous in all literature dealing with linear, hypertextual or interactive fiction. Apart from the multitude of specific propositions, in this volume we understand units as basic entities of narrative structure whose main characteristic is that they contain a certain set of actions (at least one) of a character and whose sequence is ordered according to some kind of logical sequencing.

2.2 The logical relationship between the units

The sequence of narrative units may follow different rules depending on the nature of the story and the author's personal style. For example, the sequence may be determined by a temporal order (what precedes and what follows); or it may be based on a criterion of thematic analogy (different narrative units all revolving around the theme of travel) or stylistic (the units follow each other on the basis of correspondences between words, images), or the units may be linked merely as a stream of consciousness of the narrator (see *Afternoon, a Story*, Chapter 6. Section 6.4). In interactive storytelling, each of these ordering principles must be encoded in the system through a formal representation. For example, to implement a narrative in which units are ordered according to a causal logic, the ordering rule may apply a criterion of preconditions and effects. By preconditions, we mean the states that must hold for a certain incident (an action or event) to occur. Similarly, effects are the states that result from the execution of events. This causal logic requires that, to play the unit with the action "the heroine goes into battle", the precondition "war has broken out" must hold. And then the effects of the unit "the war is won" serve as a precondition for a hypothetical subsequent unit "the heroine celebrates with her comrades". The idea that certain actions have effects that form the starting point for further actions is one of the characteristics of narrativity. It is well known in psychology that narratives are fundamental to understanding intentional behaviour, i.e., that we give meaning to actions by embedding them in narrative structures (Bruner 1991; Mateas and Sengers 1999). This logic of cause and effect corresponds to the way we experience reality: we are cognitively predisposed to perceive the world as a sequence of causes and effects. A basic rule for the orderly sequence of narrative units can be based on the sequence of effects and preconditions.

In linear fiction, this logic can be rigorously enforced by the author. Often the point of editing a story is to reorganise the parts so that they flow in the way that is seen to be most effective. The whole power of fascination of the great novels of the nineteenth century rests on such perfect structure, and – for example, when reading *Anna Karenina* – the reader has the impression that the protagonist's story not only develops along a credible and logical line, but also flows in the only possible direction, in other words, the reader perceives that Anna's specific sequence of decisions leads her to throw herself under the train.

Such a strictly logical sequence in hypertextual narratives may represent a limit, as it could lead to a rigid causal and temporal sequence of events, resulting in a telescopic development of multiple and separate narrative strands. The risk for the author of following such a structure lies in creating a graph (i.e., a network of units and connections) in which a single beginning develops in countless separate directions, resulting in an excess of unused resources, since the units of a particular narrative strand can hardly be used in another narrative strand.

One solution is to design a graph in which a reduced number of branches fully develop the narrative to one or more proper closures, while the other branches are much shorter and clearly convey the need to explore different directions. This is the case with *The Invisible Guardian* (see Chapter 6, Section 6.17), where the player has to take several decisions for each chapter of the game and thus choose between different directions of the narrative. Most of the time, however, there is only one choice that brings the story to its final closure, while the other quickly leads the protagonist to a "bad ending" where the system returns the player to the unit where the last choice was made (see Figure 2.4).

Another possible solution may lie precisely in our bias to ascribe causality to a series of incidents in sequence. This bias can be used to create a narrative in which the actions are not strictly telescopic and in which there is still a sense of a logical development of events. This is generally defined as a loose narrative where the logical connection between a series of events is implied by some relationship (thematic, temporal, etc.). However, such logical connection is left to the interpretation of the audience rather than becoming an explicit description in the story (think again of the example of *Afternoon, a Story*, Chapter 6, Section 6.4, or the exploratory model of *Myst*, Chapter 6, Section 6.8). Instead of departing from the rule that the effects of one unit must be the preconditions of another, they are interpreted less strictly to include associations regarding the state of the agents, the organisation of topics and the arousal of emotions.

2.3 Organising the multilinear project

In the case of a linear sequence of events, as in Chapter 1, Figure 1.1, we recognise a story world (in our example, a historically defined setting, a warlike and romantic genre), some dynamic elements (the narrative units, but also the agents such as the king, the queen, the enemies), and we have a predefined logical sequence (first, the war breaks out, then the king dies). In the hierarchical multilinear model (see the graph in Chapter 1, Figure 1.2), we encounter the same factors, with the only difference being that there are several logical sequences. In the hypertext model (see the graph in Chapter 1, Figure 1.4), these factors remain the same, but the number of logical sequences increases, forming a structure that appears more complex. This complexity grows exponentially with the number of units that form the network of connections.

To manage the complexity, we need a strategy to organise the narrative material (the parts of the story). The first and simple solution is to group similar events related by themes or actions (Figure 2.1). Let us assume that the first three units (white background) are part of a beginning, the others (in light grey) are part of a middle event and the last ones (in darker grey) are part of a possible ending.

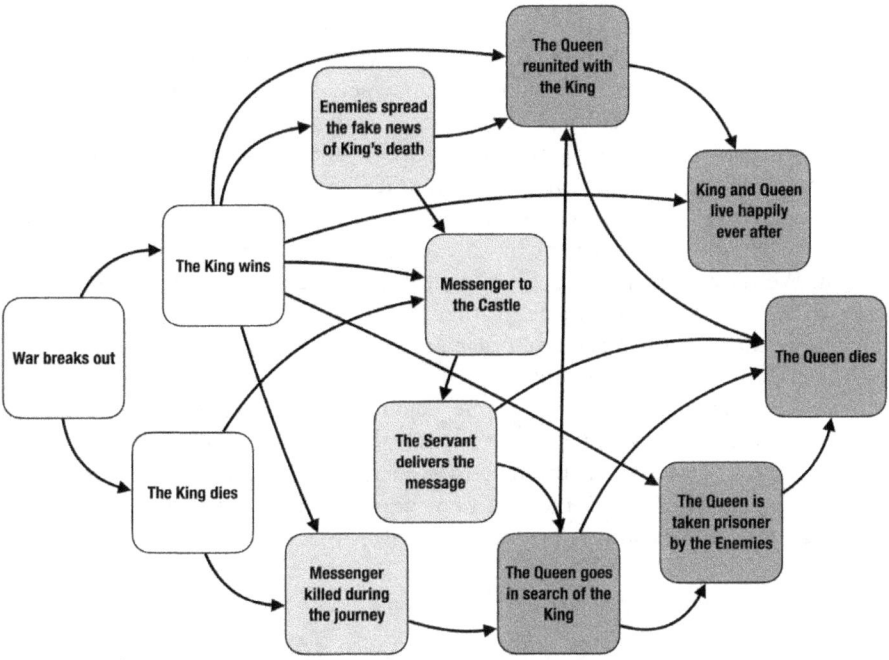

Figure 2.1 Example of tagging the hypertext

We superimpose a three-part structure on the network of incidents, as if they were three chapters, each connected to the next in a certain way (for example, a chapter begins after the king has won or respectively lost the war) (Figure 2.2). However, each chapter, for example, the one in which the state of the king (more analytically, the state of the agent king in the story world) is defined, could be articulated in different ways. For example, the king could be defeated immediately or after killing many enemies, he could die because he was betrayed, and so on.

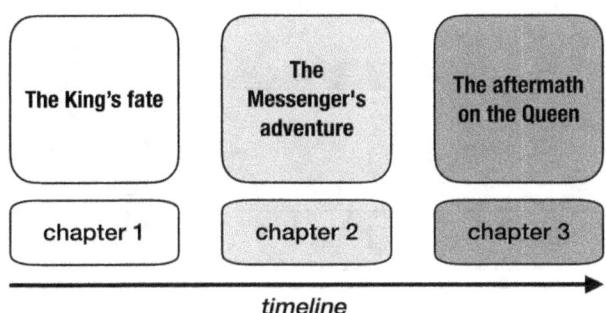

Figure 2.2 The division into parts

30 *Dynamic elements: the units*

We can think of each chapter as a multilinear or hypertextual network of possibilities leading to two different states of the world. At this point, the long and complex story of the fates of the king and queen could be a database of scenes and sub-scenes linked by specific changes of state, and each series of events could be understood as a chapter resulting from a specific and unique sequence of smaller units. In this way, we can simplify the various hypertext structures with a hierarchical structure, as in Figure 2.3. The idea of encapsulating the graph in chapters to avoid the rampant branching has proven to be a viable solution for narrative design. We have seen that *The Invisible Guardian* (see Chapter 6, Section 6.17) aims to balance the user's agency with the directionality of the film experience. Therefore, the narrative structure, organised as a graph, is divided into chapters (i. e., game levels), and in each of them the user is presented with several choices at different moments (Figure 2.4). At the beginning of the story, only one of the possible choices leads the user to the next chapter, while the other leads to a premature ending. Later, when the user has a better understanding of the situation and the characters involved, the plot branches out more decisively and the game offers several complex storylines with alternative closures.

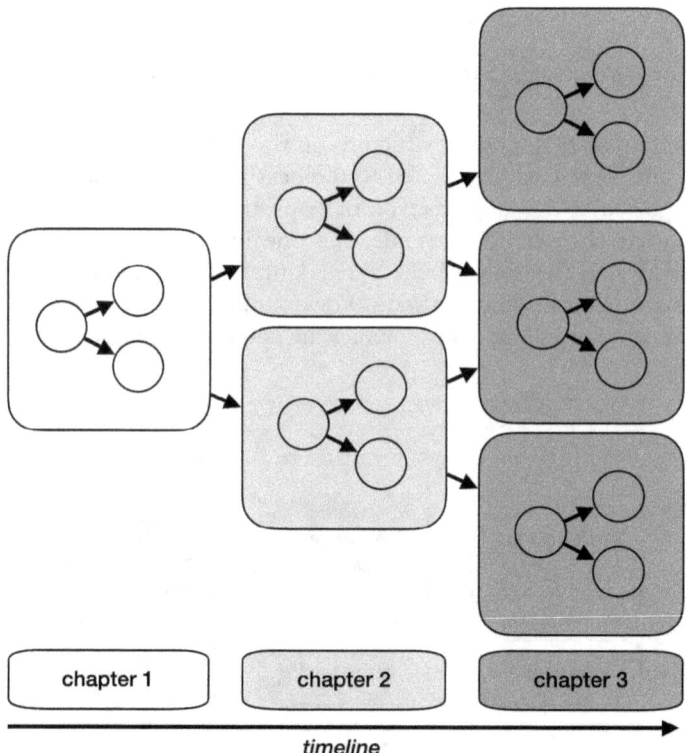

Figure 2.3 Grouping the different hypertext's units

Dynamic elements: the units 31

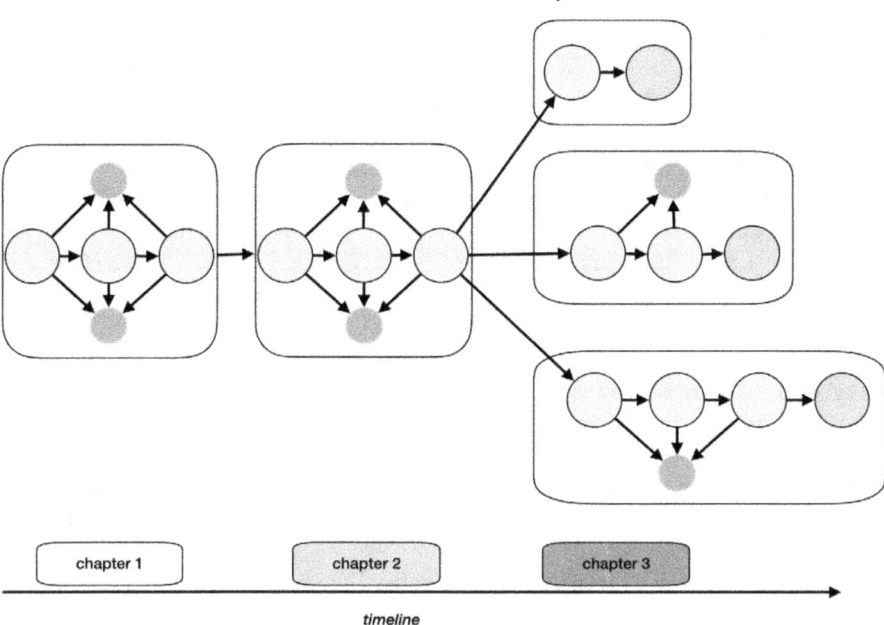

Figure 2.4 Grouping different hypertext's units and avoiding branching proliferation

2.4 What separates the units

The narrative unit can be described simply as a piece of a story. But this immediately raises the question of what distinguishes one piece of the story from another. In the broadest sense, such divisions are based on the human cognitive attitude of understanding events as finite. So when we observe a long action (but also when we think about it), we naturally tend to divide it into parts. This is our way of thinking, learning and planning.

In particular, our understanding of a story is based on being able to identify units that trigger and conclude a significant event in the plot (Lehnert 1981). In narrative, we intuitively know that the chapters of a book, the acts of a comedy or the sequences of a film tend to introduce, develop and conclude some action. This is also the reason why it is possible to induce suspense in the audience by interrupting a scene or sequence when the action has not yet been completed: the audience is kept in suspense in its expectation of the end of the action.

If the units have a beginning and an end, we can also argue that the end of one unit is such that it can be the beginning of another; and this leads to the question of what logic lines up the parts of the story.

In the case of the logical sequence of a minimal action, the rationale can be understood intuitively: reaching for the glass, for example, is followed by drinking. At the level of the story, however, the significant units usually represent more complex and articulated actions. In a story, it is not interesting that the character Bruno drinks, but that he gets drunk at a gala dinner or that he is poisoned by the murderer (perhaps the butler). In short, narratively significant actions have a greater weight and scope and cannot be linked only by a causal/temporal (telescopic) relationship where the second is a continuation of the first. Above all, the narratively significant units form the meaning of the story precisely because of the way they are sequenced and the motivations from which they spring.

Interactive narrative systems need to define both the criteria that identify the units (the database of dynamic elements) and the way in which they can be sequenced (i.e., ordered by the engine) (see Chapter 1, Figure 1.6). However, there is no clear method to delineate the boundaries of each unit.

One of the most intuitive methods might be to base it on the theme, i.e., to have a theme that encompasses the content described in the different units: a love story with a happy ending could be described in three units, such as two people meet and fall in love, she gets pregnant soon after and they move in together to start a family (Figure 2.5).

We could also rely on the characters' intentions to mark the boundaries as they shift: Alex wants to go to work, he wants to confront the boss, he wants to quit (Figure 2.6). In this case, the unit is assumed to begin when the character starts the action that follows his intention and ends when this has been achieved; or it ends when – for whatever reason – it is clear that this intention cannot be achieved.

Many of the specific solutions used in practice are based on general studies that have developed theories to define what drives the partitioning of events.

Following the observer point of view, Speer, Zacks and Reynolds (2007) propose the following definitions for the events:

- An Event is "a segment of time at a given location, that is conceived by an observer to have a beginning and an end; granularity of events can go from a second or less to tens of minutes".

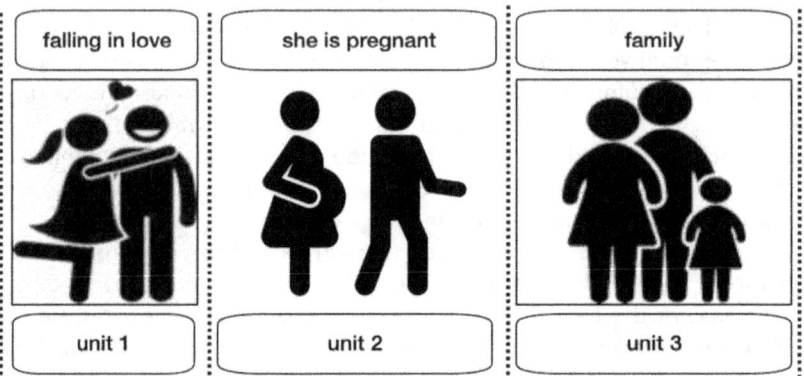

Figure 2.5 The partition of the units according to topics

Dynamic elements: the units 33

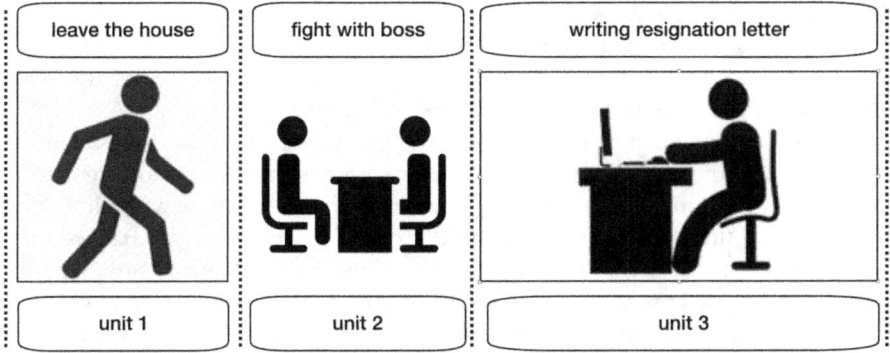

Figure 2.6 The partition of the units according to character's intention

- An Event model is "an actively maintained representation of the current event, which is updated at perceptual event boundaries".
- The Event segmentation is "the perceptual and cognitive process by which a continuous activity is segmented into meaningful events".

We know from psychology that readers structure a narrative text into a series of events in order to understand and remember the text. Relevant information for narrative encoding includes (Kurby and Zacks 2008):

- Time and Space information (as the presence of spatial changes, e.g., moving from one room to another inside a house can be meaningful);
- Objects, given the interaction of characters with elements of a scene;
- Change of Character, revealed by the changes of the subject of a phrase;
- Causes (causal relationship over activities) and Goals (new goal-directed activities), to be coded as core dimensions of Events.

However, the genre, style and theme of the story may influence the partition by different criteria. Those we have listed here are only examples. What remains important for the author is to define a consistent and effective partition system. In interactive storytelling based on exploration, we can intuit that the partition of the narrative unit is defined by the change from one place to another (as in *Adventure* in Chapter 6, Section 6.2, *Angels* in Chapter 6, Section 6.6 or *Myst* in Chapter 6, Section 6.7). In interactive storytelling based on a well-formed narrative, the boundaries between units are usually marked by a change of theme in the dialogue (*Façade* in Chapter 6, Section 6.11) or the status of the main character in the world (*The Invisible Guardian* in Chapter 6, Section 6.17).

2.5 Tagging the units: the metadata

To set the units in motion, i.e., to make the units truly dynamic elements in the composition of the narrative, it is necessary to know the role of the unit within the interactive story. This is also true for a linear story: as we know, a particular unit can be proposed at different points in the plot, resulting in different variants of its interpretation. But it is known that not all positions are possible. Sometimes the difference in interpretation by the audience can be truly sensational.

Let us consider cinema. The editing experiments carried out by Kulešov in the 1920s showed the face of a well-known actor with a neutral expression alternating with shots of various objects and people: a plate of soup, a corpse and a little girl, respectively. Although the actor's facial expression remained unchanged, the viewer could see hunger, horror or joy, depending on the following shots. The so-called Kulešov effect sees the shots as narrative units and the montage as generating the plot. From the perspective of interactive storytelling, or more generally of cinema as a database, the shots or units must contain knowledge that allows us to characterise the possible linearisation or plot. In addition to the kinds of composition we will see in Chapter 5 about storytelling systems, we anticipate here the way in which we can approach this knowledge representation in the units.

The characterisation of the content added to a digital object, i.e., a *resource* in a computer system, is called *metadata*, which is a datum about the datum. Metadata allows us to gain some information about the content without accessing the content itself. The immediate example is the *bibliographic record*, which contains the author, the year of publication, the number of pages and – very important – the position of a book in a library. Locating objects has been one of the most common goals in the use of metadata since the time of Dewey, who invented the modern library classification system in 1876. In summary, any object can be tagged with metadata and the type of metadata depends on the use of the objects within the systems. The specific use leads to the creation of a vocabulary from which labels are created to identify the objects. Typical applications are localisation, the selection or search for specific objects and, more generally, the management of available resources. In our case, the objects are the narrative units; the most important use is for ordering within a possible plot of the story. The metadata must therefore be suitable for the system that puts the units in a sequence. This is particularly important for interactive storytelling, as the units can be put together in different orders depending on the user's interactions. For example, the order of the units in Figure 2.6 is arbitrary. The three reported actions could be in any order, as in Kulešov's experiments, leading to different interpretations. Essentially, a programmed system could present them in this order, i.e., Unit01, Unit02, Unit03, based on a constraint on the order of the character's actions or even on the result of a user interaction.

The simplest metadata for the arrangement of the units is surely the insertion of an integer, modelling the constraints of the sequence. All possible plots will start with one of the units tagged with 1; units tagged 1 precede all units tagged 2; all units tagged 2 precede all units tagged 3, and so on. A graph of units is implicitly formed, with edges drawn between all units tagged i and units tagged i+1. This sequence, typical of a linear organisation of the story, can also be expressed in terms of "before" and "after", so the system that manages this kind of metadata includes a sequence function that implements a rule like the following:

If > a Unit, tagged 1 has been Presented> Then > Present a Unit tagged 2.

It is not difficult to imagine that the system could also manage other sequences, for example:

If > a Unit tagged 1 has been Presented> Then > Present a Unit tagged 2 OR Present a Unit tagged 3.

This simple logic, known in programming as conditional branching, would be sufficient to describe hypertextual stories such as the one described in Chapter 1, Figure 1.4.

A second way is to mark the role of units by explicitly defining the links to other units. The structure of the hypertext graph is subject to constraints other than the tagging with integers, and the units are not in a fixed position in the generated plot (there is no such thing as the set of first units, no set of second units, and so on). Instead, the sequence of the units follows the connections (edges) of a directed graph: a unit can only take its turn after the other units to which it is connected by an edge. This can also lead to multilinearity: many paths can be found in the graph; each path represents a plot that can be created by navigating the graph.

Finally, the tag can also indicate the content of the units. For example, one unit describes the departure to a place, another the arrival at the same place. The system may include composition rules that dictate that the departure unit must precede the arrival unit. In general, tagging requires the existence of a vocabulary from which the terms for labelling are taken. The vocabulary is in turn based on a model that describes, according to certain criteria, the story world.

Sometimes edges can also be tagged with labels that categorise the nature of the connections. For example, the tags can describe an action of the user (e.g., answer yes or no to a question, take a risk or be careful) and this corresponds to the orientation of the plot in a certain direction. The absence of edge tags may be related to a system that randomly selects the next running part of the story, but in general the tags are categorised according to the needs of the algorithm that runs the units (see Chapter 5).

For example, in the system used in the performance *DoPPioGioco* (DoublePlay) (see the description in Chapter 4, Section 4.3.2), the story is structured as a directed graph consisting of nodes (units) and arcs (edges). Each path from an initial node to an end node is a plot. The system provides sophisticated tagging of the units based on a psychological model of emotions to mark the emotional content of the unit. In this way, each unit of the story is tagged with different possibilities of logical continuations, from which the system can choose, based on the emotional tag. The system calculates the most appropriate continuation, both at the level of the story's consequentiality and at the level of the emotional atmosphere that the narrator wants to convey (Damiano, Lombardo and Pizzo 2018).

The informal annotation on the topics covered by the units can become formal tags and contribute to the generation of the plot. Using the fictional example in Figure 2.7 and the tags associated with the units, the system engine implementing the sequence could use these tags to order them and formulate the rule:

36 *Dynamic elements: the units*

Figure 2.7 Tagging the units

> Present unit tag = \ "start", if Unit tag = \ "start" was presented > Then > Present tag unit = \ "work".

In this case, as with the others, the sorting function can generate different sequences, since the tag "work" describes more than one unit, while maintaining the logic that determines the whole story (from home to work).

These are different ways of ordering a sequence of units. However, it is important that the algorithm that sorts the content can function according to the description metadata provided.

To summarise:

- Narrative units can be described by annotating the content using tags.
- Tags are categorised into functions or topics (technical features, themes, actions, characters).
- Categories are defined in relation to the goals of the interactive storytelling project and the system that implements it.

The tag system defined for the *DramaTour* project (see Chapter 6, Section 6.13), where a virtual character guides visitors through a historic house, allows users to experience an interactive story during their visit (Damiano et al. 2007). The categories used to tag the units encode the so-called dialogue functions. Here are the names of the functions and the corresponding objectives:

- *Prologue (P)*: introducing the context, the reason for the visit;
- *Socialisation (S)*: meeting the character, welcoming the visitor, providing coordinates;
- *Directional (D)*: guiding the visitor into rooms, suggesting a direction;
- *Phatic (F)*: confirming the character's presence, in the case of a long-lasting visit (the visitor sometimes may stop to carefully observe the site or wish to have breaks);

- *Ending (E)*: summarising for the final greetings, wishing a good continuation of the visit;
- *Informative (I)*: providing information and knowledge concerning the specific location of the visitor in the residence, the historical characters and events, the symbols.

The informative function, which refers to the rooms, the historical facts, the objects contained, etc., requires a variety of tags that reflect the complex nature of the content. For this reason, a metadata organisation was implemented that further specifies the informative function with tags distributed along different axes (Figure 2.8):

- *Chronological axis*: days and years, which develop along the temporal axis (12 August 1527, 1632);
- *Historical axis*: characters and facts that have had historical importance for the residence (Beatrice Langosco, the investiture of King Philip III);
- *Object axis*: objects and rooms distributed with hierarchical relations of collocation (a frame – a painting of King Carlo Alberto – the guard's room);
- *Symbolic axis*: symbols and recurring topics in the historical residence, without a particular order (love and betrayal, religious elements).

The system of multiple tags on the units creates an implicit hypertext that links the units through chronological succession, object hierarchy, similarity of topic, and so on. Depending on the narrative goals and the reactions of the user, who moves freely in the area of the historical house, the system sequences the units by traversing the axes, jumping from one axis to another, interrupting the information function with phatic units to make the user pause, or guiding the user to specific locations. The narrative goals are achieved by trying to apply as much as possible an ideal visit model that invites the visitor to walk through the different rooms and present the information in increasing detail. If the visitor moves quickly between rooms, *DramaTour* will provide more general information about the historical site. If, on the other hand, the visitor stays longer in one of the rooms, *DramaTour* will elaborate on the history of certain artefacts and also some historical gossip about the people who lived in that place (see Figure 2.8).

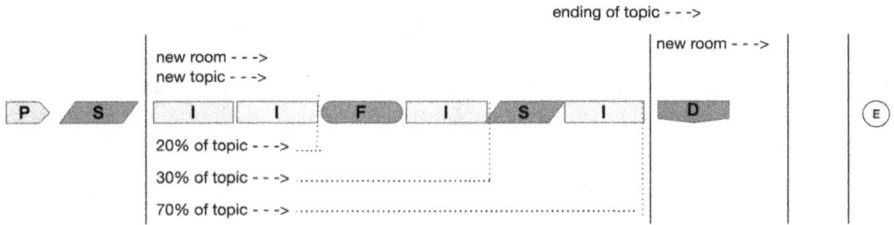

Figure 2.8 The ideal visit model for the interactive visit in DramaTour

38 Dynamic elements: the units

Another excellent example of unit tagging is the *Korsakow* system for creating interactive films, called K-films, starting from a database of units in video format (we mentioned it in Chapter 1, Section 1.3.4). A K-film project consists of minimal narrative units, called SNUs (Smallest Narrative Units), with associated keywords. A published K-movie consists of an HTML interface with a main video window that starts automatically when loaded in a web browser and other small visual elements that appear within the interface, such as buttons to load more video clips.

Each SNU is annotated with this metadata: the keywords, whether the clip must be an "initial SNU" or a "final SNU", the number of times the unit can be used in the generated plot (as referred to as "life" in video games), the possible display interface, whether the background soundtrack should be disabled while this clip is playing, whether the clip could be played in a loop, and finally, the probability that this clip is the result of keyword searches from other clips. All these attributes can be varied, so that the same unit with different values will show different behaviour in each K-film. The behaviour of the system is therefore much more complex than an explicit hypertext, since the sequence of video clips is processed in real time, starting from the user's selection. In fact, after an initial clip, the system calculates the possible sequences (based on the complex tagging) and proposes the set of possible choices; when the user selects the desired clip, a new calculation starts, etc.

What counts is the continuous multiplicity of variations between the available clips. As the film is viewed, new sequences emerge between the clips, and the viewer perceives that the work is the totality of these possible connections between its parts, and that each visualisation is always a new and different experience from the others.

2.6 Exercises

When taking the first steps in interactive storytelling, it can be helpful to draft simple short stories, with clear actions and with endings that provide closure for all possible sequences. When conceptualising the story, the author needs to be able to answer a few simple questions about the narrative: where is the story set? When? What is the state of the story world in which the narrative is set when the plot begins? Who are the agents at play? For example, we are in interstellar space in a science fiction future where a spaceship, sent by Earth to mine a valuable mineral on an asteroid, meets resistance from an alien spaceship. Depending on how these elements are taken into account, the author defines the premises and conflicts of the narrative: the spaceship's mission is threatened by the aliens. Next, the author must define the genre and style of the narrative (it is best to draw inspiration from examples with which the author is familiar), which provide a set of conventional elements for shaping the story. The author decides on either a collective protagonist (the spaceship crew, the army) or an individual (the commander-in-chief, the general) and must remain faithful to this choice throughout the narrative. Finally, the author must think of the possible endings that result from the changes that the different narrative units make from the initial state of the story's world: the spaceship defeats the aliens; the spaceship loses its cargo of valuable minerals; the aliens take over the spaceship.

2.6.1 The flow chart of dynamic elements

One way to experiment with interactive storytelling is to design hypertext narratives, that is, to build a plot as a graph of units (nodes) and connections (edges). At this point, the author must segment the story into narrative units. It is better to start with a small graph because this gives better control over the units and edges. The author needs to develop several storylines and perhaps different endings and ensure that each unit can be part of more than one sequence. It is important to keep the following points in mind: (1) limit the number of units to better control the branching of the story; (2) create alternative endings where different narrative sequences can converge; and (3) keep a good ratio between the number of units and narrative sequences.

This task can be simplified if the author already uses a pre-structured graph as a template for the narrative before writing the content for each unit. For example, the graph in Figure 2.9 has 13 possible sequences over 14 units (a ratio of 0.92). The edges are arranged to give direction (from a single unit A and two ends, units B and C) and also to avoid loops. Using a template, the author defines the specific content of each unit. It is better to start with an outline, a sentence describing the event that happens in the unit, which can later be refined to reflect the story: "The galactic cruiser *Sirius* is on a mission. It is leaving the Milky Way to approach a massive asteroid where there is said to be a deposit of valuable Klungon." Perhaps the author loves drama and only uses lines of dialogue, "Cruiser commander – *Sirius* to intergalactic base. We are leaving the Milky Way and approaching the asteroid: it looks like a colossal mass of Klungon from here." Or he/she may want to produce a short animation for each unit. Whatever the presentation, the narrative content needs to be well developed so that it is consistent across the different sequences.

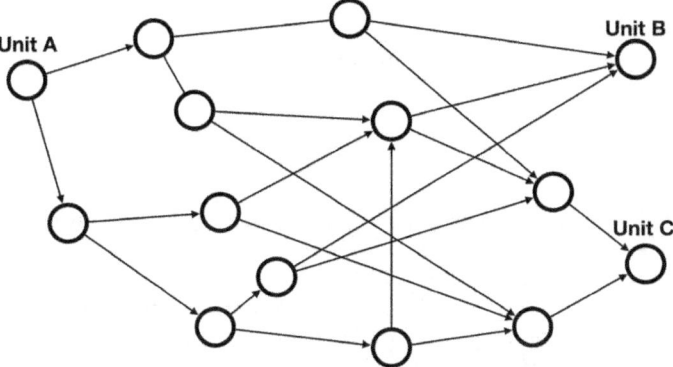

Figure 2.9 Example of graph with one beginning and two endings

40 *Dynamic elements: the units*

With Storygraphia software (https://www.cirma.unito.it/storygraphia/) the units can be connected by edges and the edges can be given labels. A navigation function makes it possible to test the possible sequences. Each time a story graph is written (i.e., saved) to a json file, another "storyprint" file is created with statistical information about the sequences and the units/sequences ratio achieved.

2.6.2 *The user actions*

The design must describe the actions of the users. For example, if the story revolves around the spaceship *Sirius*, the author may decide that the user acts as the collective protagonist (e.g., the spaceship). This will guide the creation of the edges and their description as actions. This helps the user to choose between two or more continuations with a diegetic motivation rather than as an external reader. The interactive story is more engaging if the user's choices correspond to actions in the fictional world. It is therefore desirable to devise a description for what we have so far only considered connections. To determine the possible actions of the user, the author must keep in mind what will happen in the following unit. The edge should not describe what will happen in the next unit. On the contrary, the edge can indicate choices, the result of which will be the content of the next unit. For example, if the edge leads to a unit whose content is "*Sirius* analyses the composition of the asteroid", it is advisable not to describe it with the action "analyse asteroid", but with the option "send a spaceship to the asteroid". In other words, the edge must contain an action that triggers the event contained in the subsequent narrative unit. In this way, the author leaves the results of their decisions to the users, rather than merely providing them with confirmations of their actions. The whole set of all edge descriptions, i.e., the descriptions of the possible choices, also serves to shape the character (the agent that the user is impersonating). For example, the author might decide that choices should always be "cautious and deliberate" vs "risky and impulsive"; or the author might present choices that are always guided by two or more conflicting moral values. In this way, the users see their character develop as they navigate through the story and learn that they experience agency as a diegetic action over the fictional world.

Using the software Storygraphia, users' choices can be expressed as edge labels and tested through the navigation function, possibly selecting the portion of the graph to explore.

References

Aristotle. 1998. *Poetics*. Edited by Stephen Halliwell. Chicago: University of Chicago Press.
Bruner, Jerome. 1991. "The Narrative Construction of Reality". *Critical Inquiry* 18 (1): 1–21.
Campbell, Joseph. 2008. *The Hero with a Thousand Faces*. Novato, CA: New World Library.
Damiano, Rossana, Cristina Gena, Vincenzo Lombardo, Fabrizio Nunnari, and Antonio Pizzo. 2007. "A Stroll with Carletto: Adaptation in Drama-Based Tours with Virtual Characters". *User Modeling and User-Adapted Interaction* 18 (5): 417–453. doi:10.1007/s11257-008-9053-1.

Damiano, Rossana, Vincenzo Lombardo, and Antonio Pizzo. 2018. "DoppioGioco. Playing with the Audience in an Interactive Storytelling Platform". *Advances in Intelligent Systems and Computing* 611. doi:10.1007/978-3-319-61566-0_27.

Fassone, Riccardo. 2017. *Cinema e Videogiochi*. Rome: Carocci.

Field, Syd. 2005. *Screenplay*. New York: Delta.

Freytag, Gustav. 1863. *Technik des Dramas*. Leipzig: Verlag von G. Birzel.

Horace. 1989. *Epistoles, Book II and Epistle to the Pisones (Ars Poetica)*. Edited by Neil Rudd. Cambridge: Cambridge University Press.

Koenitz, Hartmut, Gabriele Ferri, Mads Haahr, Digdem Sezen, and Tonguç İbrahim Sezen (eds) 2015. "A Concise History of Interactive Digital Narrative". In Hartmut Koenitz, Gabriele Ferri, Mads Haahr, Digdem Sezen, and Tonguç İbrahim Sezen (eds), *Interactive Digital Narrative*. New York: Routledge, pp. 11–21.

Kurby, Christopher A., and Jeffrey M. Zacks. 2008. "Segmentation in the Perception and Memory of Events". *Trends in Cognitive Sciences* 12 (2): 72–79. doi:10.1016/j.tics.2007.11.004.

Lavandier, Yves. 1994. *La Dramaturgie*. Paris: Le Clown et l'Enfant.

Lehnert, Wendy G. 1981. "Plot Units and Narrative Summarization". *Cognitive Science* 5 (4): 293–331. doi:10.1207/s15516709cog0504_1.

Mateas, Michael, and Phoebe Sengers. 1999. "*Narrative Intelligence*". In American Association for Artificial Intelligence – FALL SYMPOSIUM. Vol. 13. doi:10.1016/S0890-4065(99)80003-6.

McKee, Robert. 1997. *Story: Substance, Structure, Style and the Principles of Screen Writing*. New York: Regan Books.

Speer, Nicole K., Jeffrey M. Zacks, and Jeremy R. Reynolds. 2007. "Human Brain Activity Time-Locked to Narrative Event Boundaries: Research Article". *Psychological Science* 18 (5): 449–455. doi:10.1111/j.1467-9280.2007.01920.x.

Vogler, Christopher. 1998. *The Writer's Journey: Mythic Structure for Writers*. Studio City, CA: Michael Wiese Productions.

3 Dynamic elements
The agents

3.1 Agent and audience

In the narrative, the agents act to arouse in the audience some interest in their fate. An agent who does not elicit an emotional response from the audience is like a motionless character in a video game, practically useless, it disappears from the viewer's field of vision; at most, it becomes an element of scenography, the environment, or decoration. Of course, there are such auxiliary elements in the narrative and they are important for the overall effect: patrons in a bar, passers-by on the street, and so on. However, we will not deal with these types of characters, which, although they belong to the database of dynamic elements, are comparable to objects. As we shall see, the notion of agent can be well summarised as an intentionality whose manifestation plays a key role in the development of the narrative and the emotional involvement of the audience. However, this does not mean that the agent must always be understood as an individual character. We can also consider certain groups of people (the crowd in the stadium, an army battalion, etc.) or the elements that group them together (a battleship) as agents of the story, if they show intentional actions from which a will is inferred and with which other agents or the audience must interact.

So, an agent of the narrative is intended as a dynamic element that shows at least the following characteristics:

- having at least one intention, a goal that is the result of its own deliberation;
- performing at least one activity resulting from an intention;
- displaying emotions;
- interacting with the environment;
- interacting with other agents.

As the research and production of interactive stories have developed, the relationship with a single agent initially followed the dialogic model developed by chatbots, and has later overcome this to go further. In fact, many recent projects tend towards a social dimension with multiple agents, where the user controls the behaviour of some characters and interacts with other autonomous characters. In Chapter 2, we saw that one of the simplest forms of interactivity in a narrative is to

Dynamic elements: the agents 43

allow the audience to choose how to continue the story by selecting one of the edges in a graph of narrative units.

If the system involves the user's interaction with a single autonomous agent, the narrative content of the unit emerges from that interaction. Accordingly, the system might be able to determine the order of the units by calculating the effects of the interaction with the agent, rather than following the user's explicit choice from a list of possible continuations. For example, in one unit, the queen talks to the servant, who tells her about the battle against the enemy. Only when she knows that the king has won (precondition) can the system proceed to the unit in which she travels to her husband in view of the victory (effect). In this context, the unit is not to be understood as a given content (a text, a video clip), but as the result of a certain interaction session between the agents involved in the story (one of which is controlled by the user). The effects of the units are in fact a description of a certain state of the world of the story. Basically, the user who experiences the story influences the unfolding of events through his or her interaction with the artificial agent (Figure 3.1).

The same principle applies to interactive storytelling, where the user participates in an action (involving multiple agents), and the sequencing of the units is similar to the previous case, although the action is more complex. Essentially, the unity of the narrative emerges from the arrangement of actions between different agents (including the user). Even if the user interacts with only one of the available agents, the other agents react to what happens and the effects of the unit are still the consequences of the overall interaction. That is, all agents are involved in the action that determines the effects of that unit (Figure 3.2). For example, the sequence of beats in *Façade* (see Chapter 6, Section 6.11) depends on how the player and the two artificial agents (Trip and Grace) interact (Figure 3.2). Note that even if the player only talks to one

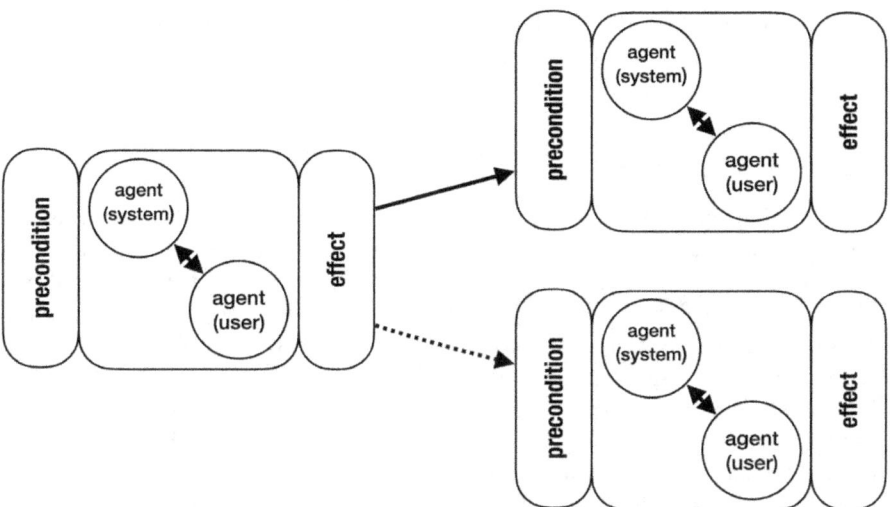

Figure 3.1 Sequencing the units by the interaction with an agent

44 *Dynamic elements: the agents*

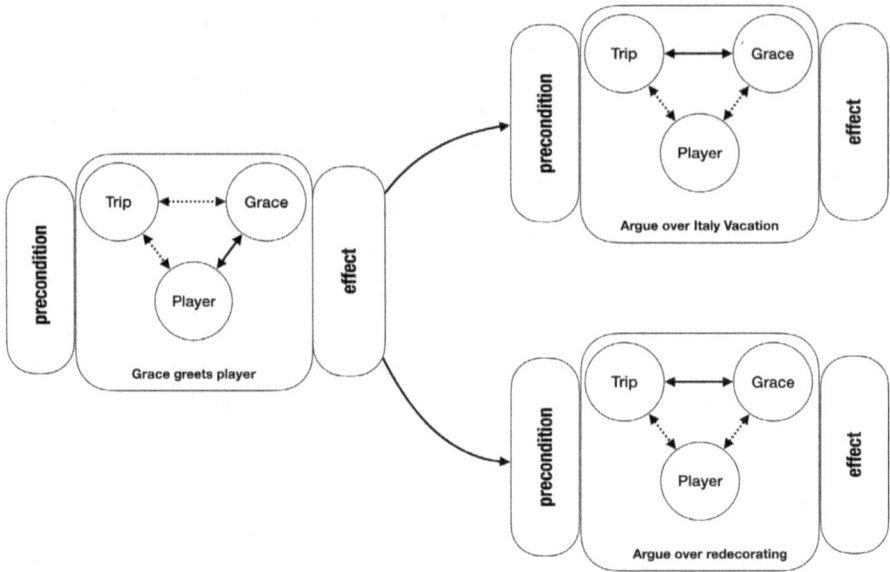

Figure 3.2 Sequencing the units by the interaction with multiple agents in Façade

of the two agents, the other will work out its own response and this will affect the sequencing of the next beat.

The interaction with a single agent could be developed as a series of sessions with a chatbot, where the end of a session coincides with the end of the narrative unit and the beginning of a new session, starting, for example, with a topic covered in the previous session. The case of multiple agents usually requires more complex programming based on the intelligent agent paradigm. Namely, in this case, the effects of a unit result from the calculation of the states in which the different agents find themselves, taking into account their objectives and the plans intended to achieve them.

3.2 Intelligent agents

While the implementation of single agents is often inspired by the conversational models typical of chatbots, the use of multiple agents in interactive storytelling draws on models derived from Artificial Intelligence (AI). The term intelligent agent (Wooldridge and Jennings 1995) is usually used for agents that are endowed with autonomous decision-making ability. The one-to-one model of chatbots allows the agent to be programmed to respond (with text or actions) to a specific action by the user (in the simplest implementations, they do not even retain memories of previous interactions with the same user). Therefore, even if we were to connect multiple chatbots together, we would simply multiply the individual interactions, as in Annie Dorsen's experiment/show *Hello Hi there* (2010), in which two screens on stage chatted about different topics, including Shakespeare's *Hamlet* (Felton-Dansky 2019).

A multi-agent model, on the other hand, can be seen as a kind of ecosystem in which each agent pursues its own goals and evolves and changes in relation to the others. But to create this ecosystem, each agent must have at least one goal, act accordingly and be able to "understand" what the other agents desire and how they behave. For this reason, intelligent agents are characterised by their ability to maintain and update at any time a representation of the state of the story world and of the other dynamic elements involved in the story. The standard model for describing intelligent agents, often referred to as the BDI model – an acronym made up of the terms Belief, Desire, Intention – is based on three basic elements: Beliefs, Goals (a term that has supplanted the more poetic but generic term "Desires") and Intentions (Rao and Georgeff 1995) (Box 3.1).

> **Box 3.1 The BDI paradigm of intelligent agents**
>
> - *Belief*: the agent's beliefs, intended as what the agent knows (in logic, the concept of knowledge is derived from that of belief), which include statements about both the state of the world and the way in which actions and events operate on it to change its state. Beliefs concern the story world facts, as well as the dynamic elements that are part of it, and their states, at any given moment.
> - *Desire*: the agent's objectives, often described as goals that the agent wishes to achieve, and which are usually described as a particular state of the world that the agent wants to bring about.
> - *Intention*: the agent's intentions are the action plans formulated by the agent, which are intended to achieve a goal, or objective, based on what the agent believes about the current state of the world, the future state to achieve, and the way to achieve it through actions.

The BDI model, developed in the 1980s from the philosopher Michael Bratman's (1987) theory of "bounded rationality", relies on a rational view of behaviour. Once the agent has formulated and adopted a goal, selecting it for active pursuit among all the available ones, he/she/it elaborates the most appropriate plan of action to achieve that goal, and intentionally executes it. Bratman's theory is inspired by folk psychology, i.e., common-sense theories of behaviour that assign meaning to the actions of human beings. Note that this feature is important for procedural authors because it ensures that the behaviour of BDI-inspired agents will be readable by a human audience, following what Daniel Dennet (1987) has called the "intentional stance" that characterises our cognition.

Action plans, then, give to the agent's behaviour that character of long-term recognisability and stability which, according to philosopher Susan Feagin (2007), underlies Noël Carroll's (2001) notion of "narrative closure". Feagin has identified in Bratman's theory the accurate representation of the particular sense of anticipation ("forward-looking") that, according to Carroll, makes a narrative compelling and leads us to perceive the character's observable actions as a consequence of the premises (their goals) and in line with the expected behaviour (the ongoing action plan that we recognise as a unity).

At the heart of Bratman's theory is the notion of commitment, which we might see as the commitment to achieve one's goals. This purely human notion has specific properties that have been formalised in Philip R. Cohen and Hector J. Levesque's (1990) logical account of the BDI model. Once committed to a goal, the agent drops it only under a certain limited set of conditions, which we can easily attribute to the narrative characters: when the agent fails without appeal (heroes are resilient; they try at all costs before giving up); when the agent finds that the goal has already been achieved (accidentally or through the initiative of another character); when the agent's motivation has ceased (namely, the goal was instrumental to the achievement of another goal that was dropped). These features alone are sufficient to explain many of the behaviours of a typical heroine in an adventure game:

1. The queen will threaten the captured enemy to learn the place where the king is held captive.
2. If the threats prove ineffectual, she will order the enemy to be chained by the neck (thus retaining the same goal, but changing the method of achieving it until she either succeeds or no method is feasible).
3. If an army explorer arrives with the information she needs, she will immediately abandon this plan (the goal of learning the location of the prison has already been achieved, regardless of her actions).
4. Moreover, when the queen learns that the war is won and the king returns home, she will immediately leave the captured enemy and embark on new adventures (the goal of rescuing the king, which was the cause of the interrogation, has been dropped, so the goal of finding the prison is also dropped).

As the above example shows, the BDI agent model assumes the ability to devise plans, a key component of artificial characters of any kind. In Artificial Intelligence, the ability of an agent to select the most appropriate sequence of actions to achieve a goal is the object of study of automated planning research. For example, suppose that Evelyn wants to go from home to the university campus: given this goal, Evelyn might plan a route that includes a walk from home to the nearest bus stop, a bus ride to the university bus stop, and finally a short walk to the campus entrance. The sequence of the three steps above can be seen as a plan to achieve her goal. Note that each of the three steps can in turn be considered as a separate plan aimed at an intermediate goal (getting to the first bus stop, getting to the university bus stop, getting to the entrance of the school). Planning can indeed be seen as a hierarchical construction that is progressively refined to the desired level of detail: for example, the bus journey includes smaller steps such as boarding the bus, stamping the ticket, finding a free spot, recognising the right stop, and getting off the bus. In real life, but also in fictional worlds, planning requires a certain flexibility: if there is no bus leading to the university stop, Evelyn must devise an alternative plan (cycling to the underground, taking the underground, walking to the university). The ability to react to unpredictable obstacles (a bus strike) is crucial to give naturalness to artificial characters but requires a more sophisticated approach that keeps track of alternatives in advance.

From the procedural author's point of view, the hierarchical nature of plans can be seen as an opportunity, as it allows the author to focus on the more abstract, general level of a character's behaviour and leave it to others (humans or machines) to describe it in detail or to postpone this task to a later time. At the same time, this example points out that some specific actions (walking, taking a bus, riding a bike) can occur in more than one plan and that we know exactly under which conditions they can be performed and why. However it is organised, it is clear that the agent's ability to plan its behaviour is based on a specialised source of knowledge in which all actions known to the agent are stored.

The combination of the BDI model, originally developed as an abstract, logical model (ibid.), with automatic planning is what characterises the architecture of the Procedural Reasoning System (PRS). Originally developed to control autonomous devices such as spacecraft, PRS has transformed the purely logical relationships between the agent's beliefs and goals described by the abstract model into a software entity capable of deliberating and executing its own behaviour autonomously, soon attracting the attention of scholars in the field of interactive digital storytelling. In PRS and in subsequent implementations of the BDI model, the bridge between the agent's goals and its actions is provided by an automatic planner. Given the agent's goal, the planner synthesises from the agent's knowledge one or more appropriate action sequences to achieve the goal. Note that in this type of architecture, the knowledge of how to behave in the world belongs to the individual agent, which allows the author to give each agent something personal in their decisions. A software implementation of this model is the language HAP, developed by Brian Loyall and Joseph Bates as part of Project Oz at Carnegie Mellon University, to program and control artificial characters living in fictional worlds, such as the cat Lyotard (Bates, Loyall and Reilly 1994).

Over the last two decades, research in interactive storytelling has made considerable efforts to develop planning systems that generate the behaviour of artificial characters. The aim of this particular area of research, sometimes referred to as "narrative planning", is to devise strategies for creating and modifying attractive action plans, intelligible by the audience and, above all, predicable and thus controllable by the author. In this context, two different paradigms have emerged, both borrowed from classical AI: Partial Order Planning (POP) and Hierarchical Task Network (HTN) planning. While these two paradigms can in principle lead to the same agent behaviours, they correspond to two different approaches to managing artificial characters. While the former, Partial Order Planning, can be seen as an implementation of theatrical improvisation, the latter, Hierarchical Planning, is more akin to the practice of directing well-designed, carefully constructed characters.

3.2.1 Planning as improvisation

In Partial Order Planning (POP), the planner synthesises plans by combining basic actions into sequences that achieve the desired goal, making it difficult for the author to anticipate all possible combinations of actions. In this case, the building blocks manipulated by the planner are basic actions (go to the bus stop, stamp the ticket, turn over a stone, etc., collectively referred to as the "action library"), which in isolation are of little importance to the construction of the character. However, this limitation is compensated by a higher variability in the generated plans, which can be advantageous from the point of view of narrative and dramatic invention.

Technically, the planner proceeds incrementally, selecting actions one at a time from the "action library" and combining them into sequences of increasing length to create a plan that makes the story world evolve from the current state to the desired state. The planner can proceed forward or backward, using rules of thumb called heuristics to effectively guide the selection of the next action. When going forward, the planner starts by adding to the (initially empty) plan an action that can be directly executed in the current state of the world. In the example above, the heroine can begin her adventure in the royal castle by executing one of the actions that are possible from there (duel, journey, etc.), but only the action of travelling to the dragon's lair puts her in a state where she can perform the action of questioning the dragon about the secret location of the treasure. After adding the first action, the planner calculates the state of the world that would result from the execution of this action, and from this hypothetical state it proceeds in the same way, adding another action, until it eventually reaches the desired state. The sequence of actions thus obtained is the complete plan. Note that in each step, when two or more actions can be applied, the plan is split and several plans are created in parallel.

Backwards, the planner starts from the desired state of the world and searches the library for actions that lead directly to that state (in our example, questioning the dragon might be a possible action to know the location of the treasure); the construction of the plan then continues by searching for other actions that match the initial conditions of the selected action. The backward journey ends when the initial state is reached, getting a complete plan.

Regardless of how you choose to build the plan (forward or backward), the plans created will have some desirable properties. First, it is possible for some actions to be performed in different orders (hence the term "partial ordering"), making the resulting plan more flexible and therefore more suitable for interactive contexts (Riedl and Young 2005). For example, a character who is supposed to seduce his/her partner might devise a plan that consists of buying a box of chocolates and a bouquet of flowers, two actions that can be performed in any order. So if the user unexpectedly changes the state of the world by moving the character to the flower shop, the plan could still be executed (first flowers, then chocolates). Furthermore, if during the execution of the plan there are unpredicted changes in the state of the world (e.g., if the character realises that the tank of his car is empty), the plan can easily be repaired by inserting the action of refuelling in the middle.

The disadvantage of this approach is that it is difficult for the procedural author to figure out all the possible sequences that can be created from the character's action library – in addition to the burden of carefully specifying all the properties of each action, one by one: who can perform it, what resources are needed to perform it (for example, for a certain kind of purchase you need a car, a certain amount of money, etc.), what are its preconditions (to buy the bouquet, you must be at the florist's), what are its effects (having the bouquet but less money in your wallet). Methods have been developed to synthesise actions from large collections of behaviours, but this does not solve the problem of controlling the generated behaviour, in fact it exacerbates it.

3.2.2 Planning as directing

As described above, in POP, great effort is put into the precise description of the individual actions in order to carefully delimit their conditions of use, since they could in principle be placed anywhere in plans. In most life situations, however, people follow a very different strategy and rely on canned recipes for everyday tasks: we do not need to plan how to get to our workplace every day unless something unexpected happens. Planning with Hierarchical Task Networks (HTN) relies precisely on this strategy: plans are not composed of small units, but described at a general level and gradually refined by adding details as the execution time approaches. Rather than describing the single actions, HTN planning describes the agent's ability to act as a series of "recipes" or pre-made plans to achieve a particular goal. These recipes, called tasks, are partially independent of specific realisations: for example, the conventional recipe for seduction might be to invite your partner, buy them a small gift, meet them at the place you have chosen, offer the gift, make a romantic proposal, etc. To compensate for the rigidity of this approach, the steps that make up a task in the HTN paradigm usually contain some limited alternatives. For example, the action "invite" can be done in person, by phone or by SMS. Moreover, some steps (or subtasks) can in turn be decomposed into sub-actions ("invite" could be decomposed into "conceiving the invitation message", "selecting the communication mode", etc.). As a result, the agent's behaviour is controlled by a well-defined set of predefined schemas (its tasks) that are interconnected and form a "network" (Aylett et al. 2007; Cavazza, Charles and Mead 2002).

From a theoretical point of view, this paradigm well represents the resource-saving strategy typical of humans, as described in Bratman's (1987) "theory of bounded rationality": in most cases, human planning consists of identifying the high-level task appropriate for the goal at hand and adapting this task to the context by making choices during execution. After all, if the protagonist leaves home to change her life and then she presents her resignation to the boss, we do not care whether she gets to the office by foot or by car.

From the author's point of view, the HTN approach provides tighter control over the character's behaviour because the definition of plans excludes the behaviours that, although possible in a combinatorial approach, would not correspond to the author's intended definition of the character. In other words, writing the character's behaviour in HTN planning requires careful planning in every respect, as the author must work out in advance the character's strategies to achieve his or her goals, despite the obstacles that may arise in the story world. This advantage, which we can relate to Aristotle's notion of the Unity of Action, is obtained at the price of two important limitations: first, the flexibility of plans is limited to the alternatives foreseen from the beginning; second, the specification of agent behaviour is more complex than in the POP alternative, where one can simply keep adding actions to the library without worrying about their use. However, this requires a coherent top-down construction of the character's behaviour: unity of actions comes at a price. Consider the example of *Façade* described in Chapter 5, Section 5.8.3 and in Chapter 6, Section 6.11: in this case, the authors had to use an HTN plan language to write the plans describing all the phases of the guest reception: the preparation of a drink, the conversation, etc., specifying in advance all the alternative realisations of these plans, which at run time, give life to the variability of the drama in response to the user's choices.

HTN planning, in the context of a BDI agent, can model the transition from a state A, in which the agent is at the beginning of a unit, to a state B (among others that we do not consider), that the agent reaches at the end of the unit. The agent selects a goal (from the set of its own goals) that fits state B. For example, the agent Frank wants to try out a new pair of skis and forms the commitment to achieve this goal. To do this, he develops a plan (skiing in the mountains) that must be broken down into subtasks in order to be completed: (1) leave the house; (2) mount the ski rack on the car; (3) drive to the ski resort; (4) put on the skis; (5) get the ski pass; (6) use the ski lifts. But the subtasks also have to be further divided again, and so on, until the level is reached where the actions can be carried out without further planning. Note again that this way of modelling plans allows intelligent agents to reformulate their actions in relation to what is happening and the behaviour of other agents only when explicitly planned. For example, if subtask (3) fails because the car breaks down, the HTN can remain valid only if plan contains an alternative way (e.g., take the train or continue the journey with a rented vehicle).

3.2.3 Scripting as planning

Although there are examples where the two main approaches to planning described above are combined, it should be clear that the choice between one paradigm and the other is an important issue in the design of an artificial agent. With some exceptions, the POP paradigm (which defines behaviour from single actions) is better suited to character-centred contexts (see e.g., Martens et al. 2013) where it is necessary to generate many alternative behaviours without the need to control the quality of the story and therefore without having to define a specific narrative or dramatic model (e.g., in the case of *Madame Bovary*, Cavazza et al. 2007).

The HTN paradigm and its variants are more useful in story-centred contexts, when one wants to emphasise the dramatic dimension of the story and direct it towards specific conflicts and outcomes. Complex multi-agent plots, such as those created to control the characters in *Façade*, belong to this category, where the behaviours of the characters who jointly carry out the invitation must be coordinated in advance and follow a predetermined sequence of high-level steps (Mateas and Stern 2005). Another typical example of this approach can be found in the work of Cavazza (Cavazza, Charles and Mead 2002), which translates the seduction strategies of the characters in the television series *Friends* into plans. In this experiment, the NPC playing the role of Ross relies on an HTN network to achieve the goal of seducing Rachel: for example, to find out Rachel's feelings for him, Ross can resort to various strategies, such as reading her secret diary or obtaining information from her friends. Once this subtask is somehow completed, the subsequent task is to attract Rachel's attention through some alternative initiatives, such as giving her a gift or sending her a message, and so on until the conclusion. Thanks to a well-specified direction, this HTN will always lead the story to a set of predefined outcomes and will do so through a predictable sequence of steps, overcoming obstacles as planned in advance. However, this is achieved at the cost of very limited variability in the user experience and may only be suitable for simple comedy-of-art-style characters.

A possible compromise between the two approaches is to restrict the development of plans to a limited number of "trajectories" compatible with the author's intended dramatic direction. This approach is exemplified by the system designed by Julie Porteous and Marc Cavazza (2009), in which the generation of plans is limited to those that enforce the constraints posed by the author to represent the dramatic curve of the story. For example, plans that would lead to "trivial" stories with no conflicts are excluded from the outset (see Chapter 5, Section 5.4.3). To demonstrate their approach, the authors applied it to the plot generation of the film *Goldfinger* (USA, 1964), imposing constraints designed to complicate the plot and make it compelling (ibid.): for example, the planner inserts a scene in which James Bond is captured by Goldfinger, creating a temporary superiority of the evil character over the good one. The creation of these events serves to build a crescendo of tension that would not be possible if the secret agent could devise his own plan to sabotage the villain without the seductions, unexpected events and reversals of fortune that arouse the audience's interest and tension. Although this example illustrates the use of constraints in the generation of a linear plot, the same approach can also be used to dynamically adapt the story to the audience's interventions, while remaining consistent with the direction set by the author.

3.3 Emotions and agents

So far, we have seen agents as the fundamental element in the construction of a story, since their intentions determine the development of the incidents in the story. Indeed, the protagonist's goals play an important role in directing the user's attention and engagement. But even more important than the deliberations themselves is the outcome of the deliberation processes, not only because of the practical changes they bring about in the story world, but also because of the intangible emotional impact they have on the characters, which is anticipated and reverberated by the audience. It is therefore necessary to include an emotional component alongside the rational model of the agent, which is responsible for describing the agent's emotional states and how they arise.

3.3.1 *The (mental) reality of emotions*

The BDI model we have proposed as a paradigm for human behaviour is based on pure rationality, albeit viewed through the lens of bounded resources and folk psychology: in the BDI model, the agent's knowledge, goals and plans are explicit and inherent in the logic of the world. However, this approach is clearly insufficient to represent the emotional component of character.

However, since the BDI model is inherently "mentalistic", i.e., derives observable behaviour from the (unobservable) mental state of the agent, it lends itself to the integration of emotions, which can be regarded as mental states of a certain type. Thus, a goal may want to achieve the state "happiness", or we might formulate a plan whose achievement requires another agent to be in the state "fear".

By casting the previous example in the BDI paradigm, the queen does the following:

- (*Belief*) *knows* the king is at war (the agent's knowledge of the world);
- (*Desire*) *wants to* see the king (the goal that belongs to the agent);
- (*Intention*) *intends to* meet him (the plans the agent makes to achieve its goals).

If we assume that the achievement of a plan brings about a certain state of the world (in this case, the queen meeting the king), we can also encode the way it affects the emotional state of the characters, namely that the plan eventually brings the queen to a state of "joy":

- (*Emotion*) *feels* joy (as a consequence of meeting the king).

Considering emotions as mental states of the agent can be a simple and effective solution to integrate emotions into the behaviour of intelligent agents, but the broader and more complex question of how to define the generation of emotions (i.e., which configurations of states of the world, successes, failures can determine which emotions) remains open. In the context of interactive storytelling, the most successful way of describing emotions is based on a family of theories called "appraisal theories" (Scherer 1982; Ortony, Clore and Collins 1988; Scherer, Schorr and Johnstone 2001): intrinsically utilitarian, appraisal theories assume that the agent evaluates ("appraises") the state of the world on the basis of its compliance with its own goals, feeling positive emotions, such as hope and joy, when they are bound to be achieved or are actually achieved, and negative emotions, such as fear or distress, if the state of the world is evolving in a direction that puts them at stake.

3.3.2 The social component of emotions

The notion of "goal" that we have used so far to describe the purposeful behaviour of agents shows a relevant limitation with respect to the definition of emotions: the agent's goals in the emotional domain cannot be reduced to the states of the world that the agent wants to achieve through action plans, but are something elusive, since they belong to the social and moral domain. In appraisal theories, the appraisal process includes not only the agent's goals but also the so-called moral standards (Ortony, Clore and Collins 1988) or moral values that determine moral emotions, such as shame and pride. Moreover, all emotions, moral or not, cross the boundaries of the self and connect agents with social and emotional ties. In addition to emotions that relate to the self (self-oriented), the agent also experiences emotions that relate to the other agents (other-oriented), for example, the queen may rejoice at her consort's victory and empathically accept his goals because of her bond with him. Or she may feel blame for the despicable behaviour of a knight who deserted, and anger in case this behaviour could harm her part.

In artificial agents, the appraisal theory of Ortony, Clore and Collins (1988) (often referred to as the OCC model) has been translated into a set of rules for activating emotions that associate each emotion type with a configuration of agent's beliefs, values and goals (Bates, Loyall and Reilly 1994). For example, the queen's belief that the king might be killed in the war determines an emotional state of fear whose intensity depends on the probability of the event. Similarly, her censure of her knight's misbehaviour determines an emotion of blame, the intensity of which depends on how censurable the behaviour is and how much intentionality she ascribes to him in pursuing it. Moral values thus become not only a secondary, accessory element of the narrated story, but a lever that the author can pull to control the characters according to a code, emotions, that is easily understood by the audience (Battaglino, Damiano and Lesmo 2013).

3.3.3 Emotions as a behavioural driver

In addition to the achievement (or failure) of one's goals, theories of emotional appraisal assume that the process of appraising the state of the world from the perspective of emotions (filtered through the agent's point of view) is influenced by a set of parameters (probability, severity, responsibility, etc.) that determine the intensity of the emotions; in parallel, emotions tend to decrease over time due to similar factors. The computation of emotional states can be integrated into BDI agents by applying the appraisal rules to the agent's beliefs, values and goals as the story unfolds (Bates, Loyall and Reilly 1994). However, in parallel with the emotions generated, the agent model must also include a way to describe how the emotions affect the agent's behaviour after they have been felt: this process, known in psychology as emotional coping, is very important for controlling the behaviour of artificial agents, as it provides the link between emotional states and their consequences at the behavioural level (Roseman 2013). Emotional states, after all, influence not only our cognition (panic, for example, can alter risk perception), but also our decisions and actions (the knight who feels remorse might try to undo the consequences of his actions by going back to the queen's court).

A paramount example of integrating the emotional dimension into a BDI agent architecture is FAtiMa (Mascarenhas et al. 2022), the agent architecture underlying the *FearNot!* system (see Chapter 6, Section 6.12), aimed at training children to respond effectively to bullying episodes through interactive storytelling (Aylett et al. 2005). In FAtiMA, the BDI agent incorporates a two-fold track for activating emotions: in addition to the appraisal process, the agent also has a set of reaction rules to generate the basic predefined affective and behavioural responses, such as the one that determines the protagonist's surrender and escape in the face of a bullying event (and which will hopefully evolve into a non-automatic, more productive behaviour in the course of the interaction with the audience). The EMA architecture (Marsella and Gratch 2009), which integrates appraisal and coping into a comprehensive model, relies on a series of emotional frames (a concept borrowed from classical AI) that handle, within a unified conceptual framework, both the activation of emotions and the manipulation of these emotions as a consequence of the ensuing behaviour. For example, the agent's control over a source of risk that endangers one of its goals (a thief entering the room and threatening the agent's life) leads to different behavioural responses depending on whether the agent has a low or high control over it: a high and uncontrollable risk factor triggers a panic reaction and a predefined aggressive behaviour; the same factor with a high controllability triggers an emotional state of fear and a more articulated, planned behavioural response (such as chasing the thief away); in both cases, however, the cause of the emotion will have been removed as a result of the generated behaviour.

3.4 Exercises

Starting from a library of actions, a plan can be synthesised in two different ways: starting from the current state of the world, adding one action after another until one obtains a sequence of actions that can bring the initial state of the world all the way to the specific configuration that is the goal state (e.g., prize won, girl met, etc.); or, taking this final configuration as the starting point, by reasoning backward, action by action, until one obtains a complete plan whose first action can be straightforwardly executed in the current state of the world.

In order to enable this kind of reasoning by a formal device (a planner that controls the behaviour of an agent intended as a dynamic element of the story), actions must be encoded according to a precise scheme that facilitates the focus of the procedure, which is to apply it to a given state of the world to determine how it will change in response. According to this scheme, we encode for each action its preconditions, i.e., the facts that must be true for the action to be executable in any state of the world, and its effects, i.e., the facts that will be true after the action is executed, regardless of the state of the world in which it is executed.

If the plan is well formulated, the effects of each action will make the preconditions of the subsequent action true, from beginning to end, or, in planning terms, from the initial state of the world to the goal state.

An assumption behind this approach is that the way we describe facts is the same when describing actions and when describing the state of the world: if the state of the world contains the fact "got key" (suppose we are describing the action of opening a door) and the corresponding fact in the action preconditions is "got pass", a formal system will not be able to match them. So, when doing this exercise, be careful about the formulation of the facts.

3.4.1 Describing the state of the world

We describe the initial state of the world of a narrative universe in which a country girl must save her little brother from a monster who has kidnapped him. To do this, she must put the monster to sleep by giving him a special dish that he likes to eat after spiking the food with a strong sleeping potion. She cannot cook the monster's favourite dish without the right ingredients, which she obtains from an old lady in return for her help, and she has to get the sleeping potion from a sadistic wizard as a prize for solving a crossword puzzle.

In Storygraphia software, states can be introduced in the PAINTING mode. They can be set as initial states by posing them as preconditions to initial units, that is units tagged with the tag "INITIAL".

3.4.2 Writing the actions

First, write down the list of actions that occur in this story, in the order that seems right to you. If you realise that some actions can be executed in different orders, write a different plan for each possible order (this is why this approach is called partial order planning, because it allows the actions in the plan to be only partly arranged according to a fixed order). After this step, consider how each action in the plan enables the execution of the next action: ideally, the effects of each action in the plan should make true the preconditions (one or more) of the following action(s): getting to the monster's den results in being at the monster's den, the precondition of feeding the monster.

3.4.3 Writing preconditions and effects

Having reflected on these relations, it will be easy to write down the list of facts that constitute the preconditions and effects of each action, for example, getting the potion, giving the potion (and getting to the monster's den between the two):

- Action: get_potion
    a   Preconditions: completed_crossword, be_at_wizards
    b   Effects: have_potion

56 Dynamic elements: the agents

- Action: give_potion
    a   Preconditions: be_at_den, have_potion, dish_ready
    b   Effects: monster_sleeping

Note that we assume that each action affects only those facts that are explicitly stated as its effects. Thus, it is not necessary to provide an exhaustive list of the facts that will be true after the action is executed. For example, if the agent is at the wizard's place when she gets the potion (be_at_wizards), it does not need to be explicitly stated that the agent will remain there after she gets the potion, since this is taken for granted.

In Storygraphia, states can be written following the guidelines defined here, and assigned as preconditions/effects to each unit. The system also computes the licensed edges when all the preconditions required by the unit (action) are satisfied by the effects of another unit (PAINTING mode).

For the sake of completeness, notice that real planning systems explicitly list also the facts to be deleted after the action has been executed. After going from the wizard's place to the monster's den, for example, the fact that the agent is at the wizard's place should be deleted from the state of the world, as it is overridden by (and incompatible with) the fact that it is now at the monster's den; for simplicity, however, we consider this minor inconsistency acceptable in the context of this exercise.

3.4.4 Simulating the execution

After encoding the actions, the plan can be tested by simulating its execution. Start by encoding the initial state of the world: again, this will be done as the list of the facts that hold in it:

- World_0:
- at_home
- imprisond_brother

Now, the first action (getting to the old lady's hut, for example) can be applied to the World_0, getting World_1:

- World_1:
- at_hut
- imprisoned_brother
- ...

... until the end of the plan. By doing so, it is possible to verify if the plan (or plans) are sound, making sure they could be manipulated by the narrative engine (the planner, in this case).

In this exercise, as well as in Section 3.4.5, Storygraphia supports this test through the Navigation mode, also by selecting the sections of the graph to be explored.

3.4.5 Starting from the goal state

As a complementary exercise, reverse the perspective and start creating the plan from the goal state: in this case, you'll need to describe it accurately as you have done for World_0, by stating explicitly all the facts that must be true in that state of the world.

3.4.6 Reusing the plan

When the action library is ready, you can think about expanding and reusing it: try to imagine alternative developments of the story and similar stories. Or try to make plans for the other characters: the old lady, the monster, etc. Alternative developments of the story create the possibility of involving the user in the story advancement, taking decisions about what the protagonist should do (and perhaps opening up different endings if alternative goal states have been encoded); plotting plans for characters allows different users to play different characters, with possibly different outcomes – try to figure out the possible interactions between them to assess the complexity of the task from the procedural author's perspective. States used as preconditions or effects provide an indirect representation of plans in Storygraphia: for a plan that licenses the action of a unit, its preconditions and effects are inserted into the unit; the effects will be missing in case of plan failure.

References

Aylett, Ruth S., S. Louchart, J. Dias, Ana Paiva, and Marco Vala. 2005. "FearNot! – An Experiment in Emergent Narrative". In Themis Panayiotopoulos, Jonathan Gratch, Ruth Aylett, Daniel Ballin, Patrick Olivier, and Thomas Rist (eds), *Intelligent Virtual Agents*. Berlin: Springer, pp. 305–316. doi:10.1007/11550617_26.

Aylett, Ruth, Marco Vala, Pedro Sequeira, and Ana Paiva. 2007. "FearNot! – An Emergent Narrative Approach to Virtual Dramas for Anti-Bullying Education" . In Mark Cavazza and S. Donikian (eds), *Virtual Storytelling: Using Virtual Reality Technologies for Storytelling*. Berlin: Springer, pp. 202–205. doi:10.1007/978-3-540-77039-8_19.

Bates, Joseph, Aaron Bryan Loyall, and W. Scott Reilly. 1994. "An Architecture for Action, Emotion, and Social Behavior". In Cristiano Castelfranchi and Eric Werner (eds), *Artificial Social Systems*. Berlin: Springer, pp. 55–68. doi:10.1007/3-540-58266-5_4.

Battaglino, Cristina, Rossana Damiano, and Leonardo Lesmo. 2013. "Emotional Range in Value-Sensitive Deliberation". In *Proceedings of the 2013 International Conference on Autonomous Agents and Multi-Agent Systems, AAMAS '13*. Richland, SC: International Foundation for Autonomous Agents and Multiagent Systems, pp. 769–776. doi:10.5555/2484920.2485040.

Bratman, Michael E. 1987. *Intention, Plans and Practical Reason*. Cambridge, MA: Harvard University Press.

Carroll, Noël. 2001. *Beyond Aesthetics: Philosophical Essays*. Cambridge: Cambridge University Press.

Cavazza, Marc, Fred Charles, and Steven J. Mead. 2002. "Interacting with Virtual Characters in Interactive Storytelling". In *Proceedings of the First International Joint Conference on Autonomous Agents and Multiagent Systems Part 1 – AAMAS '02*. New York: ACM Press, p. 318. doi:10.1145/544741.544819.

Cavazza, Marc, Jean-Luc Lugrin, David Pizzi, and Fred Charles. 2007. "Madame Bovary on the Holodeck: Immersive Interactive Storytelling". In Rainer Lienhart, Anand R. Prasad, Alan Hanjalic, Sunghyun Choi, Brian P. Bailey, and Nicu Sebe (eds), *Proceedings of the 15th International Conference on Multimedia*. New York: ACM Press, pp. 651–660. doi:10.1145/1291233.1291387.

Cohen, Philip R., and Hector J. Levesque. 1990. "Intention Is Choice with Commitment". *Artificial Intelligence* 42 (2–3):213–261. doi:10.1016/0004-3702(90)90055-5.

Dennet, Daniel C. 1987. *The Intentional Stance*. Cambridge, MA: MIT Press.

Feagin, Susan L. 2007. "On Noël Carroll on Narrative Closure". *Philosophical Studies* 135 (1): 17–25. doi:10.1007/s11098-007-9098-8.

Felton-Dansky, Miriam. 2019. "The Algorithmic Spectator: Watching Annie Dorsen's Work". *TDR – The Drama Review: A Journal of Performance Studies* 63 (4): 66–87. doi:10.1162/dram_a_00875.

Marsella, Stacy C., and Jonathan Gratch. 2009. "EMA: A Process Model of Appraisal Dynamics". *Journal of Cognitive System Research* 10 (1): 70–90. doi:10.1016/j.cogsys.2008.03.005.

Martens, Chris, Anne-Gwenn Bosser, João F. Ferreira, and Marc Cavazza. 2013. "Linear Logic Programming for Narrative Generation". In Pedro Cabalar and Tran Cao Son (eds), *Logic Programming and Nonmonotonic Reasoning*. Berlin: Springer, pp. 427–432. doi:10.1007/978-3-642-40564-8_42.

Mascarenhas, Samuel, Manuel Guimarães, Rui Prada, Pedro A. Santos, João Dias, and Ana Paiva. 2022. "FAtiMA Toolkit: Toward an Accessible Tool for the Development of Socio-Emotional Agents". *ACM Transactions on Interactive Intelligent Systems* 12 (1). doi:10.1145/3510822.

Mateas, Michael, and Andrew Stern. 2005. "Structuring Content in the *Façade* Interactive Drama Architecture" . In *Proceedings of the AAAI Conference on Artificial Intelligence and Interactive Digital Entertainment* 1 (1). Cambridge, MA: AAAI Press, pp. 93–98. doi:10.1609/aiide.v1i1.18722.

Ortony, Andrew, Gerald L. Clore, and Allan Collins. 1988. *The Cognitive Structure of Emotions*. Cambridge: Cambridge University Press. doi:10.1017/CBO9780511571299.

Porteous, Julie, and Marc Cavazza. 2009. "Controlling Narrative Generation with Planning Trajectories: The Role of Constraints". In Ido Iurgel, NelsonZagalo and Paolo Petta (eds), *Interactive Storytelling*. Berlin: Springer, pp. 234–245. doi:10.1007/978-3-642-10643-9_28.

Rao, Anand S., and Michael P. Georgeff. 1995. "BDI Agents: From Theory to Practice". In Victor Lesser (ed.), *Proceedings of the First International Conference on Multiagent Systems 95*. Cambridge, MA: AAAI Press, pp. 312–319. doi:10.1.1.51.9247.

Riedl, Mark O., and R. Michael Young. 2005. "*Open-World Planning for Story Generation*". In IJCAI'05: Proceedings of the 19th International Joint Conference on Artificial Intelligence, pp. 1719–1720. doi:10.5555/1642293.1642625.

Roseman, Ira J. 2013. "Appraisal in the Emotion System: Coherence in Strategies for Coping". *Emotion Review* 5 (2): 141–149. doi:10.1177/1754073912469591.

Scherer, Klaus R. 1982. "Emotion as a Process: Function, Origin and Regulation". *Social Science Information/Sur les Sciences Sociales* 21 (4–5): 555–570. doi:10.1177/053901882021004004.

Scherer, Klaus R., Angela Schorr, and Tom Johnstone (eds) 2001. *Appraisal Processes in Emotion: Theory, Methods, Research*. New York: Oxford University Press.

Wooldridge, Michael, and Nicholas R. Jennings. 1995. "Intelligent Agents: Theory and Practice". *The Knowledge Engineering Review* 10 (2): 115–152. doi:10.1017/S0269888900008122.

4 Display
Audience, system, emotions

4.1 Participation

4.1.1 Narratology vs ludology

In the short history of interactive storytelling, one of the issues that has divided those studying or practising this creative field for the longest and most crucial time has been precisely the use of categories, methods and definitions from narratology. It was Janet Murray who hypothesised that digital media, including video games, can be understood as tools of storytelling (Murray 2001). Others, most notably Aarseth, argued that in order to understand video games and the whole field of interactive entertainment, it was necessary to drop narratological categories and instead use those that are more derived from ludology (Aarseth 1997). This rivalry for supremacy between historically established narratology and the new ludology in such a promising field has not really come to an end. However, the latter has established itself as a scientific field of research and an academic discipline.

In practice, games that use storytelling can be expected to increasingly integrate narrative components with elements of game design, leading to a stronger narrative role for computer-controlled characters and also greater dramatic tension (Koenitz et al. 2015). At the level of theoretical elaboration, epistemological tools for the analysis of narrative fiction can be extended by the ludological perspective (Walton 1990).

In essence, the debate has led to the complementarity of the two approaches. The most widely held view is that this complementarity is the result of an increasing presence of artificial intelligence techniques in the design of games and digital narrative works:

> Advances in AI for computer-controlled characters might be particularly beneficial for providing narrative coherence in online games, to orient players' actions and to provide narrative hooks and closure. Today, narrative in multiplayer or the sandbox game is relatively rudimentary, principally because of the technical and logistical challenges in orchestrating a coherent experience for a multitude of players at once.
>
> (Koenitz et al. 2015, p. 154)

This dialogue between different schools of thought and disciplines was useful, however, because it revealed two poles, or rather two perspectives, for understanding audience participation.

On the one hand (narratology), audience participation is subject to the requirements of the narrative and thus to criteria such as organicity, structure and coherence of the experienced story. On the other hand (ludology), participation is primary and achieves its purpose precisely when it allows the best possible expression of action and control.

In any form of storytelling, the actions performed in the narrative do not merely provide information about the unfolding of events: they have the important goal of building the emotional participation of the audience. One of the most important ways to achieve this participation is to create characters with whom the audience can form some kind of bond. This has traditionally been the task of the authors of stories for all media (from print to television) and a large proportion of textbooks devote much attention to this aspect. In the context of interactive storytelling, this emotional participation must fall within the realm of the system's computational competencies. In other words, the system must process emotional data along with the other various data about the events in the narrative.

4.1.2 Interaction vs narration

The authors of interactive stories always face the age-old paradox of interactive storytelling (IS): how to incorporate interaction into a well-structured story while maintaining a satisfying and well-crafted plot for those who experience it? (Louchart and Aylett 2003; Mateas and Stern 2007; Crawford 2013). Louchart et al. ask, "How could IS authors and a system's artificial intelligence (AI) reconcile the demands of a carefully structured story experience with the necessary freedoms (movement, decisions) one would expect to grant an interactive user?" (2015, p. 185).

According to Mateas and Stern (the authors of *Façade*, see Chapter 6, Section 6.11), interactive storytelling projects have historically been based on predetermined paths with a low degree of procedurality and have therefore been forced to compromise between these two goals. They point to the earliest examples of hypertextual interactive storytelling, where the connections between events were rigidly designed to maintain a well-formed plot but which, on the other hand, offered users little control as they were limited to navigating predetermined paths with no ability to change or adapt the sequences (Mateas and Stern 2007).

Alternatively, design can go in the opposite direction, producing interactive experiences that have greater user control and a higher degree of variability, but a lower degree of coherence, rhythm and causality compared to well-formed stories (a typical example of this is the postmodern style of *Afternoon, a Story*, Chapter 6, Section 6.4). The authors of interactive narrative content may therefore choose to minimise the constraints on the arrangement of the story's units to allow for more variable sequencing and interaction. This solution (which we referred to as "loose narrative" in Chapter 2, Section 2.2), if not used sparingly, can result in sequences that lack the development typical of well-formed dramatic arcs, so that the plot appears fragmented into disjointed actions that lack direction and closure.

On the other hand, an encyclopaedic, non-procedural design approach, where the author increases variability by creating a large number of units, but all rigidly strung together to control the flow of the narrative, may not be the most effective solution in terms of resource management. The authors of the stories (from novels to television series) tend – understandably – to have strong control over the possible sequences. The most immediate solution in interactive storytelling might be – only seemingly – to define all possible plots. However, if one wants to multiply plots to increase variability and choice for the user, the most likely consequence would be to multiply the number of units to be produced. If this seems complicated for a text-based work, the task becomes much more difficult if the units are to be produced as multimedia content. The proliferation would also drive up production costs exponentially, making it virtually impossible to accomplish. In summary, the ratio between the content produced and the possible narrative sequences should be carefully weighed up.

4.1.3 Balancing the agency

One of the ways to mitigate the effects of the paradox, and also the most commonly used, is to balance two types of agency (Box 4.1).

> **Box 4.1 Agency**
>
> Although the notion of agency can generally be understood as the ability to act in the physical and social world we inhabit, the practical and theoretical development of human-computer interaction has produced a particular meaning. According to Murray (2001), the sense of agency in multimedia computer use means that one is in control, that one is in command of the situation. Over the decades, the sense of agency has become crucial to user experiences, and it is what the interactive entertainment industry pays most attention to in product design.

In the context of interactive narrative works, agency is mainly defined in two ways.

- *Local agency*: This indicates the ability to control the immediate consequences of the user's behaviour. For example, I press a handle and the door opens, I fire a gun and the target is hit.
- *Global agency*: This indicates the ability to change the overall context in which we act through a structured set of behaviours. For example, I show loyalty to a character and over time she begins to tell me certain secrets.

In many ways, local agency seems less problematic in its implementation. Even intuitively, it is not difficult to imagine a logical implementation that can maintain the relationship between the action of shooting an arrow and the effect of hitting the target. However, it presupposes a more detailed control over the execution of actions in the story world and the more so, the more the execution resembles the physical world: The action of opening a door will evoke a greater sense of agency if it is represented by the action of a hand on a handle rather than a button you have to click on the screen. A narrative that wants to combine a highly structured narrative sequence with the possibility of audience control could be structured as a combination of episodes in which the user's actions are given great freedom and immediate consequences, with less free moments in which the results of those actions are used to drive the narrative in a particular direction. This is partly the structure used by many adventure games. When the actions performed reach a predefined goal, a new clip is triggered that concludes the previous sequence and leads into the new chapter (Figure 4.1). In summary, there is a clip that introduces the story and the environment, followed by an episode in which the player has a great deal of freedom of action.

However, the question remains how to ensure that the sum of the actions carried out can influence the subsequent chapters, or even how they can emerge from the interactions undertaken so far. This is a complex problem with several and different solutions, some of which concern planning (Chapter 3) and others the automation of the action and the dynamic elements (Chapter 5).

There is no doubt that global agency has been implemented more and more over the years: consider, for example, the evolution from the very limited options players had with story elements in *Dragon's Lair* (1983) or *Mad Dog McCree* (1990), to the many and complex options available in *Assassin's Creed: Odyssey* (2018), or the consequences that behaviours have in the relationships between characters in *The Walking Dead* (see Chapter 6, Section 6.14).

4.1.4 Intensity of the process

It must be remembered, however, that agency is not the sole and comprehensive assessment of the quality of the interactive work, and it must not be ignored that agency can sometimes be fictitious, with the sole purpose of fooling consumers into thinking that they have some control over the products they consume. However, it must also be noted that the increase in agency has been made possible

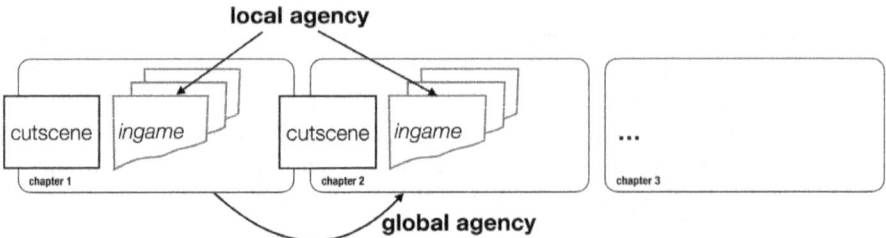

Figure 4.1 Local and global agency in a videogame structure with cutscenes

by the availability of increasingly powerful computers. That is, computers are able to process larger amounts of data and faster. This computing power can increase global agency because the system can calculate the complex dependencies that the user's choices have on the unfolding of the narrative at a high level: for example, if the user shows an attitude towards political strategy, the system could, over the course of the narrative, create the conditions for the user to embody the role of "foreign minister" rather than "army general". Chris Crawford describes the relationship between computer activity and media resources as the opposition between Process Intensity and Data Intensity or, in other words, the extent to which a program emphasises processes (algorithms, equations and branches) over data (tables, images, sounds and text). In the first case, the program spends most of its time crunching numbers; in the second case, it mainly moves bytes around (Crawford 2003). The value of process intensity corresponds to the ratio of computations to multimedia resources processed by the system. If an interactive storytelling work (a game or other type of work) only triggers the playback of multimedia content in response to the user's interaction, then we are talking about data intensity, i.e., the code does very little work and the system essentially reads bits from a memory (offline, online) and displays them through the device. If, on the other hand, interactive storytelling processes, elaborates or generates multimedia resources, then it is about process intensity. The more resources are generated in real time and with the help of algorithms, the higher the process intensity. In Chapter 5 we will see how this can be understood more precisely as the level of automation with which the narrative engine intervenes in the construction of the plot and the generation of the dynamic elements. At the current state of technological development, we can assume that there is a direct relationship between the intensity of the process and the richness of interactivity. If the system allows the user a high level of interactivity and control, then it is necessary to invest in the coding of computational processes that constantly analyse the interaction and thus support the control of the story. This means that sequences, and perhaps the resources that compose them, are created on the fly in response to the user's actions, while computational effort is devoted to maintaining narrative coherence. In *Façade*, for example, not only is the sequence of scenes in the plot created on the fly by the narrative engine, but in each individual scene the actions of the two artificial characters are organised into coherent behaviour in real time, taking into account the actions of the player. Although rich interactivity can be achieved with the increase of offline resources (data intensity), it is reasonable to conclude that a higher process intensity corresponds to a greater richness of interactivity (Mateas and Stern 2007).

4.1.5 User's action

In any work defined as interactive, the individual units must contain at least one action by the user (e.g., turning a block in the old Tetris game or moving a card in a game of Solitaire), even if there is almost no narrative. Even if it has no dramatic tension, even if it involves no interaction with fictional agents, even if it minimises the complexity of the plot, a work must contain a user action to be defined as interactive.

Therefore, user action is a pivotal element of interactive storytelling. In fact, almost all analyses of interactive works focus on describing how interaction is designed and experienced. This is because interactive storytelling works are largely determined by the actions of the participants. It is no coincidence that many human and economic resources have gone into developing more and more new interaction methods.

One of the innovations that made *Adventure* a success in 1976 (see Chapter 6, Section 6.2) was to write text commands that were not significantly different from natural language. Instead of writing a line of code or pressing a specific command key on the keyboard, one could write the action by putting together a verb and an object complement ("open door", "eat food", "kill ogre", etc.). The computer checked whether this sentence was appropriate in the game world and in the specific situation, and then prompted the next narrative content. The most important thing is that this solution simulates a natural interaction with the machine and thus with the story world. In the same way, we can understand the evolution that the video game industry has made with the introduction of physical interfaces (from the Wii® to Kinect®). The latter made it possible to overcome the dexterity problem required to use traditional gamepads and to simulate a physical interaction based on a more natural body behaviour.

This direction of interface development is known as the "bodily turn" and has been enabled by the ever-increasing integration of a whole range of sensors into our devices that capture our relationship with the physical world (movement, location, speed) (Knoller and Ben-Arie 2015). The current evolution of this trend is live and immersive role-playing games, where players engage their bodies directly into the virtual space where the story unfolds. However, it is important that users are not only aware of the action they are performing, but also of the consequences of the sequence of events, i.e., they must be able to appraise the consequences (e.g., failure or success) of the action performed as a result of a deliberation process.

Through the deliberation of the action and the evaluation of its impact, the user experiences one of the most important features of interactive storytelling (and also one of the most discussed): the "sense of control". Many of the actions performed by participants in an interactive storytelling work manifest the power of control over an element of the story. Conversely, the sense of control stems from the efficacy that users can attribute to their actions during storytelling:

> [A] reader, whether of Charles Dickens or Henry James, is likely to feel that the fictional world she has inferred from the novel is in some final sense mysterious and unknowable, beyond her grasp, beyond that of even the most willing author. By contrast, the reader of a finite interactive text is likely to feel that she can know and master this fictional universe ... The genre imitates action, rather than reflection, since if one makes a mistake and one's persona is killed, it is a simple matter to start over again
>
> (Niesz and Holland 1984, p. 122)

The sense of control enables the user to participate as an agent in the story. That is, it is not enough to 'do things', but the user must feel that they have power over the flow of events. This is an element whose central importance in a video game is also intuitively understood: players must know that they have the means to "win" and they must not, under any circumstances, find that they are winning without having intended to do so. In this case, the intention underlying the action, the guiding principle of the rational action model (which has been incorporated into the BDI model – Belief, Desire, Intention – see Chapter 3, Section 3.3.1), would indeed be missing. But in other contexts, where the nature of interaction is less traditional and structured, some new solutions and strategies open up. In the show *Best Before* (2010) by the German theatre company Rimini Protokoll, each audience member in the stalls was equipped with a gamepad with which they controlled a small ball in a three-dimensional virtual space projected onto a large screen on stage (one ball per audience member). The performance was divided into scenes and for each scene an actor invited the audience to move the ball (to go to one side, jump, etc.). Although this was already a fairly advanced form of interactivity for the context of a theatre performance with a large audience, it was quite clear that these actions did not have a significant impact on the narrative of the performance. Of course, the lack of real influence on the unfolding of events could be understood as a desire to expose as fictitious the sense of control evoked by interactive media, implying that we live in a world that deludes us into believing that we are active participants while we are merely passive consumers. In theatre performances, the responsibility for the unfolding of the narrative is often left to the actors, while interaction devices are mainly used in two ways: as a tool for the actor to control in real time certain media content (video, sound, etc.) that augments the story, or as a way to involve the audience through playful activities that somehow contribute to the construction of the story world. In this sense, Marcel·lí Antúnez Roca is a good and clear example: throughout his career, the Catalan artist and founder of Fura dels Baus has developed software and built devices that enable both types of interaction. In *Afasia* (1998), he presented a story loosely based on the *Odyssey*, commanding the content in real time; in *Pseudo* (2012), he was the storyteller, asking the audience to use various devices so to participate in the staging of Pirandello's *The Mountain Giants* (Antúnez Roca 2015; Pizzo 2016). These examples show that prompts for participation can change, depending on the context, and have different goals and outcomes, depending on whether they are mediated by a human component or fully managed by the system. However, these examples also show that in each case, beyond control over the development of incidents, participation must be implemented through meaningful actions.

The interaction strategy itself becomes an activating element for user engagement. In non-interactive narratives, one reason we engage with the story is because of the continuous unveiling, and resulting understanding of what is happening and why: that is, the compelling power of the narrative depends on the inferences we draw about the unfolding of events. This is also true of interactive entertainment, but in addition to inferences about the unfolding of events, there are also inferences here about the mechanisms that drive participation. Basically, we become involved both by discovering the content of the narrative and by discovering the ways in which we can participate.

Asking someone to click on a link on the screen, answer a call, move around a room or operate a device will result in different actions by the participant and different narratives. Just as we intuitively assume that some actions are suited to certain characters and certain environments (mastering the art of the sword is typical of a soldier in the time of the Crusades, being quick with a gun suits a cowboy in the American Wild West), so too some actions are better suited to certain types of interactive works. In other words, the story world is closely related to what is meant by the notion of "display".

In a live action role-playing game simulating a war battle, players should have maximum freedom of movement and be able to handle their weapons; in a guided tour of a historical site, it would be impractical to ask visitors to type in long lines of text to get information. It is up to the authors to determine the type of actions that users must or can perform in order to make the event they are participating in meaningful.

4.1.6 Intelligible actions

Of course, all the actions that make up a story must be comprehensible. This is intuitively true for dramatic actions: when an agent acts in a narrative (whether the action is described in a text, displayed on a screen or performed live), it is almost automatic that the action will be perceived by the audience. However, narrative actions must also be intelligible, and the audience must understand how the narrative is structured in the course of its execution: that is, a beginning as well as an ending must be experienced as such (just think of how puzzling a narrative can be if it ends with a scene that is not perceived as an ending).

Of particular importance, however, is the intelligibility of the interaction, i.e., users must understand the consequences of their decisions. Based on his own decades of experience as a choreographer of interactive dances, Robert Wechsler (2011) has summarised which features make interactivity understandable for the audience, and we have abstracted them here for the general field of interactive storytelling:

- *Education*: The bulk of information, both diegetic and extradiegetic, that helps the user experience the interactive work. This, of course, depends on the context, the coded format and the nature of the work. In some cases, the functionality of interactivity is immediately understandable (e.g., buttons to click), in other cases, it needs to be made explicit (e.g., in a live performance where the audience is invited to participate). Much depends on shared conventions, but it is important to ensure that users receive the necessary information.
- *Timing*: In interactive works, the latency between action and response, which must not exceed about half a second. Outside this limit, there is a risk that

users will not understand the terms of the local agency, i.e., the relationship between their action and the effects on the story.
- *Repetition*: By repeating an action and checking that it has the same effect on the story (e.g., if I shoot the zombie in the head, it definitely dies). This increases the user's competence and proves that what happened is not a coincidence.
- *Interaction by implication*: The type of the actions to be performed, which must be consistent with the story world. The user must feel that a certain kind of action "naturally" has a consistent effect. This creates a kind of trust in the system and makes it possible to experience more complex actions later on.
- *Intuitive logic*: The active relationship between user and story must be supported by some logic. That is, it must be understandable with the help of common cultural elements.

When designing interactions, it is important to consider whether participation is collective or individual. For example, until the 1980s and 1990s, the first examples of interactive cinema assumed the traditional configuration of the audience in a cinema: interaction was thus a collective act. With the advent of game consoles, interactive cinema became more of an individual experience, only to be shared by multiple users decades later on the Internet. The forms of individual or collective interactivity have been very diverse over the decades. Although interactivity is now an integral part of creative digital products, the modalities in which it takes place are not yet fully standardised. There are established interaction protocols for many of the devices we use (including more recent ones such as swiping across the screen), but this is not the case for interactive storytelling. For this reason, each type of interaction needs to be treated in a specific way. That is, when a particular type of interactivity is enabled by the technology and context, the design of the user's actions must clearly represent the effects of participation. In some situations where established paradigms are in play (clicking, shooting, moving, etc.), this is implicit; in other, less common situations, it is not. In an interactive museum guide, for example, it might be important for visitors to realise that their movements affect the flow of information. In a play, when we ask the audience to express their opinions in order to guide the progress of the stage action, it is also necessary to clearly show that these opinions were received and had an effect. When Marcel·lí Antúnez Roca asks the audience to play freely with the various interactive devices at the beginning of *Pseudo* (2012), he helps them to become familiar with the system, but he also confirms that their actions actually have an impact on the performance.

4.2 Writing the interaction through the units

In this section we will discuss some issues that authors need to consider when modelling audience participation using narrative units where the links may depend on various factors (unique links, rules computable by the system, user actions, etc.). In Chapter 1, we saw that the creation of the interactive narrative, in whatever form it is presented, involves the design of units, and we also saw that a large part of this task falls under the responsibility of the authors, who thus put their procedural skills to test.

The technique of writing interactive stories certainly has its roots in narrative and dramaturgy to some extent, so some of the traditional authoring skills are certainly useful. But there is a difference, which we can see from the lesson of Matt Adams, founder of the group Blast Theory (UK). The group gained international fame thanks to one of the first performances in which the audience participated in the first person in a narrative designed as a kind of video game, and thanks to a technological apparatus for interaction (see *Desert Rain* in Chapter 6, Section 6.9).

It is generally agreed that a good storyteller must have a clear idea of the direction in which the story should go. Lajos Egri (see Chapter 1) argued that the most important thing in writing a good drama is to formulate a clear premise, nothing more than the most concise answer possible to the question, "What is your story about?" But, according to Matt Adams, writing for interactivity is not primarily about having the answers ready, but about asking meaningful questions: authors of interactive storytelling works should therefore first formulate the questions that will then form the backbone of the story. In other words, it is as if *Desert Rain* was born out of the question, "What do we really know about the Gulf War?" and not out of the assertion, "The media do not reflect the reality of the Gulf War."

The idea of starting from questions is a paradigm shift because it implies the need for participation from the earliest conceptual stages. Egri's premise is assertive and puts the audience in the position of the recipient. In contrast, a project that originates from a question is based precisely on the ability to elicit a response: the audience is embedded in the project as an actuator. We do not believe that this paradigm shift can be described in a single, specific operational technique, but it certainly defines a change in the author's attitude. Nevertheless, there are some caveats to note: the questions underlying the project must be relevant to the author; they are not formulated to prove anything, but to explore possible answers; they are not rhetorical questions.

All this concerns mainly the story world and remains an inspirational principle rather than a practical guide to the implementation of the work. Nevertheless, at the general level of the conception of the work, it is possible to summarise some guidelines that can be useful in different interactive storytelling works. Below we try to break down these guidelines by type of interaction. It goes without saying that these modes can coexist within the same project.

4.2.1 Interaction by navigating the map

It is common for authors to approach interactive storytelling first with works where navigation is done by selecting links (explicitly or implicitly). We define explicit navigation when the user is asked to decide which path to take (along a predefined graph of nodes and edges) at a given moment (a decision between several options, a link to click, an action to perform). We speak of implicit navigation when the system selects the link to be activated (again in a predefined graph of nodes and edges) thanks to a calculation (e.g., in relation to the course of previous interactions). The graph is thus not only to be understood as an explicit map of the links between units (e.g., before and after), but can also be implicitly represented by a set of rules that apply, for example, to the tags of the single units (see Chapter 2, Section 2.5).

In the following, we summarise some suggestions that authors should consider in order for the narrative content to be functional for the interactive work:

- It is appropriate to define the orders of magnitude of the units that must be in proportion to the extent of the story.
- It is necessary to declare the agents (even just one) involved in the events described in the units and the actions they plan to take.
- A unit must be designed as a finite event, a small story with a beginning, a middle and an end.
- Each unit must contain a main action whose effects are represented in the fictional world and in the characters. It is useful that these effects are declared and considered as preconditions for the units that can follow in the navigation graph.
- It is necessary to define in advance the tagging vocabulary to be used, which will better describe the content of the interactive story. As we have seen, these tags can be of different types, but it is always useful that they also represent the dramatic and narrative dimension that the system will have to manage in the course of the work. For example, whether the possible sequences between units are explicitly specified or whether a sequencing engine orders the units, it is good to describe whether a particular unit represents the beginning, middle or end, or whether it marks a complication, a climax, etc. (see Chapters 2 and 5).

4.2.2 Interaction by dialogues and behaviours

The use of artificial agents or chatbots has developed very differently over the decades (see *Eliza* in Chapter 6, Section 6.1). When designing an agent's behaviours, whether through animations or dialogues, it is important that the author considers them as part of a narrative unit and that they are defined as intentions/actions. In other words, it is good to segment the behaviours into units and then have each unit answer the following questions: what is the character trying to achieve at this moment? What is the character asking the user?

Below we summarise some design guidelines:

- Regardless of the extent of the overall interactive story, the unit must succinctly express the agent's intention (e.g., the unit in which the queen sets out to reach the king must focus on her intention to find out if the king is still alive).

70   Display: audience, system, emotions

- Each unit must allow a response/action by the user that is relevant to the narrative (e.g., the user must be able to decide whether the queen meets the king or not).
- Actions within units must take into account previous interactions (e.g., if the servant has already told the queen that the king has died, it is not plausible that the queen will go looking for him).
- The agent must show some value at stake that makes the actions (of the character and the user) relevant (e.g., the queen believes in the indissolubility of marriage).

4.2.3 Interaction by physical actions

Here we summarise the broad and indeterminate area of interactive storytelling where the computer system must control the physical participation of the audience. This area includes all forms of interactive theatre and performance, role-playing games supported by motion capture technologies or virtual reality, and pervasive gaming (see *Can You See Me Now?* in Chapter 6, Section 6.10). Although these types of activities can often give the impression of a seamless continuum of action, the design of these events still requires the definition of narrative units:

- First, for each scene unit of the event, the interaction and control devices, the performance data to be collected, the type of processing, the outputs to be presented and the timing must be determined.
- For shows or events with actors or performers whose actions build a story but also allow audience participation using specific technologies, it is important to define the organisation of turn-taking that allows the system to capture and process information about the audience's behaviour. In this way, the system will be able to return the data defined by the authors (the actions to be performed, the content to be shown, etc.).
- In cases where the event foresees collaboration among audience's members, without performers or other intermediaries being present, it is important that the units clearly indicate the modalities and timing of participation.

4.3 Emotions in computational systems

Agents, behaviours, actions and units are meaningless if they do not stimulate the emotional involvement of the audience. And according to a rule that goes back to ancient Greece (perceiving others' emotions arouses our own emotions), the representation of emotions in characters is the most important means of evoking them in the audience. In other words, it is assumed that the audience empathises with the emotions portrayed by the characters. This assumption, simple as it may be, is based on a non-trivial assumption: that the audience is able to attribute emotions to the characters not only on the basis of what they express in a perceptible way (through voice, posture, facial expression, etc.), but primarily as a result of the motivations that move them. Seeing a person who experiences severe pain by placing their hand on the iron plate is likely to trigger a feeling of repulsion and an innate desire to withdraw one's hand. But these emotional states are not remotely comparable to what one feels in response to the (non-physical) pain of the heroine losing a friend after many vicissitudes experienced together: sadness, frustration, compassion, etc. In the second case, the awareness of the heroine's affection for her friend and the knowledge of her deepest goals (including the goal of keeping the people she loves safe) lead to the emotions felt by the spectator being much more intense, deeper and longer-lasting than those triggered by the vision of physical pain. The emotional aspect of the story thus confirms and emphasises the importance of the consequentiality of the characters' actions in relation to their goals. If these emotions are to be encoded in a computer system, it is necessary to agree on a list of states that the system recognises as emotions, since not all affective states that we feel can be described as emotions. For example, it is clear to everyone that physical pain is not an emotion, but a perception (which in turn can cause emotions such as distress). Sometimes the distinction is even fuzzier, as in the case of the difference between being happy about something and being absorbed in something, for ultimately both are mental states. The matter becomes highly speculative when we examine the boundary between emotions and moods: is melancholy an emotion, like anger? In the book *Film Structure and the Emotion System* (Smith 2003), Greg Smith distinguishes between two types of emotional states evoked by a film: (1) properly called emotions, characterised by fast activation, high intensity and short duration; and (2) mood, intended as an affective disposition, characterised by low intensity, slow to settle but also to extinguish, and typically associated with sensory and environmental stimuli. In Smith's model, emotions are understood as vicarious emotions connected to the characters' goals (Indiana Jones's desire to snatch the Lost Ark from the clutches of the Nazis, that of Bilbo Baggins to steal the gem from Smaug), while mood is more dependent on the expressive qualities of the film on a global level (soundtrack, editing, etc.) and is partially linked to genre conventions (the pressing editing of the opening scene of *Raiders of the Lost Ark* makes the audience immediately recognise the film as an adventure film, and the soundtrack consolidates this impression). According to Smith, the two systems work together in the film: mood prepares the ground for emotion through a sequence of affective cues, while incidents arouse intense and brief emotions, which in turn consolidate mood.

The distinction between emotions and moods, while important in distinguishing the role of emotions in the story and in its expression, does not obviate the need for a better understanding of the phenomenon for the purposes of interactive storytelling. Even if we agreed on a list of states that we recognise as emotions, we would still need to clarify which elements define each emotion (e.g., does the state of happiness only occur when an agent's plan is successful? Are there other factors concurring to determine emotions, such as the importance of the plan or the efforts made?). Without a definition of these elements, the list would be a mere enumeration of words, and a computer system would not be able to calculate and display the emotions behind these words. In order for a computer system to manage emotions, it must encompass a formal representation of those emotions. The situation is even more complex if we want to represent the multifaceted emotional relationship between audience and characters: are vicarious emotions an automatic reflex, so to speak, or are they modulated by the audience's relationship to the individual character? According to McKee, it is enough for the viewer to identify a single character who is not entirely negative in the story, even if he or she is in the most corrupt moral context, to make this character the "centre of good" that becomes the audience's emotional pivot in the story (McKee 1997). Similarly, Alessandro Giovannelli (2009), following a long tradition in media aesthetics (Carroll 2003; Currie 2009), distinguishes the notions of emotional "empathy" and "sympathy", understood respectively as the ability to empathise and sympathise with a character. According to Giovannelli, our innate ability to feel empathy for a character is a precursor to our ability to sympathise with it, fictitiously adopting its goals even if they do not coincide with our value system: "an emotion is sympathetic only when it arises from a process that leads us to empathise with the other and to assume, in our imagination its most important objectives" (2009, p. 92).

4.3.1 Coding characters' emotions

From a practical point of view, storytelling systems have dealt with the management of emotions through two main strategies: the first, exemplified by *Façade* (see Chapter 5 and Chapter 6, Section 6.11), is to assign fixed emotional values to narrative units – which in *Façade* consist of the plans executed by the characters of the drama, Trip and Grace – and constraining their selection to a predefined pattern of emotional values. In *Façade*, the planner responsible for the interactive generation of the story discards the plans, or beats, that do not match the expected emotional trend. This strategy involves the labelling of narrative units according to their emotional features, whether they are determined by the actions they contain (arguing, flirting, threatening) or by their expressive features (sounds, colour temperature, wording). Labelling all the units in the catalogue can be time-consuming, especially if the annotation scheme consists not only of simple emotional labels but encompasses several affective dimensions. However, this is compensated by the fact that once labelled, narrative units can be easily controlled by the author and reused in other systems that consider the same set of emotions.

The second strategy, especially suited to the paradigm of emergent storytelling, in which the story is built step-by-step from the interaction of autonomous agents, is to give the agents the ability to calculate their own emotions and convey them to the audience through their own expressive means (e.g., their facial expressions). This strategy, adopted for example in *FearNot!* (see Chapter 6, Section 6.12), is usually implemented by integrating into the agent model a set of rules that simulate the process of *emotional appraisal*, i.e., the cognitive process by which an agent evaluates the state of the world and determines the consequences for its own goals and values in affective terms. Each rule corresponds to a specific emotion and is activated when the corresponding conditions occur in the state of the world. For example, in the Emotion Module (EM) of the HAP system (Bates, Loyall and Reilly 1994), emotion activation rules are associated with the fulfilment of the agent's goals and ethical standards, so that the state of failure of a goal triggers an emotion of sadness in the agent, while the high probability of success of a goal triggers an emotion of hope. In the *FearNot!* system, in addition to the rules that determine the agent's emotions as a result of what happens in the story, there are also ad hoc rules for specific event types of events (reaction rules) that correspond to immediate reactions to highly relevant events (crying in response to being hit). A shortcoming of embedding emotion in the agent is that it tends to bypass the role of expressive means in the interaction with the audience: in other words, it assumes that the audience experiences the emotions of the characters in the story thanks to the goal- and value-based mechanism of empathy and sympathy mentioned above, and assumes that these emotions are adequately expressed by the characters' complex calculation of the emotions encapsulated in the agents.

When the emotion model is defined at the level of the character, it determines not only the agent's emotional response to the incidents, but also the way in which this response directs the agent's subsequent actions and thus indirectly influences the course of the story. For this reason, characters whose agent architecture incorporates an emotion generation module usually also have emotional coping mechanisms that ultimately influence their deliberative mechanisms. For example, the artificial agent playing the role of Emma Bovary in an interactive version of *Madame Bovary*, after being rejected by her lover Rodolphe (who can be impersonated by the user), feels an emotion of anger towards him and directs her attention towards alternative goals such as motherhood and family care (Cavazza et al. 2007). Thanks to this design, the audience's involvement with the character of Emma, by influencing her emotions, will also affect the unravelling of the story and give the user a sense of global agency.

4.3.2 The emotions of the audience

The generation of an interactive story, as described so far, presupposes that the system is able to manage the elements of this story in a more or less precise and articulate way. In Chapter 5, Section 5.1, we will see in particular that the system must be able to deal with the actions of the audience. In the same sense, the system can capture the audience's emotions as the interactive story unfolds and feed these emotions back into the system, thus closing the interaction loop at the emotional level. The emotional involvement of the audience can become a fundamental element in controlling the overall course of the story. However, the question of how to define or register this involvement is open and there are no specific or canonical methods for interactive storytelling.

On the one hand, resources for computing the emotions of audiences from their behaviour, whether they are immediate and situated (e.g., facial expressions and body movements) or indirect and deferred (e.g., spoken or written responses), can easily be found in the area of research usually referred to as sentiment analysis and affective computing. Sentiment analysis is usually applied to social networks because they offer a large amount of affective data in response to public events (just think of the broadcasting of events that quickly become trending topics), and also because the analysis of sentiment in texts is highly developed and certified. Through social networks, it is possible to study reactions to media products (shows, TV series, films) distributed through broadcast and streaming platforms, for example, by analysing comments and emojis in real time. On the other hand, another factor in favour of incorporating audience emotions into interactive storytelling systems is the increasingly widespread availability of devices that can capture audience affective data in real time, ranging from less-intrusive motion sensors to more-intrusive tools for measuring physical parameters such as temperature and skin conductance, not to mention software tools for extracting emotions from images captured by a simple camera (facial expression recognition). While sensors are used to detect emotional parameters suggesting a generic emotional involvement of the audience, i.e., the level of emotional activation of a subject (referred to as arousal in psychology), emotion recognition tools enable the identification of specific emotional states directly relevant to storytelling. Emotion recognition systems have recently been based on machine learning platforms trained on very large databases of images and other media representing emotions (Lucey et al. 2010). They are able to distinguish the emotional state (disgust, contempt, happiness, fear, anger, surprise, sadness) expressed by a person's facial expression in an image or stream of images (Yang et al. 2017). The measurement of affective states has been extensively studied in interactive contexts, especially in the field of video games, where the user's emotional involvement is analysed mainly on a quantitative basis (Makantasis, Liapis and Yannakakis 2021). Interest in the audience's emotional response, on the other hand, has been studied mainly in the context of so-called audience studies, where questionnaires and interviews are used to investigate in depth the audience's emotional response to a performance (Foreman-Wernet and Dervin 2013; Rofe, Geelhoed and Hodsdon 2017). In this case, however, the study of audience emotions is conducted from the perspective of the social and cultural enhancement of the performance rather than from the perspective of storytelling.

As mentioned in Chapter 2, Section 2.5, in interactive storytelling, emotions can be a category for tagging the units. For example, in the interactive performance *DoPPioGioco* (developed by CIRMA in 2019) (see Chapter 2, Section 2.5), the system navigated a graph of narrative units to identify the content to be delivered, filtering possible paths based on the audience's emotional response. In *DoPPioGioco*, each unit consisted of a video clip streamed to a screen at the back of the stage and a text recited by the performer. A camera recorded the faces of the audience during the performance of the unit displaying immediately after the prevailing emotion captured in the audience, which was projected on the floor for all to see. At this point, the performer could decide whether to endorse or oppose the detected type of emotion (using a tablet as a control interface); the system then displayed a new video clip and a new text to perform (Damiano, Lombardo and Pizzo 2018; Damiano et al. 2021). At the heart of this system was the labelling of the emotions to be evoked by each narrative unit. The story was structured as a directed graph consisting of narrative units connected by arcs, and the emotional labelling was based on the GEMEP model of emotions (acronym for **GE**neva **M**ultimodal **E**motion **P**ortrayals) (Bänziger, Mortillaro and Scherer 2012). GEMEP distributes emotions along two axes: the axis of polarity, which can be positive or negative, and the axis of intensity, which can be high or low. The two axes divide the Cartesian plane into four quadrants corresponding to four emotion families, each including three emotion types:

- positive polarity and high intensity: *amusement, pride, joy*;
- positive polarity and low intensity: *relief, interest, pleasure*;
- negative polarity and high intensity: *hot anger, panic fear, despair*;
- negative polarity and low intensity: *irritation, anxiety, sadness*.

The units in the story graph were labelled according to the emotion items in the GEMEP model. Each of the topics included in the performance was designed to evoke different emotions depending on the selected units.

In recent years, the relevance of emotions in interactive storytelling systems has gained more and more ground, pointing out the need to endow systems, no matter if they are based on the hypertext model or using generative models with some kind of computerised representation of emotions, so that the experience of the interactive story induces an intense and rich audience participation.

4.4 Cross-media contents' communication

When designing the narrative units for an interactive narrative that involves people's active participation via a device, it is also important to consider the possibility (sometimes the necessity) of the content being delivered via different media. By this we do not mean the presentation of content on media (e.g., images and sound on a smartphone screen), but the possibility that a particular narrative content can be presented in different ways: in other words, we imagine that our project content can be produced as a video, podcast, graphic animation or performance.

It goes without saying, however, that in some cases the narrative content is designed to enter into a symbolic relationship with a particular medium and makes no sense without it. A pervasive game, for example, works in relation to the real space it occupies; a story based on character chats works specifically with a phone screen. Nevertheless, it is important to examine the story's cross-media capability to determine whether the specific device chosen to represent it is relevant to its effective representation.

It is therefore useful, at least preliminarily, to consider the narrative content of the unit as abstracted from the medium. For example, the narrative could be recited by a narrator or visualised in computer graphics; the agent could be an actor on a stage or a video clip. In this way, the author remains focused on the development of the content and the possible interactivity, leaving questions of style and aesthetics of the event to a later stage.

It is like saying that before shooting a film, you must have a good script; before renting a theatre for rehearsals, you must study the text. As always, good preparation ensures that resources are not squandered in the production phase. Once the author has a rough idea of the story to be told, he/she must also have a precisely formulated story world that is, i.e., there must be a description of all the elements that characterise it (Figure 4.2).

As we saw in Chapter 2, Section 2.5, using metadata allows the system to access a description of the content without having to access the content directly. We have also seen that this metadata (i.e., the tagging system) must be based on a defined vocabulary. If the tagging system is developed according to the principle of abstraction from the media, this set of tags will remain constant, regardless of the specific technical choices made by the production in terms of the media and devices used in the final realisation.

In this way, the algorithm that manages the metadata (e.g., an engine to generate the plot by means of the automatic sequencing of the units) does not have to be completely rewritten if the contents are going to be manifested differently than originally planned. That is, if the narrative engine sequences two units by executing an instruction that checks whether the "effect" tags of one are compatible with the "precondition" tags of the other, this instruction does not need to be rewritten if the unit is presented via text, voice or video (see Figure 4.2). Many interactive stories have had a multiplatform outcome. For example, the various *Pokémon* series (see Chapter 6, Section 6.8) have been released on physical cards, game consoles and mobile devices, replicating the same world with very different interfaces and interactions.

This example illustrates two important distinguishing features of computer-assisted narrative processes. Digital media increasingly use algorithms to produce, manifest and store their content. The expansion of computer-based processes has necessitated an ever-increasing abstraction of the information contained in this content and has given rise to new formal models. This also applies to the notion of narrative: instead of seeing it as coinciding with the particular manifestation (the story is the medium in which it is written), it is abstracted into a cognitive

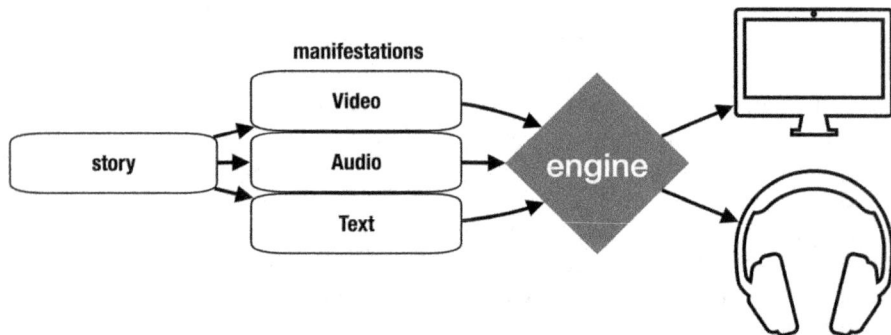

Figure 4.2 Schema of cross-media distribution of an interactive storytelling work

construct that is independent of the medium of representation (there is a story instantiated in different manifestations). A bit like our presence on social media, where we exist independently of the various avatars we use to live online. Similarly, the film on TV is one of many possible avatars in *Snow White*'s story (Ryan 2006). Conceiving an interactive story starting from the dynamic elements (units and agents) makes it possible to distinguish the latter from the engine that manages them. It also allows them to be distinguished from the way they are represented in the narrative and the way the audience interacts with them. Finally, this way of structuring the interactive storytelling project ensures that it opens itself up to cross-media distribution.

4.5. Exercises

This chapter has shown how media production and interaction design characterise the outcome of interactive storytelling. We have seen how units and behaviours of agents can be displayed by media devices and how the audience can participate in the interactive storytelling. In particular, we have focused on the tasks that authors need to consider in order to create an effective and engaging bond with the user.

The reader can design the interface of the interstellar mission of the spaceship *Sirius*: the layout for the development of the story, the audio and visual design, the decisions that the user makes.

The Storygraphia software provides an exporter for the *Twine* editor. *Twine*, which is discussed in Chapter 5, is a widely used editor for hypermedia stories that allows direct publishing on the web. In particular, it generates an HTML file that is interpreted by a browser. Once exported to *Twine*, the interactive story can be enriched with images, videos and sounds to convey a multimedia display of the story. Also, links between passages (as the units are called in *Twine*) can be enriched with media, designed to require user intervention as the story branches out, and can be augmented with multimedia support for decision-making. Finally, possibly sophisticated behaviours can be coded in Javascript, for authors with programming skills.

References

Aarseth, Espen. 1997. *Cybertext: Perspectives on Ergodic Literature*. Baltimore, MD: Johns Hopkins University Press.
Antúnez Roca, Marcel·lí. 2015. *Systematurgy: Actions, Devices and Drawings*. Barcelona: Arts Santa Mònica: Ediciones Polígrafa.
Bänziger, Tanja, Marcello Mortillaro, and Klaus R. Scherer. 2012. "Introducing the Geneva Multimodal Expression Corpus for Experimental Research on Emotion Perception". *Emotion* 12 (5): 1161–1179. doi:10.1037/a0025827.
Bates, Joseph, Aaron Bryan Loyall, and W. Scott Reilly. 1994. "An Architecture for Action, Emotion, and Social Behavior". In Cristiano Castelfranchi and Eric Werner (eds), *Artificial Social Systems*. Berlin: Springer, pp. 55–68. doi:10.1007/3-540-58266-5_4.
Carroll, Noël. 2003. "Art and Mood: Preliminary Notes and Conjectures." *Monist* 86 (4): 521–555. doi:10.5840/monist200386426.

Cavazza, Marc, Jean-Luc Lugrin, David Pizzi, and Fred Charles. 2007. "Madame Bovary on the Holodeck: Immersive Interactive Storytelling". In Rainer Lienhart, Anand R. Prasad, Alan Hanjalic, Sunghyun Choi, Brian P. Bailey, and Nicu Sebe (eds), *Proceedings of the 15th International Conference on Multimedia*. New York: ACM Press, pp. 651–660. doi:10.1145/1291233.1291387.

Crawford, Chris. 2003. *Chris Crawford on Game Design*. Indianapolis, IN: New Riders. doi:10.5555/940762.

Crawford, Chris. 2013. *Chris Crawford on Interactive Storytelling*. Berkeley, CA: New Riders. doi:10.1007/978-3-642-25289-1.

Currie, Gregory. 2009. "Narrative and the Psychology of Character". *Journal of Aesthetics and Art Criticism* 67 (1): 61–71. doi:10.1111/j.1540-6245.2008.01335.x.

Damiano, Rossana, Vincenzo Lombardo, Giulia Monticone, and Antonio Pizzo. 2021. "Studying and Designing Emotions in Live Interactions with the Audience". *Multimedia Tools and Applications* 80 (5): 6711–6736. doi:10.1007/s11042-020-10007-3.

Damiano, Rossana, Vincenzo Lombardo, and Antonio Pizzo. 2018. "DoppioGioco. Playing with the Audience in an Interactive Storytelling Platform". *Advances in Intelligent Systems and Computing* 611. doi:10.1007/978-3-319-61566-0_27.

Foreman-Wernet, Lois, and Brenda Dervin. 2013. "In the Context of Their Lives: How Audience Members Make Sense of Performing Arts Experiences". In Jennipher Radbourne, Hilary Glow, and Katya Johanson (eds), *The Audience Experience: A Critical Analysis of Audiences in the Performing Arts*. Chicago: Intellect Books, pp. 67–82.

Giovannelli, Alessandro. 2009. "In Sympathy with Narrative Characters". *Journal of Aesthetics and Art Criticism* 67 (1): 83–95. doi:10.1111/j.1540-6245.2008.01337.x.

Knoller, Noam, and Udi Ben-Arie. 2015. "The Holodeck Is All Around Us: Interface Dispositifs in Interactive Digital Storytelling". In Hartmut Koenitz, Gabriele Ferri, Mads Haahr, Diğdem Sezen, and Tonguç İbrahim Sezen (eds), *Interactive Digital Narrative*. New York: Routledge, pp. 51–66.

Koenitz, Hartmut, Gabriele Ferri, Mads Haahr, Digdem Sezen, and Tonguç İbrahim Sezen. 2015. "Beyond the Holodeck: A Speculative Perspective on Future Practices". In Hartmut Koenitz, Gabriele Ferri, Mads Haahr, Diğdem Sezen, and Tonguç İbrahim Sezen (eds), *Interactive Digital Narrative*. New York: Routledge, p. 153–158

Louchart, Sandy, and Ruth Aylett. 2003. "Solving the Narrative Paradox in VEs: Lessons from RPGs". In Thomas Rist, Ruth S. Aylett, Daniel Ballin, and Jeff Rickel (eds), *Proceedings of the IVA Conference*. Berlin: Springer, pp. 244–248. doi:10.1007/978-3-540-39396-2_41.

Louchart, Sandy, John Truesdale, Neil Suttie, and Ruth Aylett. 2015. "Emergent Narrative. Past, Present and Future of an Interactive Storytelling Approach". In Hartmut Koenitz, Gabriele Ferri, Mads Haahr, Diğdem Sezen, and Tonguç İbrahim Sezen (eds), *Interactive Digital Narrative*. New York: Routledge, pp. 185–199.

Lucey, Patrick, Jeffrey F. Cohn, Takeo Kanade, Jason Saragih, Zara Ambadar, and Iain Matthews. 2010. "The Extended Cohn-Kanade Dataset (CK+): A Complete Dataset for Action Unit and Emotion-Specified Expression". In *2010 IEEE Computer Society Conference on Computer Vision and Pattern Recognition – Workshops*. IEEE, pp. 94–101. doi:10.1109/CVPRW.2010.5543262.

Makantasis, Konstantinos, Antonios Liapis, and Georgios N. Yannakakis. 2021. "The Pixels and Sounds of Emotion: General-Purpose Representations of Arousal in Games". *IEEE Transactions on Affective Computing* 3045 (c): 1–14. doi:10.1109/TAFFC.2021.3060877.

Mateas, Michael, and Andrew Stern. 2007. "Writing *Façade*: A Case Study in Procedural Authorship". In Pat Harrigan and Noah Wardrip-Fruin (eds), *Second Person. Role-Playing and Story in Games and Playable Media*, Cambridge, MA: MIT Press, pp. 183–212.

McKee, Robert. 1997. *Story: Substance, Structure, Style and the Principles of Screen Writing*. New York: Regan Books.

Murray, Janet H. 2001. *Hamlet on the Holodeck. The Future of Narrative in Cyberspace*. Cambridge, MA: MIT Press.

Niesz, Anthony J., and Norman N. Holland. 1984. "Interactive Fiction". *Critical Inquiry* 11 (1): 110–129.

Pizzo, Antonio. 2016. "The Kaleidoscopic Career of Marcel·lì Antúnez Roca". *The Scenographer* 5: 1–10.

Rofe, Michael, Erik Geelhoed, and Laura Hodsdon. 2017. "Experiencing Online Orchestra: Communities, Connections and Music-Making through Telematic Performance" . *Journal of Music, Technology and Education* 10 (2). 257–275. doi:10.1386/jmte.10.2-3.257_1.

Ryan, Marie-Laure. 2006. *Avatars of Story*. Minneapolis, MN: University of Minnesota Press.

Smith, Greg M. 2003. *Film Structure and the Emotion System*. Cambridge: Cambridge University Press. https://doi.org/10.1017/CBO9780511497759.

Walton, Kendall L. 1990. *Mimesis as Make-Believe: On the Foundations of Representational Arts*. Cambridge, MA: Harvard University Press.

Wechsler, Robert. 2011. "Artistic Considerations in the Use of Motion Tracking with Live Performers: A Practical Guide" . In Susan Broadhurst and Josephine Machon (eds), *Performance and Technology Practices*. New York: Palgrave Macmillan, pp. 60–77.

Yang, Biao, Jinmeng Cao, Rongrong Ni, and Yuyu Zhang. 2017. "*Facial Expression Recognition Using Weighted Mixture Deep Neural Network Based on Double-Channel Facial Images*". Paper presented at IEEE Access 6, pp. 4630–4640. doi:10.1109/ACCESS.2017.2784096.

5 Engines and systems
Supporting creativity and dramatic tension

5.1 Systems and automation

In the recent literature on interactive storytelling, many system architectures have been proposed. By a system architecture we mean a configuration of programmed modules, each of which responds to a particular requirement, and which are interconnected to create a system. In the implemented systems, some components are given more or less importance, sometimes leaving some component implicit, or limiting the conceptualization to a subset of the components.

Given the reference theories and consequently the elements introduced by the composition rules, there are different architectures. For example, if the dynamic elements are units, i.e., discrete events corresponding to segments of the story, there is a module that implements a composition engine that responds to rules or simply sequences the units in an order corresponding to the possible connections introduced by the authors. The simple graph of Chapter 1, Figure 1.4 says that the unit "The King wins" can be followed by one of five units without any further selection criterion. However, this unit may involve a numerical weight calculation that depends on the units that actually preceded it in realising the sequence. The weight accumulated along the path could represent a parameter (e.g., the presence of a particular character who, depending on the path, appeared a variable number of times). Then, if the system is capable of doing so, the author could introduce a rule that automatically selects one of the following three units in plot generation depending on the proportion of the character's presence compared to other characters – less than 30 per cent, between 30 and 70 per cent, more than 70 per cent. Even this simple example makes it clear that the possible architectural solutions for the storytelling control software system are practically unlimited.

The main challenge for systems is to balance the need for a consistent progression of the story with the user's agency, which are often at odds (see Chapter 4, Section 4.1.3). The coherence of the narrative experience is achieved through a sequence of events based on the event progression, up to a conclusion. The user is free to act (within the limits set by the system), possibly introducing inconsistencies – events that cannot be generated by the system – or making the realisation of the scheduled events impossible. It does not matter if the user is unaware of the directions of the narrative or if the user maliciously wants to sabotage certain directions. The challenge is to ensure that the users feel they can influence the direction or outcome of the narrative experience, while ensuring that the experience is consistent (see the relationship between action and control in Chapter 4, Section 4.1.5).

5.2 System classification

Storytelling systems have dealt, more frequently, with the generation of plots, i.e., the intertwining of incidents (grouped into narrative units) that make up the story, but in some cases also with the generation of the database, i.e., the set of dynamic elements that make up the story's universe (e.g., agents, objects, scenarios up to the complete units to be composed by plot generation). Systems also take into account users as components of the story world, or the actions they perform. Systems typically include an editor that supports authoring and a story generation engine that evaluates and executes the possible concatenations of events and user feedback action. Some systems are more authorship-oriented, i.e., editors that support the creation of story elements (units or agents' intentions) and structures; others are systems for the distribution of interactive narratives, i.e., more audience-oriented. In general, both authorial and distribution components are present. Systems of interest can also result in linear (non-interactive) storytelling, with the automation of plot generation from the database. Finally, in interactive narrative (and in narrative in general), we need to deal with characters or agents who, to be credible, need to express intentions. In the interactive case, this is solved in software modules called virtual agents, which can be more or less autonomous in their intentions. These types of narratives, called "emerging", in cases of high autonomy, can therefore be controlled with more or less strictness.

Therefore, we have to deal with at least these three aspects (Riedl and Bulitko 2013).

- *Authorial intent*: To what extent are the author's intentions able to control the interactive narrative system? Systems range from highly constrained (strongly *story-centred*) to loosely constrained (typically *character-centred* or *emergent narrative*).
- *Autonomy of agents*: To what extent are agents autonomous? Systems range from not very autonomous characters (*totally controlled*) to systems in which the agents act totally free from the control of the system.
- *Player modelling*: To what extent does the interactive narrative system seek to model the individual differences between various users, so that it can control the narrative by preventing or responding as quickly as possible to actions that deviate from the narrative intent of the system?

Systems can be classified in many ways, starting with orientation towards the author or towards the user, respectively. We consider the approach used in realising the dynamic elements of the plot and the database respectively, starting with a high-level view of the two components. At a high level, there are systems that generate the plot starting from the elements of the database (e.g., the historical system *TALE-SPIN*; Meehan 1977); other systems generate the database starting from the plot (e.g., again the historical AUTHOR; Dehn 1981). Consequently, the pivots of systems like *TALE-SPIN* are the goals of the characters, i.e., the agents present in the database; the pivots of system such as AUTHOR are the goals of the author, i.e., the whole story from which the goals of the individual characters descend. We find the same dichotomy in story-oriented systems (story-centred), which work mainly on plot generation, taking into account both the author's and the characters' goals, compared to character-oriented systems (character-centred), which work for the realisation of the single objectives in an emergent story perspective. In general, as we will see, it is very common to see authorial goals as constraints, understood as the occurrence of certain events or the adherence to certain structures, to be addressed in the generation of the plot; in these systems there is little or no automatic database generation. In general, the database is usually poorly supported by the systems, and in the storytelling community, unlike games, the creation of the database is up to the author. One of the main reasons for this is also that the quality of the database is closely related to the quality of the story, i.e., the success of the generation technique depends on a high-quality universe created by the author.

The system model could be based on concepts derived from narratological theories, in addition to those developed in creative practice (e.g., the goals of the characters or the author). The derivation of the model from known concepts in narratology or from artificial intelligence techniques applied to dynamic elements of the plot or database is the basis of many empirical systems, as well as systems oriented to particular domains of applications (e.g., narratives built on role-play games), for which highly specific models can be devised. However, integration is a high engineering enterprise.

For a detailed description of the characteristics of storytelling systems, we refer here to the approach given in (Kybartas and Bidarra 2017), which uses a system of axes ranging from the manual creation of plots or dynamic elements to their complete automation. Most systems are obtained by characterising the components at some mid-point between the totally manual and the totally automatic implementation, with possible combinations of partial automation components. Indeed, both the composition of the plot and the creation of the dynamic elements of the database can be automated to varying degrees, resulting in a greater or less control by the author.

For the plot case, we can identify the following characterizations:

- *Manual*: No automation at all; both structure and content of the story depend on the author; the system acts as a mediator, but no decision is the result of an algorithmic execution.
- *Structural*: Structure of the plot processed by the system; events conceived by the author but sequenced by the system.
- *Schematic* (i.e., *based on some template*): The system implements a schema (or instantiates a template), which in turn produces a sequence of abstract events,

i.e., that do not refer to entities of the database; connection with story elements manually operated by the author.
- *Constrained*: Automation of the plot, including the connections between the plot and the database entities; however, possible constraints on generation (that is, certain features or structures of the plot) are introduced by the author.
- *Automated*: The author appears only in the system definition, at the programming level; none of the previous elements (structures, template instantiations, constraints) can be identified.

Similarly, though less frequently, storytelling systems can act on the database. Also in this case, some operating modes can be identified.

- *Manual*: No database automation; both the structure, i.e., the relationships between the dynamic elements, and the dynamic elements themselves are manually compiled by the author, who describes them completely; no element results from the execution of an algorithm.
- *Modifiable*: The database elements and their relationships are manually created by the author; however, the system can explicitly modify the elements, often to improve the plot generation.
- *Simulated*: It is possible to automatically generate new database items, simulating the interactions between the items of some initial pre-set. Typically, the simulation result is an initial state of the story.
- *Constrained*: Automatic generation of the database, obeying the constraints placed by the author on the plot or on specific elements that must necessarily be included (sometimes called VIP points or VIP characters).
- *Automated*: The database is fully automated, minimising the contribution of the author.

The existing systems show various degrees of the two components, depending on the application fields they are intended for. The system has a strong influence on authoring; tools, techniques and even interfaces reduce the perceived presence of the machine for the audience/user and for the authors.

5.3 Fully manual authorship

In fully manual systems, at the plot level and database level, we have seen that the author creates both the dynamic elements, including the events that can take place, and the rules of sequencing the plot in a deterministic way. These are interactive story-authoring systems that only support the creation and loading of the units that make up the database. These systems offer the author tools for creating hypertext links between the units (the dynamic elements), whether they are explicit (authored links between the units) or implicit (rules for establishing connections). The author creates the events that can occur in the story, more or less structured in atomic units, and sets the modes for sequencing the units: which units can follow a given unit and what are the options for going from one unit to the next. There are turning points in the stories, represented by options available to the user. The system does not insert any form of control to restrict the generation of the plot or database; the authors who create the narrative content can structure the story as they wish. There is no obligation to insert constraints or branching, be compliant to a model/template, or to automate certain content. Of these systems, we describe, for their popularity and variety, *Storyspace*, *Twine* and *Inform 7*.

Storyspace,[1] to which many interactive narratives are attributed, is a commercial system (Eastgate Company) that has been around since the 1990s. In the latest versions it exports to XML format, making it compatible with other tools (e.g., *Tinderbox*, a note editor). *Storyspace*'s strength lies in its interface, which allows links between units to be activated and deactivated as the reader moves between them. The creative mode supports the creation of hypertext where nodes are connected by links: it is possible to proceed both with manual linking between nodes, starting from isolated nodes (called calligraphic hypertext in *Storyspace*), and with licensing sequences from connected graphs (sculptural hypertext, i.e., removing unwanted links). In addition, it is also possible to insert constraints on the links: in this way, the system automatically reorganises the links in a significant way and avoids the (sometimes necessary) randomness in generating the paths. By inserting many links, the author can delete the incorrect ones, focusing on a few crucial issues. From a technological point of view, *Storyspace* includes a reader for the interactive story that can be distributed with the work and a variety of maps to interact with. Each node can contain text, graphics and sounds; in addition, a node can contain another map. A new link is created by drawing a line between two writing units, even if they are in different maps; links can connect entire maps as well as specific regions within a map.

Twine[2] is an open-source tool with a graphical user interface. No programming is needed; however, various forms of multimedia and interactivity can be added with simple scripting (using variables, conditional logic, images, CSS and JavaScript code). It publishes in HTML format so that stories can be played directly in browsers. *Twine* was originally developed by Chris Klimas in 2009 and is now managed by the Interactive Fiction Technology Foundation. *Twine* was used in the development of the interactive film *Black Mirror: Bandersnatch* (see Chapter 6, Section 6.16). The main tool for creating stories is the story map, where the author writes the units and inserts the links. The interface provides access to several stories, to which the one created from scratch is added with its own title; the author can insert a unit (called a passage in *Twine* terminology).

For playback, *Twine* has its own engine, which is capable of generating an HTML page, to be displayed in a web browser. Debug mode also allows parts of the story to be tested, so one can easily make corrections.

Inform 7 is a system available on many platforms and has been an open-source software since 2022.[3] The system manages both the creation of the world (including the database, in our terms) and its initial state, as well as the game rules, which shape the user's interaction with the created world (including some standard rules introduced by the system). The interface allows the writing in a controlled natural language, i.e., a language that admits limited forms of sentence composition. For example, the following statements (taken from *Inform 7* Documentation[4]): "The wood-slatted crate is in the Gazebo. The crate is a container" are "assertions" that describe the world (note that verb is always written in the present tense). Some verbs, such as "to be", "to have", and "to contain", are built in. Assertions determine the initial state of the story. In addition to such (unconditional) assertions, there are the rules of behaviour, which determine the changes in the state of the world, guiding the generation of the plot. The most common rule structures are of the following type:

- *IF rules*: They command to do something only if some "condition" holds.
- *NOW rules*: They command to change the situation, with an imperative.
- *SAY rules*: They command to say something, that is to write some text for the player to read.

A rule always starts with a situation to which it applies and then follows with one or more things to do. In the example below, the situation is "Before grabbing the box"; the player is trying to lift the box, but, wearing a hat, the latter falls into the box while the player is bending over to lift up the box (the system delivers information with the SAY keyword).

Before taking the crate:

- IF the player is wearing the hat;
- NOW the hat is in the crate;
- SAY "As you stoop down, your hat falls into the crate".

Inform 7 works with hundreds of rules, some of which are quite complex; there are also default rules that prevent unfair situations, such as putting the box inside itself or dropping something that is already on the ground (basic rules for realism).

The systems seen so far do not impose any characterising aspect on the creation of stories. However, it is possible to impose a plot structure and force the author to insert the units into that structure. They become real assistants (according to the idea introduced by Lubart 2005), trying to superimpose a narrative form on the composition. They still fall back on authorial systems, mostly aimed at the linear world. Some systems simply recall the structure of acts and scenes, inviting the author to fill in the different sections (e.g., STORYBOX 2), or they implement the form of scripts and novels to facilitate writing (e.g., SCRIVENER), without being oppressive. Storygraphia (Lombardo 2022), the authoring tool that is a companion to this book, provides environments to support well-known narrative structures (https://www.cirma.unito.it/storygraphia/; see below).

When discussing manual authoring tools, a mention is deserved for film authoring tools, that are systems describing scenarios to be visualised, then possibly shot or animated. For this reason, interfaces, instead of some hypertext, often recall storyboards and it is possible to link multimedia elements. The pioneer

European project INSCAPE (Interactive Storytelling for Creative People)[5] released a prototype of an integrated collaborative tool for interactive storytelling, which supports multiple formats and devices. As the interface is based on the notion of a storyboard, the author is invited to work at the speech level and to include graphic realisations and possibly programming code for the behaviour and emotions of the characters. The plot is controlled through possible paths on the storyboard.

Over time, the functionalities of the systems that implement graphic storyboards have been taken over by *game engines*, such as Unity,[6] which have become the industry standard application for this task and could be listed together with the storytelling systems (Shibolet and Lombardo 2022). Their specificity is storytelling in an immersive environment, such as the virtual or augmented realities, through different devices, such as stereoscopic 3D screens and headsets. Their usability has recently grown, because of the availability of 3D models in web stocks, often also provided with code for the realisation of behaviours, which free the authors from the need to have programming skills.

Finally, we also mention *Storytron*, an all-encompassing experimental system (Crawford 2013), downloadable from the GitHub repository.[7] It is a very complicated system, as its own authors declare. The notion of event is based on the verbs and the roles it requires as participants in the represented action: for example, the verb *Go* manages at least two roles, the one who goes (linguistically, the subject) and the destination place (the so-called argument of the "motion to place" frame). When the engine encounters an event, it tries to map the roles of the verb associated with the event with the participants (*actors*) of the story: the correspondence is managed through conditions and generates reactions (including the emotional ones of the participants). The actor who interprets a role has a series of behavioural options available, and one of these, the one chosen by the actor, becomes a plan. The execution of the plans, carried out by the engine, eventually generates the events.

All these systems (with some distinctions) require manual management of both the plot and the database elements. They provide generic patterns for the creation of the dynamic elements and visualisation, but usually do not intervene in decisions about the evolution of the story plot or in determining the elements that populate the story world.

5.4 Manually authored database and automation for plot generation

In this section, we group the systems that automate the generation of the plot. Unlike Section 5.3, the systems discussed here have been developed for a specific application, where the techniques have been tested directly in a story production. Furthermore, they are almost always experimental systems, not distributed widely, only applied to the specific story they were created for, often the product of a research lab.

There are many techniques to support automation in the generation of the plot. As the basis of all these approaches is the idea of constraining the shape of the plot in some way, which in manual systems is managed by the author, and to program such systems, one usually turns to formal theories that have described the "form" of stories. In the following sections, we will discuss the most common theories and techniques that have been used and how they have been applied in generation systems.

5.4.1 Plot grammars

One of the most common methods to describe the form of the plot, a template-based automation, is the *plot grammar*. By grammar, we mean a system of formal rules that define the form (in fact) of an object, in our case, the plot. The idea is to identify categories for the dynamic elements and the rules define how the elements, according to their category, can be inserted into a sequence; some sequences are legal, others are not; the rules identify the characteristics that determine the possibility that some categories are in a sequence.

A research endeavour, in the philosophical-psychological tradition, started from the universal grammar of stories, that is, the formulation of the mental structures possessed by human beings to reconstruct a story from the units of the plot and their storage in memory (a so-called *universal story grammar*) (Garnham 1983; Lévi-Strauss 1983; Andersen and Slator 1990). However, as in other areas of "weak" Artificial Intelligence, underlying the studies of Cognitive Science, the universal grammatical approach to the plot proved to be too ambitious and the actual results too limited. The hypothesised theories have not found sufficient experimental evidence (perhaps a renewed approach, with the new perspectives of Machine Learning, could be more successful). Instead, from a technical point of view, the construction of tools for the automatic generation of the plot can rely on the notion of formal grammar. Units are abstracted into categories, grammars define the behaviour of categories through rules, and thus systems can automate the generation procedures working on rules.

Among the grammars that have had some success in the implementation of plot generation systems is the model for Russian folk tales proposed by Vladimir Propp, in his book, *Morphology of the Folktale* (Propp 1968), employed, for example, in Gervás' system (Gervás 2013). At the beginning of the twentieth century, Propp identified a set of regularities in a corpus of Russian folk tales; in particular, he focused on 100 short stories, on which he carried out a systematic analysis in terms of character roles and acts that were meaningful for the development of the story. His conclusions were that, at least for that corpus of fairy tales, the number of roles and acts was limited, the sequence in which those functions were employed was always the same, and therefore all those fairy tales were instances of a single structure.

In Propp's book, the two descriptive blocks of the analysis are: a set of *roles* for the characters in the narrative (the so-called *dramatis personae*) and a set of *functions* or acts. The set of roles include elements such as the hero/victim/seeker (who goes on a journey), the instigator (who sends the hero on her/his journey), the antagonist (whom the hero faces during the story), the false hero (who competes with the hero to take credit for the actions). The set of functions include acts that compose the journey (such as the departure of the hero and her/his transfer to a place or according to indications), actions that describe the involvement of the antagonist (such as deception, when the antagonist tries to gain trust, or harm, when the antagonist strikes a member of the hero's family), phases of the struggle between hero and antagonist (such as the direct fight, the branding, the hero's wounding, or the victory, in which the antagonist loses, e.g., killed in combat). In total, there exist 31 functions and 7 key roles.

The general scheme of a fairy tale has four stages:

1. initial balance (onset);
2. initial balance break (motive or complication);
3. adventures of the hero;
4. restoration of balance (conclusion).

Each phase has functions associated with it. Functions, in turn, are grouped into categories:

- the preparatory functions A (e.g., an interdiction or a ban);
- the functions of the onset of the tale B (e.g., the harming of the hero or her/his departure);
- the functions to obtain the magic mean C (after some tests);
- the culmination of the fairy tale D (e.g., fight or victory);
- conclusion E;
- possible resumption of complications for the hero – new debut F, obtaining magical mean G;
- culmination H – and eventually second final I.

Even if the order of the sequence is always the same, some functions may not be present or be repeated to be successful (it seems that there is an adequate number of repetitions); the plot is built from the composition of the functions. To create a tale, one can take any function of category A, then one of the possible B's, then one C, necessarily followed by any D, then an E, and so on. The functions are distributed according to the *dramatis personae* following their own style and becoming stories (of course, the author should keep in mind motivations, connections, and other additional elements).

The author, in addition to this clearly procedurally deterministic description, must comply with a set of constraints: the sequential order of functions, the dependencies between functions, and the requirements of the defined functions. However, the author can take advantage of some freedoms: omission/use of functions, means by which a function is achieved, character/function assignments, linguistic expressions. Each character is compliant with a set of functions, which determine the so-called *sphere of action*: for example, the hero generally appears in the onset and performs the functions of consensus, departure, test, and reaction; on the contrary, the antagonist may appear suddenly at some point, but then re-appears and is associated with harm, fighting and hounding.

Propp's morphology, described precisely but informally by its creator, can be encoded in a formal language. George Lakoff proved in the 1970s, following Chomsky's discoveries in linguistics, that the story grammar needs a complex device to be encoded (Lakoff 1972). One possible device is a state diagram; we see an example in Figure 5.1, taken from his original article. The circles or nodes represent states, while the arrows or edges represent Propp functions. By inserting a category A event, one can go from (initial) state 1 to either state 2 or state 3; from state 2, the story moves to state 3 with a category B function and to (final) state 4 with a category D function; being in state 3 it is possible to remain there for a long time with category C events until a category D event causes the transition to state 4.

Although Lakoff's goal was to show that devices of this type and expressiveness cannot represent the whole of Propp morphology, it is quite clear how to build a formal model to move from Propp's informal description to a real program. His formal rules could describe the functions that make up a story as described by the Propp model. We can state that a story (formal category symbol Plot) consists of two sequences, the complicating one, called CS (Complicating Sequence) and the resolving one, called RS (Resolving Sequence). Each of these sequences is in turn composed of other sequences of symbols, as shown in the hierarchy in Figure 5.2.

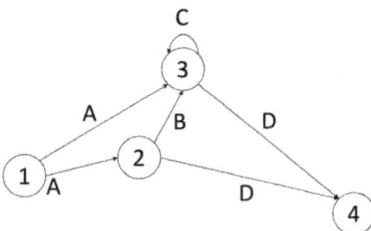

Figure 5.1 Lakoff's state diagram to represent Propp's structure
Source: Lakoff (1972).

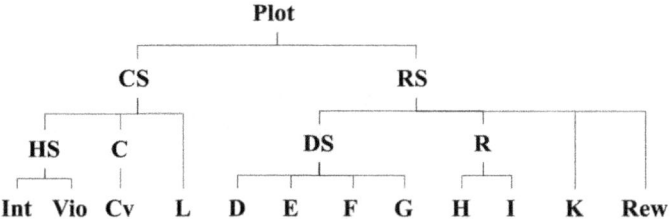

Figure 5.2 The syntax of Lakoff's grammar is represented in the form of a hierarchy
Notes: The symbols, from root to leaves, represent: Plot (Plot), CS (Complicating Sequence), RS (Resolving Sequence), HS (sequence that leads to lack of help for the hero), C (complication), DS (sequence of obtaining the magical means), R (resolution), Int (interdiction), Vio (violation), Cv (Complication due to wickedness), L (departure), D (donor who interrogates, tests or attacks the hero), E (hero who reacts appropriately), F (hero who receives the magical agent), G (hero who uses the magical agent), H (fight), I (victory), K (end of bad luck), Rew (reward).

In the actual generation of the story, one must imagine that each category symbol corresponds to a specific event that implements the scheme. Take, for example, the following specific events classified into categories:

1. Int: Ivan is warned not to leave his sister alone at home.
2. Vio: Ivan violates the warning and leaves his sister alone at home.
3. Cv: A dragon kidnaps Ivan's sister.
4. L: Ivan discovers the misdeed and sets off in pursuit of the dragon.
5. D: Ivan meets an old man who asks him a riddle.
6. E: Ivan solves the riddle.
7. F: The old man gives Ivan a horse and a sword.
8. G: The horse carries Ivan to the land of the dragon.
9. H: Ivan fights with the dragon.
10. I: Ivan kills the dragon with the sword.
11. K: Ivan releases his sister.
12. Rew: Ivan receives a medal of valour.

The story is generated by what is called a rewriting process, in which at each step a symbol, starting from the root Plot, is replaced by the sequence at the lower level of the hierarchy, until at the lowest level all the categories mentioned are completely replaced by the actual events. Traversing the hierarchy from top to bottom results in the following replacements (we use the symbol "+" to mark the concatenation of symbols; in each row, the replaced category is printed in bold):

1. **Plot** ->
2. **CS** + RS ->
3. **HS** + C + L + RS ->
4. Int + Vio + C + L + **RS** ->
5. Int + Vio + C + L + **DS** + R + K + Rew ->
6. Int + Vio + **C** + L + D + E + F + G + R + K + Rew ->
7. Int + Vio + Cv + L + D + E + F + G + **R** + K + Rew ->
8. Int + Vio + Cv + L + D + E + F + G + H + I + K + Rew

The last sequence, made up of categories, replaced by the actual events listed above, is the following story (in parentheses, the categories of each sentence):

> (Int) Ivan is warned not to leave his sister alone at home. (Vio) Ivan violates the warning. (CV) A dragon kidnaps Ivan's sister. (L) Ivan discovers the misdeed and sets off in pursuit. (D) Ivan meets an old man who asks him a riddle. (E) Ivan solves the riddle. (F) The old man gives Ivan a horse and a sword. (G) The horse carries Ivan to the land of the dragon. (H) Ivan fights with the dragon. (I) Ivan kills the dragon with the sword. (K) Ivan releases his sister. (Rew) Ivan receives a medal of valour.

The rewriting mechanism is not expressive enough to represent the stories in a correct form. In fact, as also happens in natural language, some functions are implicitly linked to each other, and this implicit constraint is not expressed in the grammar. Propp mentions two types of constraints:

- links between the categories: for example, H1, fight in open field, is linked to I1, victory in open field, or L11, spell, is linked to K8, breaking a spell;
- the necessary precondition for which some later event cannot happen unless some previous event has already occurred: for example, the hero saves from a kidnap only if a kidnap has occurred. However, some variations are allowed (saving in different forms, regardless of how the chase started).

The presence of these pairings, which sometimes occur at long intervals in the development of the story, makes the formal representation of Propp's morphology of the story with the mechanism of hierarchy in Figure 5.2 impossible. Lakoff's work demonstrated the theoretical need for more sophisticated computational devices, such as planning formalisms.

Despite this fact, the ease of (partial) formalisation and the introduction of structural simplifications and constraints on the narrative field, Propp's morphology and the notion of narrative functions have been widely used by developers of interactive storytelling systems. Grasbon and Braun used Propp's morphology to build an authoring tool for interactive fiction (Grasbon and Braun 2001): in this system, the author manually creates segments of a narrative for each of the functions defined by Propp, and the system generates a narrative guided by a Propp-based grammar. Unlike Lakoff's theoretical work, here the author ensures that illegal pairings do not occur in the implemented system. Lakoff's grammar and Grasbon and Braun's engine show two different approaches to plot automation. While both systems rely on the same underlying structure, the first approach fully automates the plot generation, while the second approach addresses the challenges of creating narrative experiences by guiding the player along a certain path in the story. The system implements a regulating function during a game/navigation/interaction session. The adjustments also concern some features of the interactive story, such as the achievement of suspense or dramatisation, or even the generation of new content to help structure the interaction into a coherent narrative experience. This tuning function is often assigned to a software module in the system, known as *drama manager* (Mateas and Stern 2007; Roberts and Isbell 2008).

Campbell's *The Hero with a Thousand Faces* (Campbell 2008), which echoes the spirit of Propp archetypal rules, has also inspired the creation of interactive fiction systems. Research centre L3i of University La Rochelle created an interactive storytelling system using a generalised plot grammar, to be customised for various stories (Champagnat, Delmas and Augeraud 2010). Again, the author must manually create the content for each of the stages of the so-called "hero's journey", while the system is mostly responsible for generating the high-level plot structure. Benjamin Colby (1973) developed a grammar aimed at the specific encoding of Aboriginal folk tales. Colby's grammar, rather than defining a rigorous sequence of events, creates a sequence that consists of three main categories of events, namely motivation, engagement and resolution. Again, the generation occurs through the application of a set of rules, with the final step assigning a specific event (called *eidon*) to each category. However, Colby departs from the sequential structure imposed by Propp to allow for a more unique and varied plot structure, without imposing a rigid order.

5.4.2 Constraints on plot generation

Template-based models are very rigid structures if interpreted in the literal sense we have seen above (with the grammar). In general, it is much more common to automate plot generation with constraints that loosely draw on a model or, mostly, introduce restrictions on plot generation. It is a bit like giving directions to someone, telling her/him to go west, avoid Columbus Avenue, recognize the destination as the yellow building with blue shutters, and respect the road signs. In other words, providing a set of constraints. This is opposite to giving the complete list of street names, together with the alternative steps in case of some obstacle (a model built on a template base).

In the case of *constraints*, the author's control is expressed through conditions (the constraints) that must be satisfied by the generated plot. As can be seen also from the simple example of the directions above, the constraints can take the form of rules for the selection of dynamic elements to fill a certain role, rules for the causal/temporal structure of events (preconditions for a certain action that must apply before the action is taken – being in front of a door in order to open it), states of the database that must hold at some point in the plot (the two lovers must meet at some point). Many storytelling systems fall into this category, sometimes in some middle ground between models and constraints. In fact, grammars are often used for a combinatorial generation of plots, which are then constrained by extra-grammatical conditions implemented in various ways. A paradigmatic case of constrained plot generation is the *DramaTour* project (see Chapter 6, Section 6.13). In this system, interactive storytelling was intended to inform visitors about a historical site through the story conveyed by a character (monologue). The visitor, i.e., the user of the story, was to be informed about the cultural heritage items of a site while moving freely around, even if a general constraint of an entry-exit direction was in place (a sort of linear development, as in the case of the Propp sequence of functions). The generation of the plot, concerning short narrative units in video format, was regulated by a set of constraints of different types. Each narrative unit, instead of belonging to one grammar category, was labelled with a set, or vocabulary of tags, which defined its behaviour, as the unit responded to specific narrative functions. The generation of the plot was therefore the result of the application of the constraints, each with its own priority, taken as input by the generation algorithm. We list them in descending order of priority:

- *Time constraints.* Since the visit had a duration limit, the development of the narrative had to take place in a certain time interval; so, some units, called

directive units, contained invitations to move quickly towards the exit, in case of a slow visitor; other units, called *phatic units*, contained distraction actions, in case of a hurrying visitor.
- *Discursive constraints*: The elements addressed in the narratives (objects, events, historical characters) were always introduced and then possibly recalled (e.g., it was necessary for the character to be credible to avoid introducing some item twice).
- *Communication constraints*: Basic social behaviours so that the character could acquire credibility and improve user engagement (e.g., greeting the visitor at the beginning and at the end, introducing himself as a guide/narrator).
- *Topological constraints*: At a certain instant during the narration, the active unit ought to refer to the room where the visitor was located (e.g., the room in which he was, the objects contained in it, a historical character linked to those objects).
- *Information constraints*: Expressed as preferences for the continuation of a story.
- *Focus constraints*:

   a   Keep the focus on the current topic (e.g., from some artwork to the artist who created them).
   b   Move the focus to a sub-topic of the current topic (e.g., from a piece of furniture to some of its details, or from an artist to her/his time, according to mereological knowledge).
   c   Shift the focus to a secondary topic with respect to the current topic (e.g., from a historical character to her/his love affairs).

Some constraints are binary (temporal or communicative constraints), while others are interpretable (informative constraints); therefore, the system may be faced with the task of choosing between several continuation units. We consider a database consisting of the following units:

- (Comm 1): Character Carletto introduces himself as a guide, illustrating the history of his family.
- (Comm 2): The character Carletto greets the visitor, hoping for a return.
- (Inform 1 – Chiablese Palace): Introduction of the Chiablese Palace, as a historic residence of the Savoy family.
- (Inform 2 – Chiablese Palace): Chiablese Palace as an office building.
- (Inform 3 – Palazzo Chiablese – Owners / 1570): The first owner of the building, a non-Savoy family lady, and her love affairs.
- (Inform 4 – Palazzo Chiablese – Owners / 1642): First Savoy family owner of the palace, Cardinal Maurizio.
- (Inform 5 – Palazzo Chiablese – Owners / Cardinal Maurizio): Maurizio leaves the cardinal role.
- (Phatic 1): Carletto polishes the medals pinned on his military uniform.
- (Directional 1): Carletto invites visitor to move because the cleaners are chasing him in that room.

Given the set of constraints above, the system could yield this sequence:

> (Comm 1) (Phatic 1) (Inform 1 – Chiablese Palace)(Inform 3 – Palazzo Chiablese – Owners / 1570) (Inform 4 – Palazzo Chiablese – Owners / 1642) ... *the visitor is languishing in the first room (in proportion to the total visit duration)* ... (Directional 1) (Comm 2).

In particular, after the initial greeting (Comm 1), Carletto takes some time (Phatic 1); then, the system gives priority to the topological tags, so Carletto addresses the building in general, which is introduced (Inform 1); then Carletto proceeds to the sub-topic of the owners, with the first owner (Inform 3), followed by the first Savoy-family owner (Inform 4); realising some delay on the visit, Carletto invites the visitor to move quickly (Directional 1); finally, he greets the visitor (Comm 2). As we can see, the labelling is composed of tags of different kinds, on multi-dimensional vocabulary: sub-topics (the owners of a building), continuation of topics (chronology). With a database of a few hundred units, the stories become interesting and varied.

In the intermediate cases, in which grammars and templates are coupled to constraints, there are more built-up algorithms that manipulate the plot generations given by the basic grammar. For example, the GESTER system (Pemberton 1989) was a plot generator that relied on a detailed plot grammar of epic narratives in ancient French. The grammar was broken down into specific events, with causes and effects, and a set of rules accounted for the relationships between characters and the objects in the story world. System Brutus used plot grammars composed with other constraints for the construction of traditional tales. Although Brutus succeeded in creating complex stories, it was limited to the domain of betrayal: these features highlighted the complexity that derives from the passage from general narrative template (such as grammars) to the generation of actual narratives (also driven by additional constraints) (Bringsjord and Ferrucci 2000).

5.4.3 Planning for plot generation

Planning has been very popular in the Artificial Intelligence community since the classical system STRIPS (Fikes and Nilsson 1971) and planners have been adapted to address plot generation. As described in Chapter 3, plans are designed to achieve goals through some listed actions. Plans can be hierarchical; the hierarchy ends when the decomposition gets to the basic actions that the agents of the system can perform and do not require further planning. Therefore, a system that makes use of planning sets up a goal and composes (or retrieves from memory) a plan that can achieve it, also given the fulfilment of the preconditions for the required actions. If a plan is at some abstract level, it is decomposed into more operational plans, until the basic performable actions. Sometimes, it is also necessary to re-plan, that is to find alternative plans. This occurs when some preconditions for the applicability of a plan are no longer valid. This feature is fundamental for interactive stories, where the user can alter the situation at hand and make a plan inapplicable.

For the plot generation process, working with planning means that a story must achieve a certain goal. This goal can take many forms and is often represented as a desired state by some of the characters in the database (e.g., "rescue of a princess kidnapped by a dragon" or "be admitted to a prestigious dance school"); it is not uncommon for a system to have multiple objectives, sub-objectives and, especially for the interactive case, changing objectives. Goals are stated by the author as a way to orient the narrative towards some direction and are often assigned to specific characters. There are many examples of planning-based plot generation systems, and even some related to database building. In general, the systems have been built empirically, with a number of successful prototypes that exposed practical problems. The relevant issues can be referred to the representation of the knowledge that is necessary to control the story development, i.e., the narrative rhythm with increasing/decreasing tension, and in general, how to use that knowledge to implement the plot generation process. In fact, this issue arises from the use of the plans of the characters instead of the narrative units and the control of the story development, to which templates and constraints have tried to answer, shifts to a more indirect level. Many approaches have therefore implemented the constraints, discussed in the previous paragraph, at the planning level, i.e., on the trajectory of the goals and, in general, the states achieved by the plan execution.

To illustrate the planning method, we report the approach pursued by Porteous, Cavazza and Charles, who made two classic linear stories interactive, namely *Madame Bovary* and *The Merchant of Venice* (Porteous, Cavazza and Charles 2010; Charles et al. 2011) (also see Chapter 3, Section 3.2.3). The specific feature of this approach is that the basis for an interactive story is a classic plot, which becomes the storage of all the possible actions. In a nutshell, the world of the linear story is modelled with planning operators, that is, the narrative units are broken down into the plans and goals of the single characters. Once this decomposition has been realised, the obtained elements, plans and goals, with the possible preconditions, can be recombined to produce more variants, changing the planning domain, at the beginning or during the execution phase. For this approach to be successful, it is important that the basic action representation of the original linear story is sufficiently generic to allow for domain variation (e.g., the basic action "reporting bad news" should be augmented in sufficient detail to cover different types of news and different types of pre- and post-conditions, the latter also called *effects*). An advantage of this approach is that it allows the system to be validated by testing the ability to generate the basic linear story in the absence of variations in the initial conditions or of dynamic changes during the plan execution. The approach is to break down the basic plot into *points of view* (or POVs) and sets of actions for each character (with constraints and goals); then, the actions are recombined taking into account the different points of view.

We take an excerpt from Shakespeare's *The Merchant of Venice*, a drama based on the conflict between two central characters: Antonio, a wealthy Christian merchant, and Shylock, a Jewish usurer. The set is sixteenth-century Venice, where trade and prosperity coexisted with racial and religious discrimination. We focus on a central element of the play, an agreement between Antonio and

Shylock, in which Shylock undertakes to lend 3000 ducats to Antonio, without interest, and the latter undertakes to repay the loan, but if he fails to repay it, he must compensate Shylock with a pound of his own flesh.

Let's see how the POVs and the actions of Antonio and Shylock are identified and formalised, considering the analyses reported in the dramatic literature. Shylock sees himself as a victim of discrimination in general and a victim of Antonio's refusal to abide by the contract (which should be enforced); his behaviour can range from revenge to conciliation. Antonio has the point of view of the ruling class, despite some contradictions, such as the need for Shylock's loan; his behaviour can range from neglect (e.g., mistreating Shylock) to conciliation.

The database of the dynamic elements, which now is about characters' goals and plans, needs to be designed from scratch. In the approach we are describing, which has a linear plot as its basis, the characters and their attributes (position, activity and honesty) can be represented as predicates of planning. Predicates, understood as expressions in the language of logic, can describe the conditions of the characters and the states of the story world. The example predicates from *The Merchant of Venice* are expressed in predicate logic, where a predicate symbol represents the relationship between the arguments in parentheses: therefore, if, in logic, we state that lives_in (antonio, venice), we mean that "Antonio lives in Venice", so the predicate lives_in, interpreted as "living in", holds between the element antonio, interpreted as the human "Antonio", and the element venice, interpreted as the place "Venice". Here are some predicates that hold for *The Merchant of Venice* story:

- Signing of an agreement between Antonio and Shylock, in which the latter undertakes to lend 3000 ducats to the former;
    - `signed-loan-agreement (shylock, antonio)`
- Shylock's reaction to the news that his daughter Jessica has escaped;
    - `reaction-news-escape (shylock)`
- Receiving, by Antonio and Shylock, of the court verdict on Antonio's default case;
    - `received-court-verdict (antonio, shylock)`

Thus, the signed-loan-agreement predicate represents what happens between the arguments, shylock and antonio. Characters' points of view, or POVs, are also represented as predicates:

- Shylock sees himself as a victim of discrimination and, therefore, victim of Antonio's refusal to abide by the contract;
    - `pov (shylock, victim)`
- Shylock has a history of mistreatment by Antonio and is bent on revenge;
    - `pov (shylock, ruthless)`

- Antonio sees himself as a loyal friend who is a victim of Shylock's insistence on enforcing the contract on the defaulting loan;
  - `pov (antonio, victim)`
- Antonio sees himself as a member of the ruling class, seeking pleasure and indifferent to risk;
  - `pov (antonio, risk-lover)`

The characters' POVs lead to the production of variants of the linear story: a certain narrative action (e.g., the signing of the contract, but also a betrayal or a challenge) is represented differently according to the perspective of each character taking part in the action. The POV represents the character's perspective with respect to the overall plot, not in a contextual way, as well as the *a priori* judgement of the character with respect to a set of events. The same narrative action will therefore have different representations according to the POV, and therefore different sets of pre- (or post-) conditions. The plot generation system will adopt the POV of a certain character, for the selection of the next narrative action at a certain point, thus resulting in different stories, depending on the POV taken into consideration. Furthermore, these variants will respond differently to the various user interactions. For example, consider the (asymmetrical) action of Shylock's loan to Antonio: Shylock lends the money, Antonio receives it. Considering the POVs listed above, there are four ways of representing this action, as seen in Table 4.1.

Table 4.1 The four ways of representing the actions in the interactive *The Merchant of Venice*, depending on the POVs

Preconditions	pov (shylock, victim) and ...	pov (shylock, ruthless) and ...	pov (antonio, victim) and ...	pov (antonio, risk-lover) and ...
Actions	loan-favour (shylock, antonio, venice-rialto)	loan-intent-revenge (shylock, antonio, venice-rialto)	loan-cautious-on-risk (antonio, shylock, venice-rialto)	loan-arrogant-on-restitution (antonio, shylock, venice-rialto)
Manifestations	Shylock, a patient victim, does Antonio a favour by lending him money	Shylock, intent on revenge, lends money to Antonio providing for the penalty	Antonio, a loyal friend, borrows the money from Shylock, fully aware of the risks	Antonio, a carefree risk-lover, borrows money regardless of the consequences
Effects	signed-loan-agreement (shylock, antonio) and serene (shylock) and ...	signed-loan-agreement (shylock, antonio) and gloating (shylock) and ...	signed-loan-agreement (shylock, antonio) and worried-about-penalty (antonio) and ...	signed-loan-agreement (shylock, antonio) and indifferent-to-penalty(antonio) and ...

The POVs of the characters lead to the production of variants of the linear story: a certain narrative action (e.g., the signing of the contract) is presented differently depending on the perspective of each character taking part in the action. The common effect is that Antonio and Shylock signed a contract for a money loan, but they differ from the other effects and preconditions because of the POVs. For example, an effect for Antonio is "indifferent to penalty" when the POV is that of a risk-lover, while he is "worried about penalty" when the POV is that of a victim. Table 4.1 also contains actions, such as planning operators, which change the character attributes. In this case, we have represented the actions in a notation inspired by the PDDL 3.0 planning language, in which the predicate of the actions (formed by a symbol and the arguments) is accompanied by the preconditions (required for the action to be executable) and its effects (or post-conditions that apply after execution). The actions are written in the form of a triple: the actual action (the third argument is the place where it occurs), the preconditions (joined by "and", which means that they must all apply) and the effects (joined with the logical "and"). The 3-dot spaced ellipses mean that preconditions and effects can be formed by a long list of predicates, joined by "and".

Once the set of actions has been compiled for each POV, it is necessary to find a way to control the generation of the plot; in other words, constraints must be placed on planning by representing desirable conditions in a narrative variant. When these conditions become true, we get at the selection of actions or operators that enrich the narrative or increase the pace or suspense. The author identifies the database predicates that fulfil these conditions and includes them as constraints (e.g., the signing of the loan agreement, discussed above). Furthermore, a constraint may only be relevant for some POVs. For example, in the context of the pound of flesh subplot, the agreement between Shylock and Antonio must have been signed before receiving the verdict of the court that resolves the dispute.

The constraints and the order in which they are applied form a precedence graph. The engine algorithm runs a cycle that includes all the constraints and selects them one at a time, taking into account the partial ordering described by the precedence graph. Once a constraint is selected, the plot generation algorithm creates a planning problem that aims to satisfy the selected constraint, given the current goals of the characters (e.g., signing the agreement). If a plan can be found, then the algorithm performs all the actions included in it; if this is not possible (no plans are available for the selected constraint), re-planning is required (e.g., in case the user has changed the state of the world or has requested a change of POV). All constraints must be considered, one at a time. Once all the constraints have been taken into account as input to the process, the final goal is addressed, possibly re-planning, in case of user interaction.

Figure 5.3 shows two stories generated for the interactive *The Merchant of Venice*. On the left with POV risk-lover for Antonio, on the right with POV victim for Shylock. Constraints selected by the generator are highlighted (A1-C1-A2-A3-A4-C2-C3-A5-C4, left, S1-S2-C1-S3-S4-C2-C3-S5-C4, right) and are preceded by the sequences of narrative actions selected to carry them out. The one on the

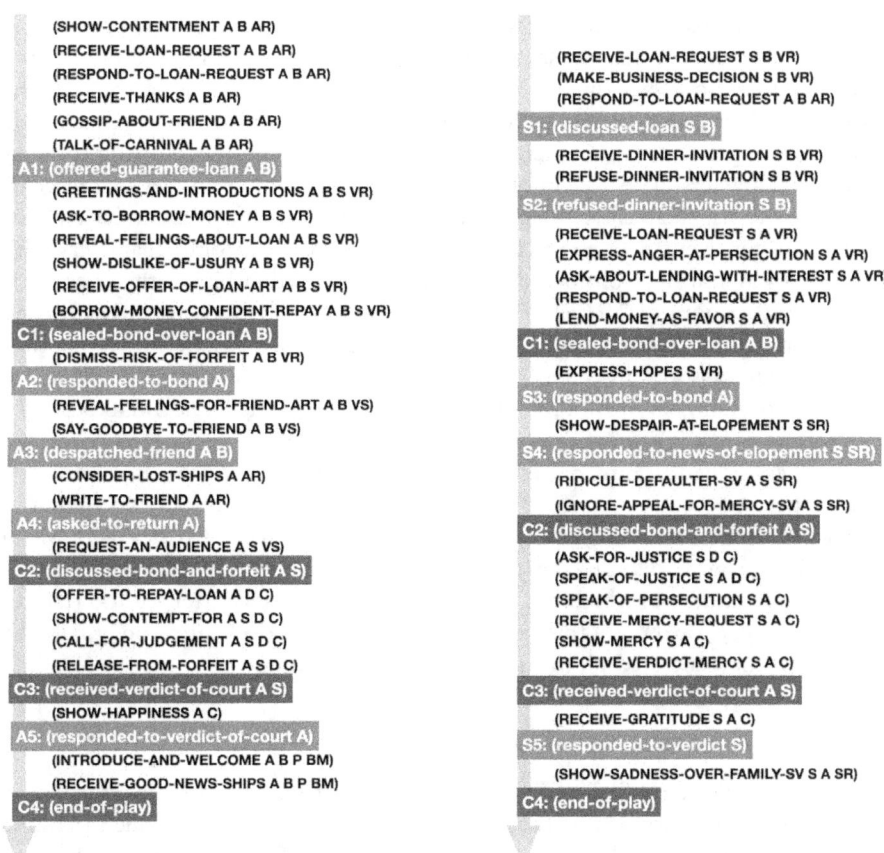

Figure 5.3 Two variants of *Merchant of Venice* interactive
Notes: Letters in italics indicate the predicate arguments, namely the characters: A (Antonio), B (Bassanio), D (Duke), S (Shylock) and the places AR (Antonio's Residence), BM (Bel Monte), C (Court), SR (Shylock's Residence), VR (Venice Rialto), VS (Street of Venice).
Source: Porteous, Cavazza and Charles (2010).

left shows a risk-lover Antonio who borrows money with confidence and continually refuses to take personal risks, even when he is taken to court for non-payment of the loan. It ends with Antonio celebrating his release. In the right-hand variant, Shylock lends money in friendship and shows mercy when Antonio defaults on the loan. It ends with Shylock receiving gratitude but showing sadness at his daughter's escape.

Finally, we address a quantitative idea of what the author has to deal with manually in this rather limited case, namely this subplot of *The Merchant of Venice* interactive. The database consists of about 200 generic narrative actions (a kind of schemata with undefined participants), which become about 1500 instantiated actions (i.e., with assigned participants). There are also about 150 constraints in the story world, of which an average of 15 are used in the generation of the plot.

100 *Engines and systems*

Planning has played a fundamental role in interactive storytelling beyond the creation of intelligent agents (see Chapter 3, Section 3.2), and has also been the terrain of numerous experiments in plot generation. For example, as early as the 1980s, the *Universe* system was developed to generate linear "soap opera"-style plots. Planning was used to generate events that aimed to cause dramatic conflicts between characters. The system also included a rudimentary model of the characters' emotions, such as well-being, mood and intelligence. These traits acted as constraints for events: for example, it could be stated that only characters with little kindness and high promiscuity can engage in relationships with other characters. Furthermore, UNIVERSE could go on indefinitely, constantly creating new twists to stay in tune with the long soap operas that inspired it: the author had to create episodes (as happens in soaps), each with its own goal, as well as setting an overall goal for the full plot (Lebowitz 1985; Riedl and Bulitko 2013). The format of the TV serial drama, probably because of its commercial pervasiveness, has continued to provide research ideas for systems that generate plots open to audience intervention. In the 2000s, *Friends* was the basis for an experiment in interactive form (see Chapter 3, Section 3.2.3) (Cavazza, Charles and Mead 2002); in the same decade, the *Gadin* system experimented with an interactive "soap opera" model in which the user was an additional character for the rules of the virtual soap opera. In this way, the user could also change and guide the creation of the generated plot (Barber and Kudenko 2008).

5.4.4 Plot generation based on dramatic tension

According to the scientific literature and the experience of practitioners, the stories with the greatest emotional participation are the dramatic stories, which organise the narrative units according to a certain progression of the story, called the *dramatic arc*. This type of description dates back to the second half of the nineteenth century, when Gustav Freytag reconsidered the traditional five-part division of the tragedy by examining the type of actions that characterised them: introduction, evolution, climax, fall, catastrophe (Freytag 1863). The crucial step was to consider the parts not as a division of the parts of the text or as interruptions that are necessary to change the setting, but based on proto-narratological categories, that is, on the narrative function they had within the story.

Today, the dramatic arc is defined according to different terminologies and with different forms (Figure 5.4). It is still widely believed that the flow of events in dramatic media must follow a tension trend that forms one or more curves. The dramatic arc is drawn from the variations of emotional tension on a timeline. The literature in this field tends to attribute a certain degree of emotional tension to the work at a given moment of its development (and therefore the notion of the dramatic arc is assumed to apply only to works whose performance foresees a certain duration). This is intuitively understandable. While participating in a story, we realise that a certain moment can also be described with an emotional degree (e.g., a great tension is perceived through the couple's argument about their relationship with their parents) or with a certain emotion (e.g., it is a happy

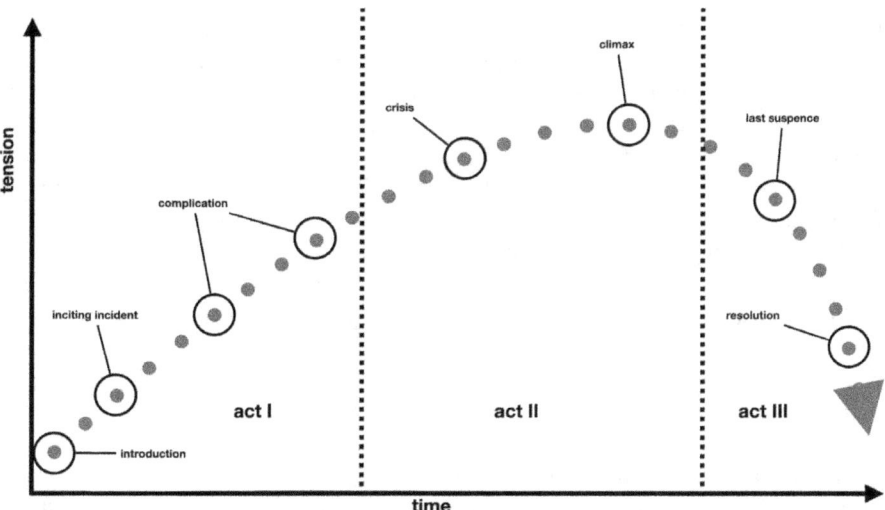

Figure 5.4 Typical example of a dramatic arc divided into three acts

moment right after the character receives the long-awaited news about being accepted into the dance academy). It is less intuitive to identify the elements that allow the audience to be aware of that emotional level or of that specific emotion. In summary, the conditions under which certain situations (configuration of events, actions and agents) lead us to perceive a certain emotional trajectory, or arc in the story, and how this arc becomes our emotional experience are not clear.

A typical element for creating dramatic tension in a story is certainly the *conflict*. The notion of conflict is pervasive in handbooks dealing with dramatic technique or film writing. The notion is eminently cultural and has changed over the centuries: conflict with destiny, conflict with duties, conflict with oneself. The different hypotheses maintain two common elements (Carroll 2003; Smith 2003; Giovannelli 2009): on the one hand, the audience's perception of emotions implies the presence of an agent, on the other hand, the emotional charge of the story takes advantage of the dramatic conflict as much as possible. Beyond these changes, it is possible to summarise the most shared characteristics that describe the notion of dramatic conflict:

- It is an opposition that arises from different objectives or values (moral, ethical, political, etc.), manifested through the behaviours of the agents.
- It can take place between different agents or even inside one agent's conscience, so the conflict can be external or internal.
- It can be between the agent and the situation in which she/he finds herself/himself.
- It is connected to some fundamental psychological trait of the agent.
- It provokes an emotional response in agents.
- It must be represented in an intelligible way, and recognisable as an obstacle.

From these traits, we understand how the notion of conflict is directly linked to the goals and behaviours of agents, which we have modelled through planning.

Dramatic tension and conflict maintain their relevance in interactive storytelling. Almost all narrative-based participatory entertainment products use conflict (video games, immersive role-playing games). And also in situations that are not oriented to drama, the notion of conflict can be useful. For example, the museum guide of *DramaTour* (see Chapter 6, Section 6.13) was more interesting because it embodied a little spider who was scared that the cleaners might find him. The protagonist of *Afternoon, a Story* (see Chapter 6, Section 6.4) is in conflict with himself because he experiences a sense of guilt, believing that he witnessed the deaths of his wife and child. Also in *Adventure* (see Chapter 6, Section 6.2) or *Myst* (see Chapter 6, Section 6.7), where the play structure is based on exploration and there is no specific antagonist role, the conflict remains fundamental as a relationship with the unknown environment and with the secrets it hides.

To illustrate how dramatic tension can be implemented in a system, we turn to *Façade*, widely acknowledged as one of the most successful interactive story systems to come out of the research community (see Chapter 6, Section 6.11). In *Façade*, the tension is a numerical level, which is calculated based on the sequence of the actions that are actually composed in the plot generation. In *Façade*, the user plays the role of a friend of a married couple (Grace and Trip) and interacts with both characters using (written) natural language together with some defined gestures. The plot generation uses constraints to ensure that specific dramatic situations certainly will occur, and the database is very detailed, to provide depth to the characters. The characters Grace and Trip are written as a large collection of *behaviours*. Behaviours are short reactive procedures that achieve the characters' goals and subgoals, written in ABL ("A Behaviour Language"), specifically developed in the *Façade* project. The system manages the execution of behaviours, in parallel or in sequence, taking into account goal success/failure, priorities, conflicts, preconditions, and context. Of particular importance in *Façade* is the handling of social interactions; behaviours are organised around a particular theme to form a *dramatic beat*; a higher-level narrative sequencer, a *drama manager* module sequences the dramatic beats. A beat in *Façade* consists of 10–100 *joint dialogue behaviours* (JDB), fragments of dialogues and behaviours shared by one or more characters; therefore, a beat is already a pre-compiled plot sequencer, and sequences its JDB with respect to user interaction. At some instant in time, only one beat is active. A JDB, which is the atomic unit of dramatic action in *Façade*, consists of a well-coordinated, dramatic exchange of one to five dialogue sentence pairs between Grace and Trip; and normally lasts a few seconds. JDBs of one beat are organised around a common narrative goal, such as a brief conflict over a topic, Grace's obsession with furnishing the apartment, or the revelation of an emotionally engaging event, such as Trip's attempt to force Grace to spend their second honeymoon in Italy. Each JDB is able to change one or more values in the state of the story or the overall level of tension in the story.

Furthermore, every single scene (beat) must adapt to the moment in which it comes into play. The dialogues of a scene can vary depending on whether they occur at the beginning of the drama, when the tension is still low, compared to a little later, when the tension has increased. Indeed, if a level of tension is very high and becomes incompatible with a certain beat, the latter may no longer take place. For example, Trip starts making drinks, but, due to what happens later, he is no longer in the mood to serve any. Finally, a beat can be played a second time if some time has passed since the first time. For example, if the player wants Trip to serve him a second drink, this should be possible. However, it is necessary to have enough structural variations yet unused, to avoid repeating the same dialogue with consequent loss of credibility. The total beats are the following 27 (in parentheses, the formal identifier within the implemented system):

1. The player arrives (PlayerArrives);
2. Trip greets player (TripGreetsPlayer);
3. The player enters and Trip calls Grace (PlayerEntersTripGetsGrace);
4. Grace greets the player (GraceGreetsPlayer);
5. Discussion on re-painting (ArgueOverRedecorating);
6. Explanation of the anniversary of the first appointment (ExplainDating Anniversary);
7. Discussion on vacation in Italy (ArgueOverItalyVacation);
8. Fight to establish drinks (FightOverFixingDrinks);
9. Phone call from parents (PhoneCallFromParents);
10. Transition to level 2 tension (TransitionToTension2);
11. Grace angry goes to the kitchen (GraceStormsToKitchen);
12. The player follows Grace into the kitchen (PlayerFollowsGraceToKitchen);
13. Grace returns from the kitchen (GraceReturnsFromKitchen);
14. Trip angry to the kitchen (TripStormsToKitchen);
15. The player follows Trip into the kitchen (PlayerFollowsTripToKitchen);
16. Trip returns from the kitchen (TripReturnsFromKitchen);
17. Trip relaunches the proposal (TripReenactsProposal);
18. Increased crisis (BlowupCrisis);
19. Post-crisis (PostCrisis);
20. Therapy Game (TherapyGame);
21. Accumulation of revelations (RevelationsBuildup);
22. Revelations (Revelations);
23. Final without revelations (EndingNoRevelations);
24. Final with self-revelations only (EndingSelfRevelationsOnly);
25. Final with only revelations of relationships (EndingRelationshipRevelationsOnly);
26. Final with both not fully aware (EndingBothNotFullySelfAware);
27. Final with both aware (EndingBothSelfAware).

As we can see, going from the beginning to the end, some beats are typical of the initial phase of the story (e.g., "TripGreetsPlayer"), some characterise the phase of rising tension ("ArgueOverRedecorating" or "FightOverFixingDrinks"), the beats of crisis ("GraceStormsToKitchen" or "PlayerFollowsGraceToKitchen"), of climax ("RevelationsBuildup") and a number of endings (e.g., "EndingRelationshipRevelationsOnly" and "EndingBothSelfAware").

The overall structure of the story is modulated to comply with a classic five-phase dramatic arc: triggering event, rising tension, crisis, climax, and conclusion. Everything happens independently of the details of each game session. The system, in fact, keeps track of the global level of tension in the story, which is influenced by the user's moves in the different moments of the social interaction. Every change in each state of the game is rendered by Grace and Trip in an emotionally expressive and dramatic way.

The drama manager is active (to select the next beat) when the running beat ends or is cancelled for some reason (while Trip and Grace are arguing about drinks, the player points out that he doesn't want to drink at all). The Beat Sequencing Language, specially developed for *Façade*, allows the author to annotate each beat with some attributes that will be considered by the process that manages the selection and sequencing. The knowledge taken into account to make the selection of the next beat consists of:

- Precondition (a test): If the precondition test is true, the beat is a candidate for selection.
- Weight (float): A static weight that modifies the probability of the beat being selected (without specifications, the default weight is 1.0).
- Test to get the weight: If the test is true, the probability that the beat will be selected is multiplied by the weight; the calculated weight takes precedence over the static weight (assigned *a priori*).
- Priority (integer, a static priority): The beats are selected for the sequence on the basis of a weighted value (among the beats in the highest priority level the system proceeds with a random extraction).
- Test to get priority: If the test is true, the beat yields the specified priority; the calculated priority replaces the static priority (assigned *a priori*).
- Effects (i.e., changes to story values): Changes to be made to story values if the beat completes successfully.

The algorithmic steps to select the next beat implement a filter on the possible candidates:

1. Initialise beat states, that can have a role in its selection.
2. Filter beats by preconditions, for all the unused beats.
3. Evaluate beats for highest priority (priority test).
4. Score the remained beats, using the effects to compare the compliance of the beat with the desired tension arc.
5. Weight the scores of the beats.
6. Randomly select a beat from the weighted scored highest priority beats.

The highest score will be awarded to the available beat whose story tension effects most closely match the short-term trajectory of the ideal story tension arc.

Now we see a possible execution log of the system reported by *Façade* authors, with a list of the beats that occur and the calculation of the next beat (Figure 5.5).

Engines and systems 105

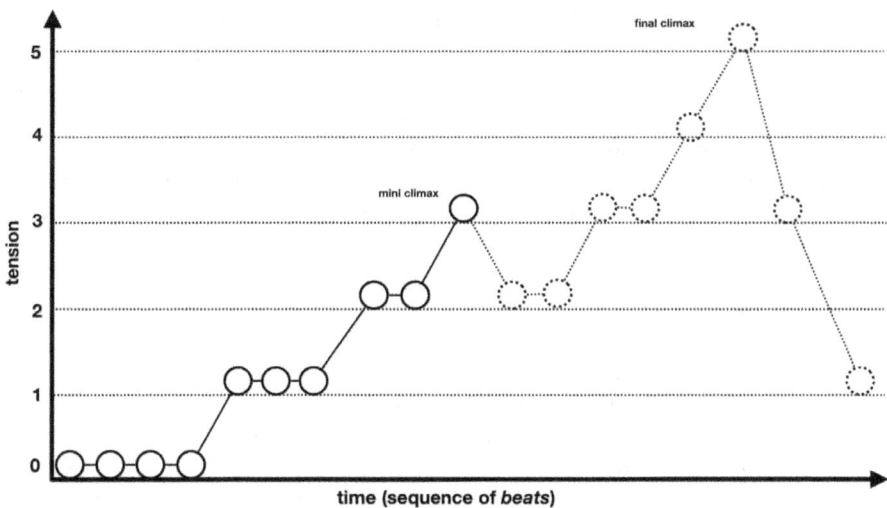

Figure 5.5 Dramatic arc of the *Façade* example execution

The player is a man named Dave. The dramatic tension is considered together with the affinity of the player with one of the two characters, Trip or Grace.

Player Dave arrives (PlayerArrives).
Trip greets Dave (TripGreetsPlayer).
Dave enters and Trip calls Grace (PlayerEntersTripGetsGrace).
Grace greets Dave (GraceGreetsPlayer). The group of beats with greetings is always made up of these four beats, in this sequential order. There are possible variations of the individual behaviours; however, the player cannot do anything to modify her/his affinity towards the characters, which remains neutral.

Dave asks about drinks (AskAboutDrinks). Level 1 tension, affinity remains neutral. The player asks for a drink, causing a priority test to increase the priority of beat AskAboutDrinks. Since this is the only beat in the highest priority, it is selected for the sequence. During the execution of the actions, some behaviour of Dave tilts his affinity towards Grace.

Discuss decorating (Decorating). The tension is still at level 1, and Dave's affinity remains with Grace. At this moment in the drama there are three beats that are candidates to be realised: discussing the decorating, explaining the anniversary of the first date, asking for information on drinks (their weight has increased, and this makes them more likely). Since the one on drinks has already been used, it is not selectable. The drama manager can still maintain the tension 1, and the affinity with Grace, so the scene on decorating is chosen. During the action the player causes a change of affinity (from Grace to Trip) and the scene is interrupted.

Holidays in Italy (ItalyVacation), healthy marriage. The tension remains at level 1, but, after the last shift, now the affinity is neutral (Dave has shown himself to be akin to both). Since two scenes with tension level 1 have already been executed, also those of the next level can be considered. Note that at this moment the desired arc level is still 1 and will reach tension level 2 after the next beat execution. Right now, the level 1 beats still have a higher chance of being selected (and in fact the one about holiday in Italy is selected), but it would not have been impossible also to execute a level 2 one. During the action, the player refuses to play the riddle game proposed by Trip on the photos of the vacation, and the affinity returns to Grace.

Grace's parents. (Grace'sParents). The tension raises to level 2, the affinity is with Grace. The desired tension is now at level 2, and the level 2 beats are more likely to be selected than the level 1 ones. This is why the one about Grace's parents comes into play. During the action, the player sides with Grace, ensuring that the affinity stays where it is.

Trip Relationships. (Revelations) Tension 2, Dave's affinity is with Grace. Since the tension is now 2, only tension 2 beats are available for the sequence; in this case, Trip's affairs are sequenced. During the action, Dave sides with Grace and keeps his affinity with her.

Mini-climax. Since two tension 2 beats have occurred, the drama manager sequences the mini-climax of part I of the drama.

Façade was one of the first interactive storytelling systems to shape the notion of a dramatic arc.

The increase in dramatic tension is also central in *IDtension*, by Nicolas Szilas (see the example description in Chapter 6, Section 6.15). This is a system for interactive drama that creates conflicts for the user and the characters, by selecting appropriate events. *IDtension* uses a set of moral values, to which each character shows some adherence. Characters with less adherence to some moral value will be more likely to take actions defined as immoral with respect to that value. This translates into a set of opposite values that form the conflict in the instantiated narrative (Szilas 2003).

Fabulator, by Barros and Musse, aims to maintain tension arcs in interactive narratives as well as to prevent the user from deviating from a canonical storyline. To avoid deviations, a planner can modify the plot in such a way as to discourage or warn the user in case of excessive deviation, with the possible risk of creating a dead end, i.e., a point from which it is impossible for the user to reach the end of the story (Barros and Musse 2008).

These examples, despite their diversity, see constraints as a means of imposing a certain level of quality or intent. Tighter constraints, or templates, lead to a more limited set of stories, for example, grammar-based plot generators are often limited to creating stories in a particular genre. Wider constraints allow for greater story variance and are often used to guide the generation process rather than explicitly controlling it. This often leads to a greater diversity of the realised stories, and in interactive stories this is used to encourage multiple experiences. Tighter constraints, however, produce more reliable results and allow for smoother or more subtle changes in the texture.

5.5 Database and automation

Even the database, that is the set of dynamic elements that form the story world (agents, objects, scenarios, ... units), together with their relationships, can be built automatically. A form of (indirect) automation is a consequence of the plot generators above: in fact, plot generators yield the database changes that result from the effects of events that actually occur and need to be traced to maintain the coherence of the story development. For example, characters who die cannot be part of the active database from a certain point onwards and cannot appear in events that occur later in the storyline. An interesting challenge is the direct automation of the database, that is, the creation of dynamic elements or the modification of existing elements. However, systems have hardly focused solely on the generation of the database. In common with the game world is the automated creation of visual elements that relate to the scenography of the narrative display, such as terrain, vegetation or entire cities, but also more significant dynamic elements. For example, text-to-image systems create 3D virtual worlds (e.g., WordsEye[8]) and, in the narrative case, select appropriate images for the text of the story (a sort of automatic illustration of fairy tales): text is typically built manually, and automation produces a corresponding (visual) world (Delgado, Magalhães and Correia 2010). Another example is the visualisation tools that take scripts as inputs, and automatically generate an animated 3D view of the space. In this case, the plot is not just text, but has a structure recognised by the engines and used by the authors for the drafting. The system automatically analyses each scene and creates characters, settings and props. Afterwards, the author can usually change the layout of the animated scene (e.g., the spatial arrangement of elements) (Liu and Leung 2006; Hanser et al. 2010; Hayashi et al. 2013). Finally, there are systems that deal with the generation of discourse, that is, the component in which the narration is expressed (the words of a text, the beats of a dialogue, the physical characteristics of a character): in this case, the database, presented by Marie L. Ryan as the notion of space, can have many dimensions and the idea is to create it automatically from plot structures (Ryan 2006). We can recall two examples here.

The *Radiant Story* system, developed for the game *The Elder Scrolls V: Skyrim*, automatically creates and places new characters or objects within the game world when creating a mission.[9] The plot structure must be created manually, using only roles instead of characters. When generating the mission, the roles are filled with the current characters and objects or by automatically creating new characters/objects that are placed in the game world. The latter are then managed with the *Radiant A.I.* technology (already provided in *The Elder Scrolls IV: Oblivion*[10]), which adapts the abilities and behaviours of the characters to the environment, based on past experiences. In more recent versions, the producers reduced the impact of the AI system on the game: "Algorithms can't come up with emotionally-fulfilling stories... yet."[11] *Gameforge* is an RPG (role-playing game) space generation system that takes a story as input and generates a database. The story is represented as a sequence of plot points, as well as the initial state of the space, which includes all the elements; then, a genetic algorithm creates potential worlds that feature the initial state provided by the author, but also elements of scenography such as terrain and city. The generation function is parametric and can favour spaces with certain characteristics (e.g., dimensions and number of places that the user can visit). In *Gameforge*, the story is seen as a set of constraints that must be satisfied by the generated world (and the resulting database) (Hartsook et al. 2011).

However, most systems address plot and database conjointly during the generation step. These systems generally yield the so-called *emergent narratives*, where the author has no strict control over the story development.

5.6 Emergent narratives: joint automation of plot and database

Systems that implement joint automation of plot and database usually generate emergent narratives, i.e., stories that emerge from the interactions of the dynamic elements of the world. These are almost always sophisticated virtual agents whose interactions and conflicts should eventually lead to some form of storytelling. Often these systems exercise weak control over the outcome. Narrativity here is to be understood as a sequence of events that are causally motivated according to Abbott's definition. The resulting stories are always unique, as the author usually has little or no influence on the storyline and only intervenes in the creation of the initial state of the database (Abbott 2002). Furthermore, since the database and the storyline influence each other, some researchers tend to make changes to the database as this would improve the actual generation of the plot (Riedl and Young 2005). Planning-based systems are widely used because they can modify the database to support plot generation. There are also systems that generate new database items based on constraints imposed by the author or motivated by events in the plot. Then there are the simulations of story worlds that are created manually but can be modified or enriched. And, finally, there are systems that work on the basis of user actions.

5.6.1 Constraints on the plot and modifications of database elements

The constraints expressed on the plot, as we have seen before, can be used to modify the elements of the database. There are many ways to create or modify the elements of the database. Here we look at the ones that have received some attention.

Revision of the initial state

A typical modification of the database is to calculate the initial state of the system, i.e., the situation in which the dynamic elements are at the beginning of the story. In the case of a plot grammar, the hierarchy of expansion rules on the far left provides the category for the initial unit (e.g., an Interdiction for Propp); in the case of a set of constraints, these must be applied to determine which unit type can start the story or create a new unit that satisfies the constraints; in the case of character planning and conflict, it is necessary to determine the initial state of the characters (even if this is only their spatial position in the world). In the literature, this problem is often referred to as "revision" of the initial state, since by default a system always contains an initial state created to cope with cases where there are no interactions that change it.

The *Fabulist* system is a planning-based plot generator that merges the goals of the author and the characters (Riedl and Young 2006). In the case of a database modification, it uses an initialisation algorithm that generates an initial state that satisfies some aspect of the plot. In particular, the system uses abstract rules for generating the plot that do not include the details of the actual narrative situation. The algorithm models the world, taking into account the requirements of the generation rules. For example, if a hidden weapon is to be placed in the game world, it must be ensured that a certain character will eventually be able to find it and assassinate their rival. Therefore, the rules state that the position of the weapon (which is an undetermined piece of information) is constrained in some way and some positions are forbidden (because it would be impossible for the character to find it); during plot generation, the system places the weapon in a position that meets the constraints and then updates the database. These changes are very limited as they only apply to spatial details, as in this example.

The late commitment

Late commitment is a database modification technique inspired by improvisational theatre. Improvisation allows actors/characters to change or generate new content for the database that is useful for fulfilling a specific purpose. For example: a character wants to fight another character and proposes to pull out the weapons (which the system has created from scratch) at the time of the fight. The system checks that there are no violations of consistency in the world (a Masai warrior might not use the bazooka), makes the change and creates the weapons. The late-commitment approach thus uses consistency as a constraint to ensure that any change is transparent, i.e., the user should not notice that changes have been made as if the database had never been redefined. This approach has been implemented in the *Virtual Storyteller* system, which basically also implements a Story Director. The Story Director is an agent that works with a formal model of the plot (which can be expressed, e.g., by a grammar) and a simulated understanding of the narrative. The Story Director can selectively trigger events within the simulated game world and combine them so that the result is a narrative. The Story Director can also act on the game world and introduce new characters or change the goals of the characters to improve some of the qualities of the resulting storyline (Swartjes, Kruizinga and Theune 2008).

Users' actions

When creating or modifying the database elements, the systems can also take into account the encoded user actions that participate like the other dynamic elements of the database. The mediation technique used by the Mimesis system to modify the plot or database has the purpose of bringing the users' actions in line with the default plot (a similar concept to the interactive *The Merchant of Venice* described above). There are two types of mediation. Reactive mediation intervenes when the user performs an action that could prevent the current plot from being implemented. In these cases, the system re-plans the narrative to either allow or force the user's action to fail (e.g., causing a weapon jam, if the user intends to shoot a main character in the story). Proactive mediation, on the other hand, aims to predict the user's future actions and changes the world of the story in advance to make the attempt even impossible (e.g., locking a drawer with a gun to prevent the user from shooting the character) (Riedl, Saretto and Young 2003; Harris and Young 2005). *TALE-SPIN*, one of the very first story generation systems we mentioned at the beginning of this chapter, works by providing the characters in the database with goals and attitudes (Meehan 1977). The system models simple stories and simulates the events that occur when a character tries to achieve a goal. The characters' goals are derived from their personalities and are tracked by the system, which modifies the content of the database to ensure that the characters' goals are achieved. *TALE-SPIN* was also one of the first AI systems to emphasise the importance of narrative aspects, such as uniqueness and coherence, and their direct connection to the content of the database, which in turn depends on the role and depth of the characters.

5.6.2 Plot and database modelled with constraints

In these cases, the systems contain constraints that can be used to find non-ad hoc solutions to continue generating the plot despite the adverse events and update the database accordingly. Some approaches are now discussed.

Engines by analogy

Some systems have explored the creation of fictional events that can be added by the storytelling engine during the plot generation process. Such events are created when the planner is faced with a situation where it is impossible or difficult to achieve the next goal of the story. In such situations, the system uses analogy-based reasoning to find a case consisting of steps similar to those required to achieve the current goal (Li and Riedl 2011). Through analogy-based reasoning, we can access a large archive of successful cases and analyse the similarities between the current case and the archive cases, retrieving the case that is most similar to the current case. At this point, the engine implementing a reasoning by analogy detects the two sequences of events that are comparable and inserts some missing events to complete the solution and adapt it to the new context. For example, the action of beating a donkey with a stick can be used to create the action of killing the dragon with a sword. The rules for transforming predicates (from hit to kill) and attributes (stick to sword, donkey to dragon) do the work. Li and Riedl refer to such missing events as gadgets, and the system reasons about how a gadget should be used in the context of an event sequence in which events that occur immediately before and after the gadget are in place. These events form the behaviour of the gadget, which is represented as a temporally ordered sequence of actions. Starting from a goal taken from a story (e.g., the character Bob needs to be infected with a flu virus), the system constructs the gadget's behaviour by working backwards towards the goal, using actions and entities from different examples. As we saw with *The Merchant of Venice*, the goals are logical predicates (e.g., infected by (bob,virus)), an action is an operator that tests some predicates as preconditions and asserts some predicates as effects. The Gadget Generator works with a conventional story generator which provides goals that the gadget must achieve. The goals are first used to identify elements of the world. For example, an object can be mentioned in a goal: the target world implicit in infected-by(bob,virus) includes concepts such as viruses, a character named Bob, and actions such as coughing and healing. The system creates the second input world by retrieving an object from its knowledge base and searching for items that achieve predicates similar to the specified goal. The retrieved element is the prototype of the gadget. The second world includes the element, its behaviour, the actions performed and the entities to which the behaviour refers. For example, the behaviour of a wireless phone is linked to the entity "voice", which becomes part of the second input world. At this point, the two input worlds merge into a new world called blend world. In particular, the gadget's behaviour is constructed by selectively adapting actions from one world to the other. This adaptation, called *projection*, is driven by the goals and, via plan representation (see Chapter 3. Section 3.2), by the actions that achieve those goals; plans thus require preconditions, i.e., predicates. These predicates must hold for the action to be carried out. Whenever an action is introduced into the blend world, its preconditions are also added to the world. Actions continue to be projected to meet goals until all goals are met or determined as a fundamental property of the gadget itself. The projection of actions is achieved by various methods:

- The action is projected from input world 1 to the blend world as is (no change is needed). For example, action *Speak-into* performed by entity *Alice*, on entities *voice* and *cup1*, speak-into(alice,cup1,voice), i.e., "Alice speaks by putting her voice into the cup of the wireless phone".
- The blend action is obtained by taking arguments from both spaces, by analogy. For example, action *Cough-Into* and entity *virus* are projected from world 2, but *Cough-Into* includes arguments *Alice* and *cup1* from world 2, after mapping *Cough-Into* with *Speak-into* due to the analogy similarities. The blend action is *cough-into(alice,cup1,virus)*, i.e., "Alice coughing the virus into the cup of the wireless phone".

However, the blend action can be obtained from a merge with illegal arguments and can create a new (illegal) action. For example, action speak-into(alice,cup1, voice) produces as consequence the predicate transmit(phone,Alice,Bob, voice), that is, "The phone transmits the voice from Alice to Bob". Having projected action `cough-into(alice,cup1,virus)` by analogy, we can now achieve `transmit(phone,Alice,Bob,virus)` by replacing voice with *virus*, i.e., the transmission of a wireless phone now transmits viruses instead of voice. Note that this occurs because the algorithm knowingly ignores the rules of the microworld, producing an illegal assignment of parameters and achieving the goal of an imaginary telephone device capable of transmitting flu viruses from one person to another.

Authorship support

The database generation can be done in mixed mode, which assists the author in the creation process. In this case, the author can specify the goals for the development of the plot and the system will automatically generate the goals of each character. This should bring the plot generation closer to the author's ideas, as the encoding of the characters' (possibly conflicting) goals is rendered in a formal way. In addition, the system simulates different users and allows the analysis of possible paths through the story to highlight the author's possible discrepancies between the plot actually deployed and the plot the author had in mind (Si, Marsella and Pynadath 2007). Swanson and Gordon's (2008) system aims at a mixed-initiative approach supported by crowdsourcing knowledge extracted from internet blogs. The author and the system take turns writing the text: the system selects a line of text from a database of lines extracted from internet blogs that should correspond to the author's intended story. The line of text entered by the system can generate as many new database items as the lines entered by the human author. This approach is perhaps closest to Lubart's original vision of working with a computer as collaborator, although results have shown that stories generated using such a method have generally been incoherent (Lubart 2005). In Section 5.6.3, we will discuss other co-creation systems that occupy an intermediate status and also lean towards fully autonomous creation but rely on techniques that will be introduced therein.

The *Scheherazade* system also aims at generating interactive narratives using crowdsourcing methods. Some anonymous authors were asked to provide linear stories for a bank robbery, which were then combined into a final story. This storyline contains branching situations in cases where human authors have created alternative events after a shared event. The aim of this system is to create stories that have the knowledge and creativity of human authors without having to integrate this knowledge into a story generation system. In fact, the system here mainly automates the final combination of all the different plots and worlds into one final story (Li, Lee-Urban and Riedl 2013).

5.6.3 Full plot automation and database simulation

We now turn to the complete automation of the plot, accompanied by a database created by a simulation. That is, starting from an initial seed, the system creates a story world, governed by some combination rules, and produces the effective database of dynamic elements. The combination rules are then shared with the automatic plot generation so that the newly created elements remain consistent.

Cognitive systems of writing

The system *UNIVERSE* implemented the creation of story worlds, focusing particularly on the automatic creation of characters with their histories, family relationships and interpersonal relationships (Lebowitz 1985). Michael Lebowitz's aim was to study the cognitive processes of human authors in the story generation process and to implement a program that could generate consistent storylines for soap opera-type stories that were theoretically unending. Storytelling in *UNIVERSE* is the expansion of goals, until the actual events that can be generated. Goals can be character goals and author goals. Character goals need to be monitored to maintain consistency (a process similar to that of the *TALE-SPIN* system); author goals control the storytelling algorithm, typically goals that instantiate high-level structures. For example, an author's goal might be to cause Lucy to double-cross Lawrence. Two precedence graphs illustrate how the author's and characters' goals relate to each other and to events that have already occurred. Then, the system selects an author's goal to expand, and continues this process recursively, until all goals are converted into actual events, and the system produces the text with natural language generation methods. Incidentally, here we highlight an important component of the process, namely the generation of actual discourse; this step relies on natural language generation, which has greatly improved in recent times, with language modelling techniques (Perera and Nand 2017). To ensure the validity of the generated characters, the story of the fictional world is simulated, using existing characters and/or creating new (cause-motivated) characters: for example, the system can automatically generate children for married characters whose characteristics can be used in the desired storylines. The system could also enforce temporal coherence: for example, if the plot requires a new character for a storyline based on an affair, the character must be born several years before the story's narrative time to ensure that their age falls within the correct range to maintain story consistency. To ensure consistency of character, information is stored in a person frame: traits and goals typical of stereotypes, values used to override values inherited from stereotypes, names that behave like programming variables or identifiers. Finally, to tell a compelling story, the system includes interpersonal relationships for the characters arranged on four scales, namely positive/negative, intimate/distant, dominant/submissive-to, attractiveness. Finally, *UNIVERSE* creates the characters by running a simple simulation of their past lives and creating spouses, children and other assorted characters as needed. The creation of characters is cyclical, keeping a queue; each character is removed in turn from the queue and *UNIVERSE* steps through their life, creating spouses and children; when the present is reached, the system specifies further details, such as occupation and other descriptive traits from the stereotype. The selection of specific events is somewhat arbitrary and is constrained by various character traits. For an example character created by *UNIVERSE*, see Figure 5.6.

```
Name: JESSICA DONADIO (&PER7)
Born in: 1918
Marriages:
  DOUGLAS DAVIDSON [&PER0] [1951/1959]
  - MARK DAVIDSON [&PER8]
  - RENE DAVIDSON ROGERS [&PER9]
  IVAN SCHAAD [&PER14] [1959/1967]
Interpersonal Relationships:
  EX-SPOUSE    DOUGLAS DAVIDSON [&PER0]      -5/-5 // 4/4 // 0/0 // 4/4
  DIV-MOM      8/4 // 4/4 // 6/2 // /        MARK DAVIDSON [&PER8]
  DIV-MOM      8/4 // 4/4 // 6/2 // /        RENE DAVIDSON ROGERS [&PER9]
  EX-SPOUSE    IVAN SCHAAD [&PER14]          -5/-5 // 4/4 // 0/0 // 4/4
               BRUCE SMITH [&PER45]          /-4 // / // 6/-4 // /
History: REVENGE/1964 [&PL7]
Stereotypes: MASSEUSE PARTY-GOER EGOMANIAC
Trait modifiers: (PHYS-APPEARANCE -1) (AGE A)
Overall description:
  WEALTH 6
  PROMISCUITY 7
  COMPETENCE 7
  NICENESS 0
  SELF-CONFIDENCE 8
  GUILE 7
  MOODINESS 5
  PHYS-APPEARANCE 5
  INTELLIGENCE 4
  GOALS (BECOME-FAMOUS MEET-FAMOUS-PEOPLE ASSOCIATE-RIGHT FIND-HAPPINESS)
  AGE A
  SEX F
```

Figure 5.6 A sample UNIVERSE character
Source: Lebowitz (1985).

Figure 5.6 shows Jessica Donadio, born in 1918, features her interpersonal relationships from marriages and with her offspring: in fact, she has stereotypical ex-spouse relationships with her two ex-husbands, Douglas and Ivan, as well as a divorced mother (DIV-MOM) relationships with her two children, Mark and Rene. For each relationship, there are up to four pairs of numbers shown, representing the four scales mentioned above: for example, the relation between Jessica and Douglas on the positive/negative scale has -5 (the ex-spouse stereotype). One additional non-encoded interpersonal relationship, with Bruce, arose from a past revenge event (in 1964); Jessica has negative feelings about Bruce (-4), but he is in a position of power over her (6).

Modifiers are used to make individual traits with respect to the stereotypes, e.g., physical appearance and age. Descriptive traits are self-explanatory: not nice, astute, self-promoting goals.

A similar context, in terms of representing the human creative process, but with a more productive effect, is *Mexica*, a system based on a cognitive model of how humans write (Pérez y Pérez and Sharples 2001). *Mexica* is a constraint-based model that operates through the interaction of two phases: engagement and reflection. There are four types of constraints:

1 *Story world constraints*, organised per character and registering the effects of events (e.g., used to update the consequential states of the actions).

2 *Knowledge constraints*, built from archived stories and encoding content and rhetoric (e.g., tensional constraints to create sequences of events that combine degradation-improvement processes).
3 *Guidelines*, updated through the appraisal of the story (e.g., detecting that the current story lacks improvement-degradation processes, i.e., that the story is boring, triggers guidelines requiring interesting actions to occur).
4 *General constraints*, basic beliefs about the story world to be satisfied (e.g., effects of one action modify the story-world context of at least one character).

Engagement and reflection alternate their interventions in a loop: engagement filters the set of next possible actions according to guidelines created during reflection, after measuring the novelty and interest of the story in progress with respect to an archive of abstractions of the story. It is argued that this simulates human behaviour, namely the employment of schemata to constrain story generation: for example, "if a person is asked to write a Sherlock Holmes story, he probably will retrieve events related to detectives, gangs, bad and good boys, etc." (ibid., p. 11). The final output of generation consists of predefined sentences assigned to the actions of the characters (many to one) so that the story can be varied in the final output.

Large Language Models for discourse generation

Generating an acceptable output discourse is one of the major weaknesses of symbolic AI systems such as *UNIVERSE* (1984) and *Mexica* (2001), as these techniques perform poorly without appropriate creative human intervention. Recently, there have been great improvements in language generation achieved by statistics-based large language models. Large Language Models (LLMs) are models of several gigabytes trained on very large amounts of text (up to petabytes). The creation of the well-known GPT-3, for example, includes 175 billion parameters, i.e., values that the algorithm updates when learning from training data (Brown et al. 2020). These techniques can be applied in a variety of contexts, including translation, question answering, chatbot conversations, auto-completion and cloze tests in reading comprehension. The key to their application successes is their ability to adapt to the desired tasks by using only what are called prompts, i.e., verbal descriptions of the tasks: prompts for translation, for example, some pairs of the desired inputs/outputs, e.g., the prompt "English: How are you? French: Comment allez-vous? English: Hello! French:" is likely to yield the output "Bonjour!" (Wu, Terry and Cai 2022, p. 1).

The LLMs have been used to automate the generation of stories, both for the plot and for the database of dynamic elements, as completely autonomous modules or in collaboration with human authors. The advantage of such models is that they generate credible texts. However, with regard to the aforementioned tasks, the generation of narrative texts is more challenging, as larger texts are needed and consistency over long stretches as well as coherence over sequential segments is more difficult to maintain.

The *Dramatron* system implements a hierarchical approach to story generation (Mirowski et al. 2022). The system starts with a summary of the central dramatic conflict, called the logline, which is provided by the author. From the input of the logline, which is used as a prompt, *Dramatron* uses the LLM Chinchilla (but any other LLM that accepts prompts is also acceptable) to generate a title for the story, a set of characters, a set of scene summaries organised into a plot, the descriptions of the settings, and finally the dialogue organised into the scenes listed in the plot. *Dramatron* can work autonomously until the end. However, the user/author can intervene at any stage of the hierarchical generation by requesting alternative generations, editing/rewriting the output text or replacing some speeches. The final script can thus be generated completely autonomously (although user evaluations are less than enthusiastic) or with human assistance (and users/authors report appropriate assistance at various stages of generation).

Spindle also relies on a prompt-based LLM (Calderwood, Wardrip-Fruin and Mateas 2022). It is geared to co-creation and the generated stories are targeted to the *Twine* framework, namely choice-based interactive fiction. Therefore, *Spindle* does not create linear plots, but interactive, branching narratives. The generation pipeline consists of condensing the narrative context (or logline in *Dramatron* terms) into a compact prompt representation that feeds the pre-trained language model, namely GPT-3. This model is further fine-tuned. *Spindle* is a mixed-initiative tool where the user takes turns controlling the language model: Since *Twine* narratives consist of "passages" and hyperlinks between passages, *Spindle* performs narrative compression at the request of the user/author to elaborate an understanding of the current thrust of the story, and uses this understanding to determine the generation of the next passage. To begin, the human author creates the title and then the Start passage. At some point during creation, all outlined passages are in a to-do list. Each time a passage is selected, the user/author decides whether to draft the passage body in a text editor or request a system generation, taking into account the narrative context of the passage; then the author reviews the written passages, generates new passages (which are added to the to-do list) or concludes the writing.

Authoring as (re)telling on a database

We conclude this section with another possible work flow for automating story generation through database simulation, and here again we can see some examples of co-creation. *Dwarf Fortress* is a construction/management simulation game with a procedurally generated fantasy world (or database, in our terms). In this world, the user/player has indirect control over a population of dwarves with the goal of building a fortress. Although the game has received some complaints about its complex gameplay, it is a long-lived game that has inspired other well-known games (such as *Minecraft*), and has been developed as freeware since 2002 and was first released in 2006, and survives on donations. It is an emergent story with an open ending and no main goals (one of the criticisms). At the beginning of the game, users introduce some constraints for the generation process of the fantasy world: a site for the world (where the fortress should be built), in terms of the size of the world, the presence of forests or minerals, continents, oceans and islands, and so on. The database is procedurally created via generative geology, meteorology and biology, simulating the evolution of the civilisations that inhabited the world over centuries, down to the individual lives of the current inhabitants, without the need for manual intervention. The process results in a coherent world with internally consistent tradition and history. *Dwarf Fortress* is a colony management or adventure game (can also be played in turns): the goal is to build a successful fortress that can withstand monster attacks and generate wealth while taking care of the dwarves. Creatures, dwarves and monsters are modelled in detail, down to the body organs and fluids, are made of different materials (metal, stone, fire), have minds and personalities, abilities, short- and long-term memory, and emotional states.

The features of an endless management game, which proceeds by generating events as in real life, have triggered the use of these environments as sorts of expressive tools for the creation of stories (practices referred to as retellings, Eladhari 2018). It happens that emergent narratives are the result of extensive play that embellishes the course of events by adding new details created by the possibilities of the game environment, or by commenting on the flaws/limitations of the game as a storytelling tool. There are even proposals to consider such games (called Interactive Emergent Narratives) as playable narrative media, namely as "narrative instruments" that, like musical instruments, require a player to operate (Kreminski and Mateas 2021). Games like *Dwarf Fortress* have a strong narrative texture, such as the recurring "gradual rise followed by sudden precipitous decline" arc (a particular form of the arc of tension seen earlier), and this characterises the game with a very desirable attribute, and its "instrumental voice" is successful because it provides a perceptible marking on the event structure.

However, returning to some of the tools for automatic generation or co-creation of stories presented above, we can consider *Dwarf Fortress* as composed of roughly two modules (from the point of view of emergent narrative), namely the game engine, which curates a particular telling of game events (and this presupposes a narrative mood due to the database structure), and the simulation engine, which produces the internal raw material that becomes narrative only after the narrative has been curated by humans. Indeed, as suggested by James Ryan (2018), we can make a distinction for these cases where the co-creation features a human that creates and some system that generates (mostly by simulation) the database. *Bad News* is an experimental game that is a combination of social simulation and live performance and has won numerous awards at international festivals and events. The actual creation task is carried out through the improvisation of human actors and audience/players based on a simulated database (Samuel et al. 2016). This is a one-to-one performance: one performer and a one-person audience (the player). The player is introduced to an environment through some initial instructions, a procedurally generated town, with a simulated history of over a century. The game consists of conversations between the player and the inhabitants of the city (the so-called Non Player Characters or NPCs), all interpreted by a single actor who plays by improvising on the information provided by the database. As the player moves through the city, the performer is informed by the database about the area the player is exploring and its inhabitants. Each performance features a different generation of the city. This guarantees a new game, both for the player and the actor. The purpose of exploring the city is told to the player at the beginning: his goal is to inform a particular resident (an unknown resident who will be identified during the exploration) that some of her/his relatives have recently died elsewhere.

The database is created shortly before the start of the game using the AI software *Talk of the Town* (Ryan 2018). The simulation is about a fictional small American town from its founding in 1839 to the year 1979. This simulated chronology creates towns (a database) with about 50 businesses and several hundred residents (the dynamic elements), with their physical appearances and personalities. The simulation, which runs over time, requires residents to make decisions about where to go based on their personalities, their social and family networks, and their daily routines (which may take them to work, to run errands, to visit a lover, or to play a sporting game). If many characters are in the same position, there is a chance that they will share information and implement knowledge transfer from one character to another. In their simulated interactions, the characters exchange knowledge about their current state, which is described by a (database) record of occupation, home address, physical description and family ties.

However, as time progresses in the simulation, the characters' confidence in some knowledge item wanes, if it is not continually reinforced; so, for example, friends who have been estranged will slowly begin to forget the details of each other's life. While this happens, characters may unknowingly spread false information or even lie, i.e., intentionally spreading false information. After nearly a century and a half of this simulation, the characters get a complete, if sometimes factually inaccurate, view of the town they live in and the people who populate it. In addition, the characters get married, have children, quit jobs or start new ones, set up businesses, move out of town and die. Birth, death and marriage rates, baby names and types of businesses that are started or close come from historical US census data; real historical events such as world wars and natural disasters are not modelled beyond their influence on the data. A child's personality is built on that of her/his parents. Every type of business has a range of jobs to fill (e.g., retail establishments have cashiers, managers, caretakers, etc.) and hires for these positions consider personality, age, work history, family and social ties; family businesses feature frequently in *Talk of the Town*.

The simulation contains no model, no grammar and no explicit constraints of narrative (e.g., events with dramatisation priority), but a narrative-inspiring world emerges from the simulated database. By simulating more than a century of history, *Bad News* characters fit into rich social contexts brought to light through player interaction and actor performance. This means that it is the responsibility of the simulation algorithm to discover interesting elements, and that of the actor to gently guide conversations to points where these elements can naturally come up.

When done well, a large part of the joy of playing *Bad News* – for players and actors alike – is discovering the wonder in the seemingly normal lives of these simulated characters.

5.7 General considerations regarding storytelling systems

We conclude this section with some general considerations. After the previous long section on emergent narratives, a general objection to the whole concept of interactive storytelling arises. It has been long and often said that a feature of interactive storytelling is that it does not end. "Interactive fiction is, in principle (if not in practice) with an undefined, infinite end" (Niesz and Holland 1984, p. 121). A dialogue with a chatbot could only be interrupted by a crash of the human system (the user faints) or of the computer system (an online connection failure); a narrative intelligence system could continue to produce stories and variants as long as it is powered and functioning.

As usual, statements of principle collide with practice. While some game adventures have seen so many editions over the years that they do indeed seem endless, it goes without saying that every story in every edition is structured to come to a conclusion that conveys a sense of narrative closure. Of course, the same game adventures are designed to allow the audience to play multiple sessions, but that does not mean there are not many instances where, once you reach the end, you start all over again. The infinite mode, the ability to last over time but not end, is typical of games based on the puzzle model, where after solving one puzzle we move on to the next without an end.

And this is the model of game environments, where the well-structured narrative is replaced by exploration of environments and solving of puzzles. In the war game, where our online avatar plays countless adventures allying or conflicting with other avatars, the game may never end, but the individual stories do. Every time we start a fight, every battle, every level of the game will be a story that begins and ends. And that means that the story may be more or less built on a model of actional closure, depending on how much narrative there is. But in any case, it is appropriate to define the parts of the action, so that they reflect a dramatic development.

In fact, when we design the development of an interactive narrative, it is good to keep in mind that the emotional participation of the public can develop within two polarities that identify two macro approaches to narration:

- *Dramatic narration*: The audience is involved with the actions that happen to the several agents, the consequences of the actions performed, possibly including their avatars.
- *Exploratory narration*: The audience is intrigued by the unfolding of facts, by the knowledge of the story space, acting on what the system allows them to do or by discovering the possibilities of going against the system.

These are also two cognitive attitudes that interactive storytelling induces in the audience and in the way they perceive their interactivity with the story. Although they are not mutually exclusive, the authors of interactive storytelling need to be clear about what kind of attitude they want to induce and at what time. The tension arc integrates interactive storytelling as the product approaches the dramatic model, but it is not limited to the latter. And that's because tension design is not just about the dramatic model. Exploration of a space can also be designed in a compelling, intriguing way if it is designed to create emotional tension in the audience. For example, the discovery of some locations in the fantasy world of *Myst* may be accompanied by higher moments of tension; or a guide to a historical site might consider a particular environment as the climax of the visit. Interactive narratives on a hypertextual map may assign greater emotional tension to some units in order to induce a peak of emotional involvement.

It is understood that more and more interactive multimedia works are approaching the models of television series and films, seeking solutions that, albeit in a different form, re-propose the management of the viewer's tension. One of the tasks of the engine is to generate the ordered sequence of units or the sequence of behaviours of the agents, it becomes increasingly important that this happens, considering how the emotional tension of the story and of the audience. evolve, respectively. The sequencing engine in *Façade* (see Chapter 6, Section 6.11) for example, took into account the dramatic arc and also selected beats based on their ability to increase or decrease tension. The *IDTension* system provided a narrative sequencer that calculated the effects of possible actions and sequenced them, again with the aim of creating dramatic tension effects. These examples show that the formal description of emotions is essential to provide the system with the necessary instructions so that the tension increases and decreases in a non-random way.

5.8 Exercises

In this chapter we have reviewed the systems for storytelling, including authoring tools, which support the story-writing process through the representation of the dynamic elements, and storytelling engines, which generate the plot, starting from the dynamic elements and sometimes also the dynamic elements from abstract descriptions. In the exercises here, we focus on the plot generation. As we have seen, the graph of the units can be constrained in several ways for the plot generation. Therefore, the author must take into account the operational behaviour of the engine to develop a notation that constrains the sequencing of the units. We address three approaches, that correspond to the grammar-based categorization of units, the precondition/effects annotation of units, and the dramatic tension of units.

5.8.1 The form of the story, or the application of a template

Approaches based on templates, structures, or grammar provide fixed schemata that the unit sequences must comply with. The simplest one is that every story has a beginning, a middle, and an end. In general, each story is made up of parts with specific characteristics. For example, the beginning is characterised by not assuming any other incident has been told. Then, the template, structure, grammar, or schema provide a syntax that defines the composition: for example, one schema can implement the positional schema above (first, the beginning units, then the middle units, and, finally, the end units). In this exercise, the reader is invited to experience how Lakoff's grammar of Propp morphology can constrain the unit writing and sequencing. The author must write units according to the characterisation provided by the following 11 categories:

1. Int: Interdiction
2. Vio: Violation
3. Cv: Complication due to evil
4. L: Departure
5. D: Giver interrogating, testing, or attacking hero
6. F: Hero reacting appropriately
7. G: Hero receiving magical agent
8. H: Fight
9. I: Victory
10. K: End of bad luck
11. Rew: Reward

As remarked above, many units can correspond to each category, depending on the possible branches that the story develops. So, if we take the spaceship story in a mission for Klungon, the introduction of an Interdiction event is

> The interstellar command has ordered spaceship *Sirius* not to cross the borders of the galactic empire.

The next category, Violation (Vio), can show the spaceship venturing beyond the borders, and the one after that CV (Complications due to evil) could be the attack of the aliens. In order to get a multilinear story with this grammar, multiple units per category are required. That is to say, Vio units can describe different actions (finding an ally in the army of the galactic empire, attacking and defeating the imperial squad, etc.), but they all have the same narrative function (violating the interdiction).

In this type of design, the units are not placed in succession only on the basis of connections (manual or logical, as in the previous examples) but according to the ordering established by the grammar. The labelling of the units according to the 11 categories also defines their sequence. However, we can decide that a specific unit, in one of the categories, can be reached only through a limited number of paths or that some categories are not implemented. A way to do this is to identify the narrative lines by giving them a name. A possible solution to encode this choice is to tag the individual with a tag representing a narrative line. Then, to keep the number of stories high, it makes sense that the same units can be part of multiple storylines. For example, if we have created three units with the function

Cv, we will be able to decide that two of them can be part of both the narrative lines labelled "A" and "B", respectively, while the third can only be part of line "C ".

This approach can easily be implemented in most editors through tagging, thus implementing the list of 11 categories as special tags. In order to keep both the Propp category vocabulary and some other relevant tagging vocabulary (such as, e. g., the one for narrative lines), Storygraphia provides a specific interface, in Propp (PRP) mode, with a background reporting the 11 categories, ordered from left to right, and an interactive menu that implements the annotation of a unit with one of the Propp categories. The unit is then positioned on the x axis according to the Propp function assigned.

5.8.2 The constrained plot generation: preconditions and effects annotation

The generation of the plot can simply traverse the edges created explicitly by the author. However, in this case, the author compiles a graph by mentally building up the states of affairs that must hold in the story world before some unit comes into play and the states of affairs that hold after some unit has been executed. This work can be effectively carried out by the engine, once the states of affairs that must precede and will follow the unit execution are written in some constrained format.

In the systems described in this chapter, these constraints are usually given as states of the story world expressed in a logical format. For example, `loan-favour (shylock, antonio, venice-rialto)`, i.e., "Shylock gives Antonio a loan as a favour in Venice Rialto", is formally read as:

> the predicate loan-favour, interpreted as relation of giving a loan as a favour in some place between a person who gives the loan and a person who receives the loan in some place, and holding in this case between the entity shylock, interpreted as the person Shylock in the story world, namely the person who gives the loan as a favour, the entity antonio, interpreted as the person Antonio in the story world, namely the person who receives the loan, and the entity venice-rialto, interpreted as the area of the city of Venice in the story world, namely where the loan giving takes place.

States become the preconditions and effects of the units, and their annotation decides the connections of the units. Specifically, we can annotate the units with their preconditions, i.e., the states that must necessarily hold for the actions contained in the unit to be performed. Similarly, we can annotate the units with their effects, i.e., the states that hold after the executions of the units, and likely produced by the actions occurred in the units to be relevant for the story development. The latter comment is of paramount importance for the causal connection of the story incidents: preconditions and effects must forcibly not be related to fortuitous events, but preferably related to actions intentionally performed by agents in the unit incidents.

States are snapshots of the story world at a given moment; therefore, we must avoid verbs that suggest any process (go, do, etc.) and use stative verbs (be, have, lives in, etc.). For example, the precondition of the initial unit in which the action of the spaceship is to search for the precious ore could be "Spaceship *Sirius* is on a mission."

Preconditions and effects, which are preferably expressed as logical formulae, but any other constrained formal language is possible (depending on the engine), also define the logical consistency of our hypertext narrative through the coherence of unit connections. Specifically, when all the precondition states of a unit are satisfied by the effect states of another unit, the two can be connected. Therefore, the graph edges are not plotted by the author, but automatically plotted by the engine. The author manages all the possible connections that define the story graph implicitly, by writing states and annotating units with states in precondition or effect positions. Also, if the author wants to plot the connections by hand, it can be advantageous to test their coherence through an annotation of the preconditions and effects, since it is not immediately feasible to mentally compute all the connections that are logically possible for some unit (thus, increasing the graph connections) or that are logically licensed for some unit (thus, reducing the graph connections). Therefore, the precondition/effects constraints can work as an automatic test for the consistency of a story graph.

We can review the narrative features of the units of the spaceship story in search of Klungon and augment the unit descriptions with preconditions and effects to build a logical backbone for the narrative. We enforce the annotation of precondition/effects states on units to test the coherence of the connections that have been established manually by the author. These are the incidents occurring in Unit02:

> An alien life form, which is hidden among the samples from the asteroid, manages to take over the ship's controls and disable them.

Working with minimal precondition/effects annotation, we can introduce two states, one precondition and one effect of Unit02:

- *Precondition state*: "The probe has inspected the asteroid and brought samples on board."
- *Effect state*: "The ship is damaged and out of control."

The incidents occurring in the unit cannot take place if those preconditions are not present and the effects are the direct effect of those incidents. The description of the unit can be as sketched as the above or be refined in detail, such as:

> *Sirius* scientists are analysing the stone samples taken on board by the probe. Suddenly, a pile of stones collapses. A worm-shaped being sneaks out of the pile, jumping very quickly onto the wall of the ship. The hooked tail seriously hurts Dr. Spike in her neck.

Dr. Wuang: "Yon, plug the wound; I'll try to catch it!" The worm, near the door, exits the lab and enters the command room. Here the crew is committed to a manoeuvre to pull the ship out of the control of the asteroid's gravitational force. The worm moves wildly. It accidentally breaks three engine levers and hides in an air duct. The ship is out of control, and the worm is in some unknown point in the ventilation system.

This approach can be implemented in editors that can represent conditions through units, such as *Twine*, though not typically as a logic-based engine. Storygraphia provides a specific interface for preconditions and effects. Each unit is graphically augmented with a menu reporting the precondition and effect states. The engine underlying Storygraphia automatically connects pairs of units that are coherent with the precondition/effects continuity. The appropriate operating mode is called the "painting" (PTG) mode: all units are disconnected unless some unit, with its effects, satisfies all the preconditions required by another unit.

5.8.3 The dramatic tension of the story

The decision on the next unit to be sequenced can be handled by approximating the ideal curve of a dramatic arc, a well-known structure in narrative and drama. As we saw in Section 5.4.4, each story fragment, or beat in the case of *Façade*, is annotated with a numerical measure of the dramatic tension that can be experienced when in use. The engine selects the next fragment to play on the basis of the trend of the curve, that is identifying a fragment that increases the current tension value, if the curve is going up, or a fragment that decreases the tension value, if the curve is going down. Approximations form the variations on a rigid sequence and depend upon user behaviour. We are generally talking here of fragments and not of units because, as happens in *Façade*, deeply investigated above, beats are not predetermined story units but contain variations that depend upon the characters' autonomous behaviour.

Once we assume a curve like the one in Figure 5.4, we need to distribute the units along the curve by assigning them a straight numerical value or a calculation method that encodes the type of conflict occurring within a unit. Therefore, the x coordinate responds to the position of the unit in the unfolding interactive story and the y coordinate represents some tension value of the unit due to conflict. The key point is to conceive units with diverse emotional tensions. For example, in the case of *Façade*, the arguments about the drinks were plausibly considered to have a lower tension value than the arguments about Grace's parents.

The dramatic arc model assumes that the narrative sequence starts from units with a low emotional tension value, to grow (more or less steadily), through units of greater value (approximations through equal or slightly lower values are possible), up to a point where the story reaches the peak of tension, to move then (more or less rapidly) to the conclusion with a brief succession of units with (more or less) decreasing values.

The hypergraph connects multiple narrative lines, all approximating the dramatic arc. However, the developments can be many, and the units can be included in different paths. In the spaceship mission story graph, the unit of maximum tension (i.e., the final attack of the aliens) can be the peak of many paths. It is important to put links according to some (albeit informal) criterion by considering the attribution of the tension value, in order to rank the unit on a scale. For example, we can take the effects of unity as a possible referential system: the more the effects put some protagonist's goal in danger of not being achieved, the more tension rises; then, when that goal is achieved or drops, the tension drops too. Alternatively, we can evaluate the conflict that occurs in some unit: the direct opposition of two protagonists marks the highest point of the dramatic arc. It is not fundamental what is the criterion that is adopted (there are many possibilities in the literature and the practice of storytelling); however, it is important that we create an explicit one and write units whose succession creates a dramatic arc that is consistently evaluated on the criterion. For example, in the case of the spaceship mission, the battle for the control of the ship raises the tension from the exploratory mission to the asteroid. The re-establishment of control with some losses is balanced with a tension for the missed approach to the Klungon resources but rises with an explicit opponent for the acquisition of the resource.

This approach can be implemented in editors that can annotate units with numerical values or include code that the engine will execute at each sequencing cycle. Storygraphia provides a graphic background for the dramatic arc. The tool assigns a vertical position to a unit on the basis of the annotated tension and its value. Each unit can be assigned a defined tension (e.g., arguing about how dangerous an alien mineral is) and is positioned on the y axis on the basis of the corresponding tension value, an integer from 1 to 100.

Notes

1 http://www.eastgate.com/storyspace/ (accessed 30 October 2022).
2 https://twinery.org (accessed 30 October 2022).
3 https://ganelson.github.io/inform-website/ (accessed 30 October 2022).
4 https://ganelson.github.io/inform-website/book/WI_1_1.html (accessed 30 October 2022).
5 http://inscapers.com (accessed 30 October 2022).
6 https://unity.com/
7 https://github.com/storytron
8 https://www.wordseye.com (accessed 31 October 2022).
9 However, there are some concerns about the actual result with respect to the original promises: https://www.alteredgamer.com/tes-5-skyrim/116302-whats-new-in-skyrim-new-radiant-ai-and-radiant-story/, 2011 (accessed 31 October 2022).
10 https://venturebeat.com/games/dimming-the-radiant-ai-in-oblivion/, 2010 (accessed 31 October 2022).
11 https://www.gamesradar.com/remember-skyrims-radiant-ai-its-got-the-potential-to-revolutionise-rpgs/, 2018 (accessed 31 October 2022).

References

Abbott, H. Porter. 2002. *The Cambridge Introduction to Narrative*. Cambridge: Cambridge University Press.

Andersen, Sandy, and Brian M. Slator. 1990. "Requiem for a Theory: The 'Story Grammar' Story". *Journal of Experimental & Theoretical Artificial Intelligence* 2 (3): 253–275. doi:10.1080/09528139008953726.

Barber, Heather, and Daniel Kudenko. 2008. "Generation of Dilemma-Based Interactive Narratives with a Changeable Story Goal". In Ulrike Spierling and Nicolas Szilas (eds), *Interactive Storytelling. ICIDS 2008.* Berlin: Springer, pp. 214–217. doi:10.4108/icst.intetain2008.2477.

Barros, Leandro Motta, and Soraia Raupp Musse. 2008. "Towards Consistency in Interactive Storytelling: Tension Arcs and Dead-Ends". *Computers in Entertainment* 6 (3). doi:10.1145/1394021.1394036.

Bringsjord, Selmer, and David A. Ferrucci. 2000. "Artificial Intelligence and Literary Creativity: Inside the Mind of BRUTUS, a Storytelling Machine". *Computational Linguistics* 26 (4): 642–647. doi:10.1162/coli.2000.26.4.642.

Brown, Tom B., Benjamin Mann, Nick Ryder, Melanie Subbiah, Jared Kaplan, Prafulla Dhariwal, Arvind Neelakantan, et al. 2020. *"Language Models Are Few-Shot Learners"*. Paper presented at Advances in Neural Information Processing Systems 2020 (NeurIPS), December.

Calderwood, Alex, Noah Wardrip-Fruin, and Michael Mateas. 2022. "Spinning Coherent Interactive Fiction through Foundation Model Prompts". In Maria M. Hedblom, Anna Aurora Kantosalo, Roberto Confalonieri, Oliver Kutz, and Tony Veale (eds), *Proceedings of 13th International Conference on Computational Creativity (ICCC'22)*. Association for Computational Creativity.

Campbell, Joseph. 2008. *The Hero with a Thousand Faces.* Novato, CA: New World Library.

Carroll, Noël. 2003. "Art and Mood: Preliminary Notes and Conjectures". *Monist* 86 (4): 521–555. doi:10.5840/monist200386426.

Cavazza, Marc, Fred Charles, and Steven J. Mead. 2002. *"Interacting with Virtual Characters in Interactive Storytelling"*. Paper presented at First International Joint Conference on Autonomous Agents and Multiagent Systems Part 1 – AAMAS '02. doi:10.1145/544741.544819.

Champagnat, R., G. Delmas, and M. Augeraud. 2010. "A Storytelling Model for Educational Games: Hero's Interactive Journey". *International Journal of Technology-Enhanced Learning* 2 (1–2):4–20. doi:10.1504/IJTEL.2010.031257.

Charles, Fred, Julie Porteous, Jonathan Teutenberg, and Marc Cavazza. 2011. *"Timeline-Based Navigation for Interactive Narratives"*. Paper presented at ACE '11: Proceedings of the 8th International Conference on Advances in Computer Entertainment Technology. doi:10.1145/2071423.2071469.

Colby, Benjamin N. 1973. "A Partial Grammar of Eskimo Folktales". *American Anthropologist* 75 (3): 645–662.

Crawford, Chris. 2013. *Chris Crawford on Interactive Storytelling.* Berkeley, CA: New Riders. doi:10.1007/978-3-642-25289-1.

Dehn, Natalie. 1981. "Story Generation After *Tale-Spin*". In *IJCAI-81. Proceedings of the 7th International Joint Conference on Artificial Intelligence.* Vancouver: Morgan Kaufmann Publishers Inc., pp. 16–18.

Delgado, Diogo, João Magalhães, and Nuno Correia. 2010. "Assisted News Reading with Automated Illustration". In *MM'10 – Proceedings of the ACM Multimedia 2010 International Conference,* New York: ACM, pp. 1647–1650. doi:10.1145/1873951.1874311.

Eladhari, Mirjam Palosaari. 2018. "Re-Tellings: The Fourth Layer of Narrative as an Instrument for Critique". In Rebecca Rouse, Hartmut Koenitz, and Mads Haahr (eds),

ICIDS 2018: *Interactive Storytelling*. Cham: Springer International Publishing, pp. 65–78. doi:10.1007/978-3-030-04028-4_5.

Fikes, Richard E., and Nils J. Nilsson. 1971. "Strips: A New Approach to the Application of Theorem Proving to Problem Solving". *Artificial Intelligence* 2 (3–4):189–208. doi:10.1016/0004-3702(71)90010-5.

Freytag, Gustav. 1863. *Technik des Dramas*. Leipzig: Verlag von G. Birzel.

Garnham, Alan. 1983. "What's Wrong with Story Grammars?" *Cognition* 15 (1–3):145–154. doi:10.1016/0010-0277(83)90037-9.

Gervás, Pablo. 2013. "Propp's Morphology of the Folk Tale as a Grammar for Generation". In Mark A. Finlayson, Bernhard Fisseni, Benedikt Löwe, and Jan Christoph Meister (eds), *Workshop on Computational Models of Narrative 2013*, vol. 32. Dagstuhl, Germany: Schloss Dagstuhl-Leibniz-Zentrum für Informatik, pp. 106–122. doi:10.4230/OASIcs.CMN.2013.106.

Giovannelli, Alessandro. 2009. "In Sympathy with Narrative Characters". *Journal of Aesthetics and Art Criticism* 67 (1): 83–95. doi:10.1111/j.1540-6245.2008.01337.x.

Grasbon, Dieter, and Norbert Braun. 2001. "A Morphological Approach to Interactive Storytelling". In M. Fleischmann and W. Strauss (eds), *CAST 2001. Living in Mixed Realities: Conference on Artistic, Cultural and Scientific Aspects of Experimental Media Spaces*. Schloss Birlinghoven: FhG – Institut Medienkommunikation (IMK), pp. 337–340.

Hanser, Eva, Paul McKevitt, Tom Lunney, and Joan Condell. 2010. "SceneMaker: Intelligent Multimodal Visualisation of Natural Language Scripts". In R. Goebel, J. Siekmann, and W. Wahlster (eds), *Lecture Notes in Computer Science (Including Subseries Lecture Notes in Artificial Intelligence and Lecture Notes in Bioinformatics), 6206 LNAI*. Berlin: Springer, pp. 144–153. doi:10.1007/978-3-642-17080-5_17.

Harris, Justin, and R. Michael Young. 2005. "Proactive Mediation in Plan-Based Narrative Environments". In T. Panayiotopoulos, J. Gratch, R. Aylett, D.Ballin, P.Olivier, and T. Rist (eds), *Intelligent Virtual Agents. IVA 2005, 3661 LNAI*. Berlin: Springer, pp. 292–304. doi:10.1007/11550617_25.

Hartsook, Ken, Alexander Zook, Sauvik Das, and Mark O. Riedl. 2011. "*Toward Supporting Stories with Procedurally Generated Game Worlds*". Paper presented at 2011 IEEE Conference on Computational Intelligence and Games (CIG'11), pp. 297–304. doi:10.1109/CIG.2011.6032020.

Hayashi, Masaki, Steven Bachelder, Matéo Grippon, and Masayuki Nakajima. 2013. "*Interactive TV by Text-To-Vision*". Paper presented at 2013 International Conference on Cyberworlds. doi:10.1109/CW.2013.78.

Kreminski, Max, and Michael Mateas. 2021. "Toward Narrative Instruments". In Alex Mitchell and Mirjam Vosmeer (eds), *Interactive Storytelling*. Cham: Springer International Publishing, pp. 499–508. doi:10.1007/978-3-030-92300-6_50.

Kybartas, Ben, and Rafael Bidarra. 2017. "A Survey on Story Generation Techniques for Authoring Computational Narratives". *IEEE Transactions on Computational Intelligence and AI in Games*, 9: 239–253 .doi:10.1109/TCIAIG.2016.2546063.

Lakoff, George P. 1972. "Structural Complexity in Fairy Tales". *The Study of Man* 1: 128–150.

Lebowitz, Michael. 1985. "Story-Telling as Planning and Learning". *Poetics* 14 (6): 483–502. doi:10.1016/0304-422X(85)90015-4.

Lévi-Strauss, Claude. 1983. "Structure and Form: Reflection on a Work by Vladimir Propp". In Monique Layton (ed.), *Structural Anthropology*, vol. 2. Chicago: University of Chicago Press, pp. 115–145.

Li, Boyang, Stephen Lee-Urban, and Mark O.Riedl. 2013. "*Crowdsourcing Interactive Fiction Games*". Paper presented at International Conference on the Foundations of Digital Games, Chania, Crete, Greece, May 14–17, 2013, pp. 431–432.

Li, Boyang, and Mark O.Riedl. 2011. "*A Phone That Cures Your Flu: Generating Imaginary Gadgets in Fictions with Planning and Analogies*". Paper presented at Intelligent Narrative Technologies IV - Papers from the 2011 AIIDE Workshop, pp. 41–48.

Liu, Zhi Qiang, and Ka Ming Leung. 2006. "Script Visualization (ScriptViz): A Smart System That Makes Writing Fun". *Soft Computing* 10 (1): 34–40. doi:10.1007/s00500-005-0461-4.

Lombardo, Vincenzo. 2022. "Storygraphia: The Constrained Tool for IDN Authoring Education". In Mirjam Vosmeer and L. Holloway-Attaway (eds), *Proceedings of the International Conference on Interactive Digital Storytelling (ICIDS 2022)*. Cham: Springer Nature. pp. 590–597. doi:10.1007/978-3-031-22298-6_38.

Lubart, Todd. 2005. "How Can Computers Be Partners in the Creative Process?: Classification and Commentary on the Special Issue". *International Journal of Human-Computer Studies* 63 (4–5 Special issue): 365–369. doi:10.1016/j.ijhcs.2005.04.002.

Mateas, Michael, and Andrew Stern. 2007. "Writing *Façade*: A Case Study in Procedural Authorship". In Pat Harrigan and Noah Wardrip-Fruin (eds), *Second Person. Role-Playing and Story in Games and Playable Media*. Cambridge, MA: MIT Press, pp. 183–212.

Meehan, James R. 1977. "*Tale-Spin*. An Interactive Program That Writes Stories" . In *Proceedings of the 5th International Joint Conference on Artificial Intelligence*, 1, pp. 91–98. San Francisco: Morgan Kaufmann Publishers.

Mirowski, Piotr, Kory W. Mathewson, Jaylen Pittman, and Richard Evans. 2022. "Co-Writing Screenplays and Theatre Scripts with Language Models: An Evaluation by Industry Professionals". *ArXiv*, September: 1–102. doi:10.48550/arXiv.2209.14958.

Niesz, Anthony J., and Norman N. Holland. 1984. "Interactive Fiction". *Critical Inquiry* 11 (1): 110–129.

Pemberton, Lyn. 1989. "*A Modular Approach to Story Generation*". Paper presented at EACL '89: Fourth Conference on European Chapter of the Association for Computational Linguistics, pp. 217–224. doi:10.3115/976815.976845.

Perera, Rivindu, and Parma Nand. 2017. "Recent Advances in Natural Language Generation: A Survey and Classification of the Empirical Literature". *Computing and Informatics* 36 (1): 1–32. doi:10.4149/cai_2017_1_1.

Pérez y Pérez, Rafael, and Mike Sharples. 2001. "*MEXICA*: A Computer Model of a Cognitive Account of Creative Writing". *Journal of Experimental \& Theoretical Artificial Intelligence* 13 (2): 119–139. doi:10.1080/09528130010029820.

Porteous, Julie, Marc Cavazza, and Fred Charles. 2010. "Applying Planning to Interactive Storytelling: Narrative Control Using State Constraints". *ACM Transactions on Intelligent Systems and Technology* 1 (2): 1–21. doi:10.1145/1869397.1869399.

Propp, Vladimir. 1968. *Morphology of the Folktale*. Edited by Louis A. Wagner. Austin, TX: University of Texas Press.

Riedl, Mark O., and Vadim Bulitko. 2013. "Interactive Narrative. An Intelligent System Approach" . *AI Magazine* 34 (1): 67–77. doi:10.1109/MCG.2006.59.

Riedl, Mark O., C. J. Saretto, and R. Michael Young. 2003. "*Managing Interaction between Users and Agents in a Multi-Agent Storytelling Environment*". Paper presented at International Conference on Autonomous Agents, pp. 741–748. doi:10.1145/860690.860694.

Riedl, Mark O., and R. Michael Young. 2005. "*Open-World Planning for Story Generation*". Paper presented at IJCAI'05: 19th International Joint Conference on Artificial Intelligence, pp. 1719–1720. doi:10.5555/1642293.1642625.

Riedl, Mark O., and R. Michael Young. 2006. "Story Planning as Exploratory Creativity: Techniques for Expanding the Narrative Search Space". *New Generation Computing* 24 (3): 303–323. doi:10.1007/BF03037337.

Roberts, David L., and Charles L. Isbell. 2008. "A Survey and Qualitative Analysis of Recent Advances in Drama Management". *International Transactions on Systems Science and Applications* 4 (1): 61–75.

Ryan, James. 2018. *Curating Simulated Storyworlds*. Santa Cruz, CA: University of California Santa Cruz.

Ryan, Marie-Laure. 2006. *Avatars of Stories*. Minneapolis, MN:University of Minnesota Press.

Samuel, Ben, James Ryan, Adam J. Summerville, Michael Mateas, and Noah Wardrip-Fruin. 2016. "Bad News: An Experiment in Computationally Assisted Performance". In *Lecture Notes in Computer Science (Including Subseries Lecture Notes in Artificial Intelligence and Lecture Notes in Bioinformatics), 10045 LNCS*. Berlin: Springer, pp. 108–120. doi:10.1007/978-3-319-48279-8_10.

Shibolet, Yotam, and Vincenzo Lombardo. 2022. "Resources for Comparative Analysis of IDN Authoring Tools". In Mirjam Vosmeer and Lissa Holloway-Attaway (eds), *Proceedings of the International Conference on Interactive Digital Storytelling (ICIDS 2022)*. Cham: Springer Nature, pp. 513–528. doi:10.1007/978-3-031-22298-6_33.

Si, Mei, Stacy C. Marsella, and David V. Pynadath. 2007. "Proactive Authoring for Interactive Drama: An Author's Assistant". In *Intelligent Virtual Agents. IVA 2007, 4722 LNCS*. Berlin: Springer, pp. 225–237. doi:10.1007/978-3-540-74997-4_21.

Smith, Greg M. 2003. *Film Structure and the Emotion System*. Cambridge: Cambridge University Press. doi:10.1017/CBO9780511497759.

Swanson, Reid, and Andrew S. Gordon. 2008. "Say Anything: A Massively Collaborative Open Domain Story Writing Companion". In *Lecture Notes in Computer Science (Including Subseries Lecture Notes in Artificial Intelligence and Lecture Notes in Bioinformatics), 5334 LNCS*. Berlin: Springer, pp. 32–40. doi:10.1007/978-3-540-89454-4_5.

Swartjes, Ivo, Edze Kruizinga, and Mariët Theune. 2008. "Let's Pretend I Had a Sword". In Ulrike Spierling and Nicolas Szilas (eds), *Interactive Storytelling. ICIDS 2008*. Berlin: Springer, pp. 264–267.doi:10.1007/978-3-540-89454-4.

Szilas, Nicolas. 2003. "*IDtension*: A Narrative Engine for Interactive Drama". In Stefan Göbel, Norbert Braun, Ulrike Spierling, Johanna Dechau, and Holger Diener (eds), *Technologies for Interactive Digital Storytelling and Entertainment: TIDSE 2003 Proceedings*. Darmstadt, Germany: Fraunhofer IRB Verlag, pp. 187–203.

Wu, Tongshuang, Michael Terry, and Carrie Jun Cai. 2022. "*AI Chains: Transparent and Controllable Human-AI Interaction by Chaining Large Language Model Prompts*". Paper presented at Conference on Human Factors in Computing Systems. doi:10.1145/3491102.3517582.

6 Examples of interactive storytelling
Description and analysis

6.1 1966: *Eliza*

Description

The *Eliza* software was developed in 1966 by Joseph Weizenbaum in MIT in Cambridge, MA. It is considered one of the first attempts to simulate an artificial agent capable of carrying on a conversation in natural language. The software was able to respond with short lines of text to utterances typed by the user. *Eliza*'s responses were output to a printer almost immediately after the user typed the text. As the author explains, the name *Eliza* was inspired by the protagonist in Shaw's *Pygmalion*, "to emphasise that it may be incrementally improved by its users, since its language abilities may be continually improved by a 'teacher'" (Weizenbaum 1966, p. 36). The software parsed the phrases and sentences typed by the user and used some decomposition and assembly rules based on a few keywords that triggered the selected response. The system was based on a database of *Eliza*'s answers, created by the author; the input functioned as a query that activated the algorithm. The algorithm's task was to select the output that most closely matched the user's input text. Obviously, it was a fairly simple system (especially compared to today's systems), but it could give the impression of a conversation. There is no doubt that the system had no knowledge of the meaning of the conversation (there was no formal model of the user or the topics discussed). The system described by the author, in a nutshell, works as follows. The input text is read by the software and inspected for the presence of a keyword; if such a word is found, the sentence is transformed according to a rule associated with the keyword; otherwise, a content-free remark or, under certain conditions, an earlier transformation is retrieved; the text so computed or retrieved is then printed. For example, the sentence, "I am very unhappy these days" is heard by someone with a limited knowledge of English and therefore only the first two words "I am" are understood, while the rest of the sentence (although heard) makes no sense. The listener who wants to appear interested might reply, "How long have you been very unhappy these days?". The system has applied a kind of template to the original sentence, part of which matches the two words "I am", and re-uses the rest of the phrase "very unhappy these days". The system has a composition rule associated with the

DOI: 10.4324/9781003335627-6

template: the rule states that any sentence of the form "I am BLAH" can be transformed into "How long have you been BLAH?", regardless of the meaning of BLAH (ibid., p. 37). *Eliza* had several composition rules for each template that matched the user input and therefore produced different answers. For example, if the user entered, "I am [phrase] (e.g., a very nice guy)", *Eliza* could answer "Are you often [phrase]?" or 'Why do you say you are [phrase]?". Or, if the input was "You [single word, e.g., hate] me", the output could be "Why do you think I [single word] you?". The trick was to carry on the conversation using the contents produced by the user.

Analysis

The system saves the contribution of the algorithm and produces the pleasant feeling of being heard. The most important intuition in *Eliza*, however, was the ability to exploit the inevitable cluelessness of the machine. An adult with average education can usually hold a conversation on a variety of topics, change the subject, express an opinion, gain new information and perhaps even change their beliefs in the course of the conversation. These qualities make a conversation interesting, but in *Eliza*'s times they were an almost impossible task for a machine. Normally, we can converse with someone we do not know about topics we do not know and still give the reassuring feeling that we are listening and participating in the conversation with thoughtful responses. To achieve this effect with the help of a machine, the most important thing for Weizenbaum was to drastically limit the context of the interaction. Above all, he recognised that the confinement of the relationship to the machine within certain limits had to appear motivated and credible to the user. He brilliantly solved the problem by drawing on the conversational model of Rogersian psychotherapy. In this type of therapeutic session, the focus is on the patient and their conversation. This type of dialogic interaction with natural language is one of the few cases where it is believable that one of the two can pretend to know almost nothing. The session is designed to induce the patient to elaborate a discourse about his/her own emotions and feelings, and it is acceptable for the therapist not to express opinions, conjectures, etc., but to confine himself/herself to echoing the patient's thoughts. This setting was absolutely suitable for the system because the computer never had to declare anything and therefore could not contradict itself. This is, so to speak, a simple solution based on a dramaturgical trick: the limits of the machine corresponded to the characteristics of the therapist's character. In other words, the computer was cast for a role that corresponded to its abilities. And since *Eliza* is a therapist, the system was able to shift the weight of the conversation to the user, thus subverting the very reason for which it was created: chatting. Probably this clever balance of software coding and character representation was the reason why many people were really fascinated and thought this artificial agent was almost alive.

- *Story world*: the psychotherapy session. This model of dialogic interaction contains an implicit description of the character represented by the chatbot. It also contains the principles that govern the assembly rules for dealing with the textual content produced by the user, as well as some more general associations, such as that between "mother" or "son" and a response that refers to "family".

- *Dynamic elements*: the set of possible answers stored in the database defines the total units used by the system. It should be noted that these are not explicitly described as units in the system, but rather are created from text fragments. These fragments are only part of the narrative unit, which instead comprises the user's input as a whole. Note also that these units are designed and produced for the specific display that the system uses: the text. Because the system is based on natural language processing, it requires a display capable of rendering a line of text (regardless of the different renderings that a text may have, whether on paper, on a monitor, or through a text-to-speech module). These minimal conversational units can be dynamically retrieved according to the user's input (Box 6.1). In other words, the dynamic elements can be described as a table of predefined keywords and rules.
- *Engine*: the system contains a parser that analyses the text entered by the user and implements the relationship between the elements in the table. In this way, the system can process the list of responses (the dynamic elements) and apply the specific rules to each interaction with the user.
- *Display*: the medium is the text gathered by the assembly of partial units contained in the database and the words entered by the users. In the first version, the user interacted via a teletypewriter that wrote the answers on a sheet of paper. Later, there were new implementations of the system with a text-based interface on a monitor.

Further details

There are still web implementations of *Eliza* that allow you to try out the chatbot, available at: https://www.masswerk.at/elizabot/eliza.html. Weizenbaum's paper on *Eliza* can be accessed at: https://web.stanford.edu/class/linguist238/p36-weizenabaum.pdf.

Box 6.1 Example of a chat with *Eliza*. U = User; E = Eliza.

U: Men are all alike.
E: *In what way?*
U: They're always bugging us about something or other.
E: *Can you think of a specific example?*
U: Well, my boyfriend made me come here.
E: *Your boyfriend made you come here?*
U: He says I'm depressed much of the time.
E: *I am sorry to hear that you are depressed.*
U: It's true. I am unhappy.

> E: *Do you think coming here will help you not to be unhappy?*
> U: I need some help, that much seems certain.
> E: *What would it mean to you if you got some help?*
> U: Perhaps I could learn to get along with my mother.
> E: *Tell me more about your family.*
> U: My mother takes care of me.
> E: *Who else in your family takes care of you?*
> U: My father.
> E: *Your father?*
> U: You are like my father in some ways.
> E: *What resemblance do you see?*
> U: You are not very aggressive but I think you don't want me to notice that.
> E: *What makes you think I am not very aggressive?*
> U: You don't argue with me.
> E: *Why do you think I don't argue with you?*
> U: You are afraid of me.
> E: *Does it please you to believe I am afraid of you?*
> U: My father is afraid of everybody.
> E: *What else comes to your mind when you think of your father?*
> U: Bullies.
> E: *Does that have anything to do with the fact that your boyfriend made you come here?*
>
> (Weizenbaum 1966, pp. 36–37)

6.2 1976: *Adventure*

Description

Adventure is considered the forerunner of the genre of video games later called "adventure". The work, which is entirely text-based, is set in a fantasy world. It was originally developed by William Crowther around 1975; later, in 1976, it was improved and publicly distributed thanks to Don Wood of Stanford University. The game placed the user in a world populated by different creatures, where there were different objects to operate and where different events could take place. The user had to enter commands on the computer keyboard, but these commands were simple lines in natural language (usually a combination of verbs and nouns, such as "examine building"). The phrases were parsed by the system and if the sequence was recognised within the possible list of commands, the associated procedure was executed and a new specific description was displayed on the screen; otherwise, the system prompted the user to reformulate the phrase (Jerz 2007). To navigate this text-based world, the user had to solve some riddles and puzzles and fight various creatures, always having a clear list of possible commands at hand. The plot revolved around the exploration of a huge cave filled with both treasure and danger. The goal was to collect as much treasure as possible and get out alive. The user could explore the cave and handle objects. Each appropriate user's command triggered a new textual description of the situation (the environment, the available objects, the user's location) and possibly the event triggered by the user's choice, as if the computer were acting as a storyteller (Montfort 2003). The system was based on a structure organised by location and a map that served as a graph with nodes through which the user could move from one place to another using movement-based commands ("go", "exit", etc.). Each node could be the place for further exploration by selecting objects or looking at details of certain elements. Originally, the game was available for free on ARPAnet, the forerunner of the internet. Later, in the years when the video game industry was emerging, some commercial versions of the game were released. The first commercial version had a graphical interface and was called *Adventure* (1979), developed by Warren Robinett for the Atari VCS 2600, and became a milestone in the history of video games. Then Tim Anderson, Mark Blank, Bruce Daniels and Dave Lebling (from MIT) created *Zork* (1979) and founded Infocom, which became a leading video game company for the adventure genre (Egenfeldt-Nielsen, Smith and Tosca 2008, pp. 57–58).

Analysis

Adventure is considered the first example of an interactive narrative and was the origin of the video game genre of the same name. The game was specifically inspired by the author's passion for cave exploration, and the game's node map resembles Mammouth Cave in Kentucky. More generally, the game's conception was the result of the fascination with Tolkien in those years and the growing popularity of fantasy role-playing games and *Dungeons & Dragons* (Montfort 2003). In these systems, the game experience focused more on puzzles and riddles than on plot development. On the one hand, the user had to solve puzzles while exploring an unknown environment; on the other hand, the interaction appeared as a kind of metaphor for the work of a programmer. In other words, the same machine became a place of exploration. According to Crowther, people liked *Adventure* "because it's exactly the kind of thing that computer programmers do. They're struggling with an obstinate system that can do what you want but only if you can figure out the right thing to say to it" (ibid., p. 92). *Adventure* is an example of a narrative based on the pleasure of exploring. Since then, this model has evolved while still retaining the idea that the user's participation is not so much about doing actions or following a well-formed sequence of events, but rather about uncovering a mysterious world and overcoming obstacles along the way. Indeed, a similar structure was repeated in later adventure games with graphical interfaces. But regardless of how the environment was presented, navigating the map always involved moving from one narrative unit to the next.

- *Story world*: the map describing the setting of the adventure, the genre-related traditional conventions, the sum of the rules associated with each location,

Examples of interactive storytelling: description and analysis 135

object and character. This set of instructions provides the description of the world that the player enters during the game session. The story world also includes the types of actions that intuitively can be executed, hence the commands that are available to the user.

- *Dynamic elements*: these are the locations, actions and the table in which they are connected. This adventure game is based on a list of locations and other entities organised in a database to respond to the user's query. When the user is at a particular node on the map, the command "Go North" triggers the selection of a particular item (a new cave, a character, etc.) from the list and its display on the screen (as a text description). If the same command is given from another node on the map, another item from the same list is triggered.
- *Engine*: this implements the table for linking commands and elements in the system and accordingly sends instructions to the display for visualisation. In this case, the software sequences the narrative elements (mostly the parts of the cave) according to the user's choice and selects the actions (commands) that are available in a given situation.
- *Display*: this renders the text-based descriptions and allows user input as plain text (which is then interpreted by the engine). The user interacted with the game via the keyboard and thanks to a monitor on which the descriptions were printed. Both input and output were always and exclusively text-based.

Further details

A lengthy description of the original game can be found at: http://www.digitalhumanities.org/dhq/vol/001/2/000009/000009.html

Along the years there have been many different implementations of the original game. An online version is available at: https://quuxplusone.github.io/Advent/.

6.3 1978: *Aspen Movie Map*

Description

This was the first example of interactive virtual navigation in a real environment using video footage and photographs. The project was led by Andrew Lippman of the Architecture Machine Group and coordinated by Nicholas Negroponte and MIT. The project was funded by DARPA, which had already supported similar projects because of its interest in virtual environments for military training in inaccessible areas; nevertheless, the *Aspen Movie Map* was overall an academic research project and had no direct commercial goals. The virtual playback was made possible by the recent invention of laser discs that could be controlled by a computer. The entire project was stored on various discs containing video, sound, images and even computer graphic animations; the contents were accessible via a purpose-built control system. The experience was available to a single user at a time. The interface (in the simpler implementation of the project) consisted of a video monitor that allowed the user to move through the streets of Aspen,

Colorado, famous for its ski resort, in two different seasons: Winter and Summer. The film was shot with a 16mm camera mounted on a jeep that moved through the streets, taking a shot every 10 feet: these shots formed the basis for the virtual visit. Photos, paintings and other historical documents (building façades, public spaces) were also added. The control system allowed access to the content at the user's choice. The visitor watched the recorded video sequences and controlled the speed of movement. The images were presented in first-person perspective, but visitors could switch to aerial perspective on the graphic map of the city to better understand where they were. Additional information (text, audio, photos) was available for the places visited, including some computer graphics and historical insights into specific buildings (Lippman 1980). This project received great media coverage as it was the first to present a virtual visit to an existing place via a video interface with images of real locations. It was so famous that in the following years and before other companies entered the "mapping" business (such as Google), "moviemap" became the word to describe the process of filming and simulating interactive journeys using a spatial interface for a multimedia database (Naimark 2006).

Analysis

The user experience of accessing the system was primarily focused on gaming and entertainment, but had a strong influence on various practical innovations and spawned a long line of research and experimentation that led to interactive maps and 3D visualisations and our everyday use of topographies and visualisations that allow us to "visit" remote locations (like the well-known Google Street View). Geo-satellite tracking technology has certainly driven this research direction, but the idea of immersivity remains a core element in simulating the user's presence in a remote space. In *Aspen Movie Map*, locations were organised as spatial units and the sequence was determined by the user's choices. The focus was on interactivity, but this did not preclude narrativity as an emergent quality. At the end of each visit, the user had completed a journey that could be understood as a narrative. In other words: narrativity was the result of an exploration that followed a schema that was just emerging in the gaming field in those years and that was to have great success in the following years with the development of VR and immersive technologies (such as 360° visors).

- *Story world*: the city map (i.e., the boundaries of the area to be explored) implicitly provides the rules for navigation. This includes the set of shared information about urban space and driving.
- *Dynamic elements*: the entire archive of videos, sounds and photographs, including computer graphics. The laser discs stored the indexed content and the system included a table describing the available elements and their relationship to each other (the photo frames' sequence, the link between a photo frame and a historical image, the hotspots where selection is possible). This index enables the system to retrieve the corresponding content after the user has made a selection.

- *Engine*: this implements the table that links commands and effects and gives the monitor the correct visualisation instructions. The engine takes care of the speed of the visit and the correspondence between the different multimedia contents. It also selects the actions (commands) that are available in each specific situation (e.g., at a crossroads you can choose where to go).
- *Display*: the monitor shows the images and the navigation commands. The user interacts directly with the screen by touching a few simple directional commands on the lower part of the monitor.

Further details

The raw video content of the laser disks is stored and available at: https://archive.org/details/ASPEN4. A list of the disks' content (with some video frame pictures) is available at: https://www.domesday86.com/?page_id=3028. Naimark's web page contains a brief description of the project with links to few papers, available at: http://www.naimark.net/projects/aspen.html. A video description of the project is available at: https://www.youtube.com/watch?v=Hf6LkqgXPMU.

6.4 1987: *Afternoon, a Story*

Description

This work is generally known as the first hyperfiction. Author Michael Joyce published it with Eastgate Systems, which also supplied the Storyspace editing software (see Chapter 5, Section 5.3 and http://www.eastgate.com/storyspace/). The work was published before the great development of hypertextual navigation for the World Wide Web. It was based on navigation through units of text (called lexia) and readers could move from one unit to the next using fixed links created by Joyce. There were no external links. The story was told from the point of view of the protagonist Peter, a writer who has just been divorced from his wife Lisa. One morning he witnesses a car accident. This event is the starting point for his thoughts, which form the core of the narrative. Peter believes that he saw his wife and son Andy die in this car accident. Then he feels guilty for not having done anything to help. The plot follows the protagonist's trials and tribulations, but because of the hypertext structure, it has no predetermined order in the sequence of events. Therefore, many other events, even if relevant to the afternoon referred to in the title of the story, may not be shown in all possible reading sessions. It is in the nature of the work that it is almost impossible to summarise the plot in an exhaustive synopsis. Each reading yields a different story. The work aims to break down the traditional structures of the nineteenth-century novel and is based on post-structuralist notions such as the absence of wholeness, the lack of a unified progression and the obliteration of the idea of closure. The reading ends when the reader reaches some unit that has no connection to what follows, even if the narrated event has no sense of closure at all. Finally, the work does not unfold a plot based on action, but follows the tradition of psychological fiction and stream of consciousness. Sometimes the same lexia recurs more than once during the reading (e.g., "I want to say that I may have seen my son die this morning"), which helps to establish the protagonist's paralysed state of mind. The event he witnessed is meant to trigger a series of mental associations that flow freely without cause-and-effect constraints. Many narrative units are a reflection on the two other main characters in the story: Wert, his ex-wife's new boyfriend, and Lolly, a secretary and prostitute. The flow of narrative units can baffle or confuse the reader, so that he/she in turn has the same experience as the protagonist wanders in his thoughts. Nevertheless, these features, together with the lyrical and evocative tone of the writing, make this hypertext an icon of the genre (Ensslin 2007, pp. 69–72).

Analysis

On the one hand, *Afternoon, a Story* manifests the historical correlation between the fashion for the rhizomatic in postmodern fiction and the new possibilities offered by the digital revolution of hypertext. On the other hand, it is a work that shows, after a few decades, that this new form of fiction has not caught on with mainstream audiences. Nevertheless, this was one of the moments when it became clear how closely some formal elements of the new digital creativity were linked to the contemporary philosophical debate (Douglas 1993). From *Finnegans Wake* by James Joyce to *The Garden of Forking Paths* by Jose Luis Borges to the works of Italo Calvino and Umberto Eco, solutions that questioned the relationship between author and reader and challenged the difference between subject (the experience) and object (the work) were tried out in fiction. Undoubtedly, the possibilities offered by digital tools to overcome the idea of the novel as a book fuelled these tensions. *Afternoon, a Story* sparked a debate about cyberliterature, about reader authorship and – even more – about storytelling as an act of participation and collaboration. Since then, it has been argued that fiction can be interactive not only as a playful experience (as in video games) but also as an aesthetic experience.

- *Story world*: here the cultural references to post-structuralist fiction play a key role in the formation of the world for the reader who navigates the story. The elements of real contemporary life, the beliefs about the psychological attribution of the described events, the portrayal of different states of mind, are all central to the understanding of the work. Clearly, there are some conventional clues about the navigation of the hypertext that are understood as the story progresses.
- *Dynamic elements*: the list of narrative units (lexia) and the table linking one to the other. This table allowed the system to recall the unit according to the reader's choices.
- *Engine*: this implements the table where the commands are associated to the list of units and prints on the monitor the unit to be read.
- *Display*: the monitor shows the narrative unit and allows the selection of possible continuations.

Further details

The story is available for purchase on: http://www.eastgate.com/catalog/Afternoon.html.

6.5 1987: *City in Transition: New Orleans, 1983–86*

Description

The idea of an interactive documentary film arose on the occasion of an urban renewal plan for New Orleans, Louisiana, USA, with the aim of using it as a teaching tool in the Urban Planning course at MIT. The project was conceived and directed by Glorianna Davenport, who was in those very years experimenting with the use of networked computers in education (Project Athena; Arfman and Roden 1992). Director Richard Leacock provided the nearly three hours of video footage. Added to this were images of people and places, maps and various other documents, including demographic and economic statistics. All the content was stored on various laser discs and accessed through a single user interface via a video monitor. The upper left part showed the video, while the lower left part contained the navigation and editing controls. The right part contained the interface for querying the database. Indeed, the whole contents of the project had been organised in a database that could be queried by the user (Mackay and Davenport 1989). Thus, the system did not display a predefined sequence, but the user could freely explore the content. This exploration consisted of personal editing of the media, which was possible by selecting and ordering a series of icons representing different content and even by adding new content (comments, information) (Davenport 1988). The system was first used in the MIT programme and later developed further thanks to testing and feedback. The educational purpose of the project was to develop students' analytical skills in relation to urban planning. However, it also became known as one of the first examples of database narrative, where people had access to different types of media and texts that could be freely arranged in a user-defined sequence.

Analysis

In this system, the information that would have been organised in a traditional linear narrative was segmented and archived in a database. The storyline, which in a documentary is usually the director's point of view, became a working field for the user. The project marked a turning point, as the interaction with the media was no longer focused on exploring an environment or handling a certain set of objects. In this case, the user was not put into a certain mode of participation in the story (like the character in an adventure game, for example), but was expected to build the story itself. The basis for this system was not only the new laser disc technology, but also a new paradigm of database narrative. Within this theoretical framework, content was organised and described so that it was available horizontally rather than in hierarchical order: for example, when the user searched for information about a person, the system returned all related content (text, video, photos, etc.). In addition, all content was archived so that it could be retrieved and edited as a narrative unit. This allowed the user to create, modify and delete sequences and links fluidly and intuitively.

- *Story world*: the context is limited to the urban renewal of New Orleans, which establishes a general and implicit link between all the materials in the archive. Furthermore, there are two basic concepts: the first is the multimedia archive, i.e., a database that organises different media; the second is the narrative editing that the user does with the help of the system.
- *Dynamic elements*: the entire content of the multimedia archive (the so-called item, such as footage, photos, texts, their description and tagging). While the laser discs allow storage and access to a large amount of multimedia content, the system contains tables to index this content with the correct tags. The tables can be supplemented with further data (e.g., further historical content), but also with the links that users create as part of their individual editing of the content. It is important to note that the system also contains the interaction history of the users as dynamic elements.
- *Engine*: this enables queries in the archive and implements the consequent sequence in the editing; it selects the various actions of the user according to the content at hand and instructs the display for visualisation.
- *Display*: the video monitor provides both the control interface and the final output. The speakers play the audio content accordingly.

Further details

The Interactive Cinema research group was discontinued in 2004, yet there is a web page with a short description of the project and links to a few papers about the project, available at: https://ic.media.mit.edu/icSite/icprojects/NewOrleansInTransition.html.

6.6 1991: *Angels*

Description

Nicole Stenger is a French-American artist who was artist-in-residence at the Human Interface Technology Lab (Hitlab) at the University of Washington in Seattle. She worked there on some VR research topics in 1989 and is probably the first artist to work in VR (Morie 2012). Her momentum towards virtual reality is clearly summed up by a motto at the end of her essay "Mind Is a Leaking Rainbow":

> According to Sartre, the atomic bomb was what humanity had found to commit collective suicide. It seems, by contrast, that cyberspace, though born

of a war technology, opens up a space for collective restoration and for peace. As screens are dissolving, our future can only take on a luminous dimension! Welcome to the New World.

(Stenger 1991, p. 58)

Angels (or "Les Recontres Angéliques", recalling Stenger's French origins) is a journey into a virtual paradise. The user's experience begins in a dark background scenario where the only thing animated is a colourful carousel with some geometric objects (actually shapes typical of early VR environments). The objects are gateways to other VR environments. The geometric shapes are stylised hearts, actually angel hearts; the environment shows the hand (as in modern VR applications); the user can touch one of the three angel hearts in the carousel; the order in which the hearts are touched determines the order in which the three virtual worlds appear. The duration of each session varies from about 30 seconds to 2 minutes and 30 seconds. The voices of the angels ask the users to interact with them, which opens up a story.

The story is about two ethereal beings who seek each other out and come together to form a single being that completes each other. The viewer/player inhabits the environment together with the virtual characters and interaction is limited to travelling in empty space (except for the carousel) to reach out and touch the hearts of the angels. The love encounters with the two creatures are very intense (despite the simplicity of the forms) and the user can participate by entering the three scenes, which can be called bliss, loss and fusion, respectively, according to their content (a three-segment dramatic arc with six possible stories). Each touch of a heart opens a new world. As each path is completed, the user returns to the spinning carousel to make a new selection.

The original music, an electronic composition by Diane Thome, played a major role. Each virtual world had its own theme, and the composer was faced with a rather challenging and unusual task: the order of the narrative was not fixed in advance, and no specific duration could be assigned to each section, as the sections could be interrupted at any time. The solution was to compose a "reference loop", which is common in interactive multimedia content but not in stories: "the shadow-like transit time between participating environments was always associated with a much more generalised, ambient, less motivic music than that which accompanied the highly coloured environments themselves" (Thome 1995, p. 29). The music piece had a duration of about 10 minutes, according to Stenger's decision to anticipate the optimal duration of a participant's experience. Each environment was assigned a specific music loop to better respond to the needs of the narrative. The music was directly and closely related to the visual material: in fact, the images and music associated with each environment remained fixed.

Analysis

In the late 1980s, the few researchers and practitioners of virtual reality were not concerned with making art. In fact, the agencies that funded research at VR focused on practical issues such as training systems or basic research into the physiological and psychological effects of VR. There was no funding and no lab looking at the artistic potential of VR and its immersive sensory experiences. However, some artists were interested in VR as an artistic medium and were determined to gain access to VR equipment and software. Therefore, they had to convince scientists and technocrats that there were valid reasons to create content for these systems. Some artists were very determined and fortunate to work in government and academic laboratories that had access to the VR technology for their creative endeavours. However, this was not always acknowledged by the larger artistic community. Also, the artists' contributions were often seen as peripheral to the scientific aspects, as they lacked the empirical vision of VR. Although these artists were rarely included in the published records of the laboratories, or even exhibited to a wide audience, some were given access to scientific conferences that developed an artistic track. Stenger's work *Angels* is considered the first immersive VR film. The project was funded by the Prix Villa Medici. It was developed in 1989–1991 at MIT when she was a Research Fellow at CAVS (Center for Advanced Visual Studies) and the Visual Arts Program, employing the Advanced Visualizer, of the Wavefront company, running on an IRIS workstation from Silicon Graphics, the most prominent computer graphics company at the time. Then it was developed at Hitlab (UoW), using the Virtualization interface and Body Electric software from VPL ("Virtual Programming Language", the company of Jaron Lanier, the scientist who is said to have coined the term "virtual reality"), also running on IRIS. Finally, it was recorded on video in January 1992. It was exhibited at the Siggraph 1992 Art Show, hosted by the annual ACM Conference on Computer Graphics. The film immersed viewers through three senses: visual perception, auditory perception and touch, implementing the principles of VR, according to Tom Furness, the founder of Hitlab. The VR equipment consisted of a Head Mounted Display (or helmet) with Eye-Phone, a 3D audio system (Crystal River, a pioneering company working on binaural audio) and the VPL Dataglove. The latter was a non-tactile data glove, meaning it only detects hand movement but not actual touch. For this work, Nicole Stenger designed computer images, spoken text and a specific narrative, which was not common for early VR applications. *Angels* together with *Chambers* (2001) and *Dinasty* (2009) form the *VR Trilogy*. It has been shown in video form at various exhibitions in the United States and Europe (e.g., Biennale des Arts Eléctroniques in Paris) and on French and German television.

- *Story world*: similar to many early video games, the story world is very simple, and allows a virtually infinite exploration of a space inhabited only by a single carousel that captures the player's attention. The active objects located in the carousel are the only meaningful presences in the world. The actions carried out by the objects are simple coordinated movements that convey the general mood of the scene, bliss, loss and fusion.
- *Dynamic elements*: this is an interactive story based on units; the units are the individual environments; the user decides on the order of the environments by

selecting the heart (a simple graph with one level, i.e., all nodes are at a distance of 1 from the initial environment, the root); the units consist of simple actions.
- *Engine*: a simple visit to a graph that triggers each environment depending on the user's choice; the content of the unit does not require any intervention by the engine, as it is predetermined; the system only takes into account the user's exploration.
- *Display*: a VR device consisting of a head-mounted display for immersive visualisation, 3D spatialised audio with music composition and a data glove for touching the virtual objects without feedback.

Further details

More documentation and a video clip of the 3D environment can be found at the Digital Art Archive, available at: https://www.digitalartarchive.at/database/general/work/angels.html.

6.7 1993: *Myst*

Description

This was produced by Cyan, the company founded by Robyn and Rand Miller; it was a milestone in the video game industry and is credited as the reason sales of CD-ROM-equipped PCs increased. But it was also a turning point in the evolution of interactive storytelling, bringing computer-based interactive adventure to mainstream audiences. The game introduced graphics that were very realistic for the time to depict settings and locations and to suggest an enchanted world in which the player could experience a kind of immersion. All the images (about 2500) were pre-recorded and showed Myst Island and other lands to be visited. The player had to explore the world, without haste, almost in contemplation, while discovering the navigation rules. The graphics were presented in such a way that they always suggested a first-person perspective, thus casting the player as the protagonist of the events. At the beginning, a book described the mysterious Myst Island, to which the player was magically transported immediately afterwards. The only possible action was to explore the place. The graphical interface allowed the player to move around with the mouse and operate certain objects, but offered no explicit instructions or commands such as menus or tags. The island houses the ruins of a library of which only two books remain, a red book and a blue book. Trapped in these books are two fictional characters, Sirrus and Achenar, sons of Atrus. The latter is presented as the author of more magical books that have the power to transport the player from one place to another. Sirrus and Achenar blame each other for the death of their father and the devastation of the library. Both plead for freedom, but as some pages are missing from the books, their message seems incomplete and confused (Wolf 2011). After this introduction, the action began and the player discovers more and more elements of the mysterious world. By solving a series of riddles and puzzles, the player come into possession of five missing pages of the book, hence the brothers are set free and present the player with the final and ultimate decision. Namely, they advise against opening a green book because it is supposedly a trap. On the contrary, this book led to the place where Atrus was held captive. If the player decides to open the green book, Atrus ask him/her to find the last page that would eventually bring him justice (Wolf 2012). From here, four different endings were possible, involving Atrus' freedom and revenge as well as the player's character imprisonment. As with most other games of the time, this was a single-player game that did not take advantage of the internet, which was already gaining momentum. Probably the nature of the game, which was based on a well-structured narrative, would have made it more difficult to manage multiple actions simultaneously (Egenfeldt-Nielsen, Smith and Tosca 2008).

Analysis

Myst remains important because it pushed the adventure genre forward, focusing more on the narrative experience than dealing with high-paced events to enjoy violent action. The puzzles help to create an atmosphere of mystery in the world, which in turn was designed to evoke a participatory attitude in the player, closer to the more traditional engagement with storytelling. Even a theme such as the creation of a library, that helps to complete the adventure, provides an atmosphere that attracts lovers of storytelling and literature. The *Myst* player did not need to have quick reflexes or great eye-hand coordination, but rather the ability to solve puzzles and an attitude of deductive reasoning (ibid.). This was probably the reason why the game attracted both male and female players, opening up a field for both sexes that was long thought to be only for males. *Myst* represented an excellent balance between the nature of participation and the pleasure of a well-designed story. It also exploited the possibilities of multimedia PC and merged text and images into an experience that took place in a unique fictional space between films and books. In other words, it was a game where the reward was the true richness of the experience rather than scoring points through a clever sequence of quick actions. This was highlighted by Janet Murray, who writes that, unlike what usually happens in video games, the "losing" endings of the game are much more satisfying than the "winning ending" because of the way incidents are sequenced toward a dramatic effect:

> The superiority of the losing endings of *Myst* suggest a basic opposition between game form and narrative form. How can we tell significant stories in a form that always has to end happily? How can we impose endings that yield complex story satisfaction on a form that is based on win/lose simplicity? Many would argue that computer-based narrative will always be game-like and that such dissatisfactions are therefore inevitable. But when looked at more closely, games and stories are not necessarily opposed.
>
> (Murray 2001, p. 142)

- *Story world*: the general fantasy context (as developed in books, and also in films such as *Never-Ending Story* from 1984) provides the basic reference. This is true for many games, but here it is of particular importance because the genre conventions help the player to become familiar with the story world. There is also the map with all the navigable locations, which is explicitly included in the design, even if it is not immediately communicated to the player. Furthermore, given the spread of the video game at the time, the story world can rely on the common new standards of human-computer interaction.
- *Dynamic elements*: the stored content (graphics and video clips) and the texts are the basic element of the system. There is also a table that defines the relationships between the dynamic elements and between the dynamic elements and the actions. The whole archive can be seen as a set of narrative units that the player can activate. The course of the story depends on the exploration. Therefore, the archive also contains the player's interaction history, which updates the table for the possible actions to be performed.
- *Engine*: this implements the possible actions at a given moment of the game, according to the table updated in real time. Consequently, it instructs the display to visualise the available content and commands for the player.
- *Display*: the computer screen provides the interface for the commands (interpreted by the engine) and the appropriate graphics, while the speakers play the synchronised sounds and music.

Further details

A detailed description of the game and its history is available at: https://en.wikipedia.org/wiki/Myst. There is a recent VR implementation of the game that if faithful to the original story.

6.8 1996: *Pokémon*

Description

The term "Pokémon" is a fusion of the words Pocket and Monsters. It refers to the many species (1008, according to a recent count) that populate the *Pokémon Universe*. Satoshi Tajiri, the game's creator, was inspired by his childhood hobby of collecting insects. A weedle, for example, is an insect larva with a worm-shaped body divided into yellow to brown spherical segments. Like some natural insects, it hides in grass and bushes, eats leaves and has a sharp stinger on its head. Players, who take on the role of Pokémon trainers, perform three actions, collecting, training, and battling. Specifically: (1) they collect the Pokémon species in a (fictional) region where a game is taking place to complete the so-called regional Pokédex; (2) they complete the national Pokédex by transferring Pokémon from all regions, and (3) they train a team of strong Pokémon to compete against teams of other Trainers. The ultimate goal is to win the Pokémon League and become a regional Champion. A wild Pokémon can be captured by throwing a Poké Ball at it. Unless the Trainer shows a lack of experience, the captured Pokémon is owned by the Trainer, who can send it into battles against other Pokémon and possibly collect more wild Pokémon in the process. Each generation of the nine releases in the main *Pokémon* series has introduced a new region. Regions consist of many locations (mainly cities) that the player explores to meet the challenges (Gyms, i. e., battlegrounds, or other competitions). The regions from the main series are based on a real-world place. For example, the Hoenn region is based on Kyushu in Japan and Kalos in France. There is a single player mode and a multiplayer mode with a number of NPC (non-player characters) Trainers. A Trainer must follow a path through a number of regions where she/he encounters creatures and battles opponent Trainers. In some versions of the game, there are eight powerful Trainers, referred to as Gym Leaders. The Trainer must defeat them all in order to compete against the region's Pokémon League, which consists of the "Elite Four" talented Trainers. Finally, the winning Trainer challenges the reigning Regional Champion. The Trainer who wins this final battle becomes the new reigning champion. The game has been developed for several platforms, starting with the Nintendo Game Boy in 1996, and becoming an Augmented Reality experience with *Pokémon Go*, which peaked at 232 million players in 2016. There have also been several *Pokémon*-themed fan VR games.

Analysis

The *Pokémon* series (1996–) was a huge success worldwide. It was originally released for the Nintendo Game Boy (from 1989). It was inspired by several earlier games in terms of collecting, training, battling, and exchanging. For example, the *Megami Tensei* series (Namco and Atlus, 1987–) pioneered the "collecting" and "training" elements of Goddesses, as well as *Makai Toushi Sa-Ga* (Square, 1989) and *Mother* (Nintendo, 1989) as RPG implementations on the Game Boy. And, finally, the "capsule monsters" or *Capsule Kaiju* of Ultraseven (the third release of the *Ultraman* Series), which are monsters that exist in a capsule most of the time and only materialise when someone uses them. If one follows the guidelines suggested by Henry Jenkins in his blogs (Jenkins 2009a; 2009b), *Pokémon* can be considered a prime example of transmedia storytelling, as it distributes its fictional elements across multiple media and has the purpose of creating a coordinated entertainment experience. Transmedia examples include: *Pokémon Trading Card Game* (with more than 43 billion cards sold worldwide since 1996), 23 feature films (since 1998), one of the longest-running anime series (more than 1,000 episodes, seven series in Japan, 22 seasons internationally, since 1997 in Japan, 2003 in the Western world), a fan-developed *Pokémon* VR game for Oculus Quest headsets (2020), a virtual theme park (available for one month in August 2020). Roles and goals of Pokémon can be enacted by players in their daily lives: the Pokémon experiences of travelling, catching and completing a series of quests can be transferred to real life. Some releases included devices that can be carried in the pocket and used to collect Pokémon points at every step. And trading cards can be collected, traded with friends and used in battles. Transmedia storytelling is the aesthetic form for this era of collective intelligence (ibid.). *Pokémon* fans have created several websites that explore the *Pokémon* universe in depth and comprehensively, cosplay at conventions, create videos and even a *Pokémon* VR game. It is also true for *Pokémon* that each individual game is accessible in its own right while providing a unique contribution to the overall narrative. Overall, *Pokémon* builds a complex fictional world that supports multiple interconnected characters and their stories. It constantly creates new characters that have some relationship to the animals of Earth, but sometimes go beyond our natural rules. There are several spin-offs of the game series, all consistent with the complex fictional world that is constantly being expanded (e.g., each new series creates new regions). The *Pokémon* storyline is simple: some people, the Trainers, hunt the wild, magical Pokémon; then they train these creatures for battle; Trainers and the respective Pokémon join forces to fight other Trainer/Pokémon teams. The themes addressed are fairly universal, namely coercion, education, friendship, cooperation and conflict. Pokémon are many (see Bulbapedia; https://bulbapedia.bulbagarden.net/, the community-driven Pokémon encyclopaedia, since 2005), each with a particular aspect, superpower and personality; in some iterations of the *Pokémon* series, they also bond with their respective Trainers (another strong narrative feature). The *Pokémon* game employs a kind of sparse storytelling, with stories hidden within the *Pokémon* world. As Caroline O'Donoghue (2020) has observed, these stories are revealed in bits and pieces as the game progresses: they seem "half-written, allusive, full of hints and easter eggs", extras to be discovered. The game provides clues that give the impression that a story is underway to keep interest alive. These clues are shared by players on forums and create myths about certain facts or characters. For example, an elusive Pokémon called Mew was a hidden extra in one of the games. Mew is a pink, bipedal, mammal-like Pokémon with triangular ears. "Mew is said to have the DNA of every single Pokémon contained within its body, allowing Mew to learn and use any attack" (see Bulbapedia). Because it was number 151 in a 150-character game and never appeared, it created a myth about the game's background and fans spread various theories about how to find Mew (a widely acknowledged solution was that Mew was hiding behind a small lorry that could only be accessed by trading with another player). *Pokémon* is analysed in transdisciplinary contexts. Here are three examples. Bainbridge (2014) considers the game in its behaviours related to the conservation and consumption of nature at the same time, as a reflection of Japan, a nation caught between economic development and environmental protection. Buckingham and Sefton-Green (2003) analyse the relationship between structure and agency in *Pokémon* to place it in the broad context of children's media culture and suggest pedagogy as an alternative tool for analysis. Finally, Jordan (2004) examines the impact of *Pokémon* on children and concludes that, of the various media components, the video games and card trading drive the brand, while cartoons and films have been the most influential on children's subconscious development (explored through Pokémon characters and stories).

- *Story world*: the story world is a complete game multi-environment with geographical regions, cities with different activities, intentional characters, Trainers with goals and actions, Pokémon characterisations through aspects and behaviours, battlefield environments, path travelled by Trainers. The consistency of the environments is maintained across all media, creating an enduring fictional world shared by millions of players and fans.
- *Dynamic elements*: the behaviours of the characters, implementing simple personalities and reactive environments that update the state of resources and the hierarchy of players; elements are organised into a structured universe where creatures are defined by their morphological features and abilities in combat. Tasks and goals are clearly defined by their adaptation to the region and the characteristics of the battlefield.
- *Engine*: this is a constraint-based approach with some templates that define paths and sequences in general (e.g., the sequencing of Pokémon to defeat enemies in a Gym). It implements the general rules of the game by suggesting enemies and Gyms along some paths. It also provides time for exploration and interaction with the mentor characters.
- *Display*: the multimodal mode of the *Pokémon* saga brings with it a multitude of interfaces, from physical cards for trading and playing to mobile devices connected to GPS and operated via touchscreens. The graphics are very simple, although they implement a 3D environment and have recently included GPS positioning for use on mobile devices.

Further details

The world of *Pokémon* is described at length in Bulbapedia, the community-driven *Pokémon* encyclopaedia, since 2005 available at: https://bulbapedia.bulbagarden.net/. A video of the recent (2020) Pokémon VR Theme Park! – Pokémon Virtual Fest Gameplay can be found at: https://youtu.be/pIbFs0OKHFI.

6.9 1999: Desert Rain

Description

This live performance is a mix between installation, film set and video game. It was developed by Blast Theory in collaboration with the Mixed Reality Laboratory at the University of Nottingham in the UK and has become a benchmark for an interactive event where the narrative content is created by the same participants. In each run of the performance, six people are sent on a mission in a virtual world to find as many human targets as possible. After entering the performance venue (usually a disused warehouse), the participants are led into a bare room where they are asked to leave their personal belongings, take off their outer clothing and wear a uniform, an anorak. They are briefed about the mission: they must find six people (identified by name and photo), navigate through the virtual world within a given time and cooperate with each other. Next, each player is given a headset/

microphone and led to a fabric cubicle with a personal footpad to stand on. Each player stands in front of a rain curtain of falling water about 2 metres high and 2.5 metres wide, on which a rear projection shows the image of a motel room. Each footpad functions like a kind of joystick; each player can navigate through the different motel rooms in the virtual world by shifting their own weight on the surface.

In each motel room there is a TV device playing the Gulf War coverage of CNN news. Eventually the projection changes and the players find themselves in an open desert landscape. Now the players can hear each other over the live audio link, mixed with the voices of the actors (who watch the player unseen from behind the rain curtain) giving instructions as needed. As they explore the desert, the players can see each other (when they meet), represented as avatars with text labels (likewise they can see the target). Eventually, each player arrives at a virtual doorway labelled with the name of their target. Once having crossed the doorway, the new virtual environment represents a rotating virtual cylinder, with a sign saying, "Wait here". Now one of the performers physically steps through the rain curtain, approaches the player, hands him/her a plastic swipe-card and walks back through the curtain without speaking. Now all the players are back in the virtual world, which is an underground bunker with a labyrinth of narrow corridors. Together they have to find the exit before the 30 minutes are up. The exit only opens when all the players have found their targets. If they succeed, a performer reappears to guide the players through the rain curtain - the reward for success. If they fail, the rain stops before they are led to the next stage. The final part takes place in the physical world. The six players go through a narrow corridor and climb up a sand-covered ramp to enter a physical replica of the virtual motel room (designed with wallpaper-sized photos on the wooden walls). Using the swipe card previously obtained, each player can activate a TV set in the room and watch a video of an interview with their target. Each video offers a different perspective on the Gulf War. The six targets are: an actor who was on holiday in Egypt at the time; a soldier who served in the Gulf War and one who was bedridden and followed the war on TV; a peace worker setting up a peace camp; a reporter in Baghdad; and an actor who played a soldier in a TV drama about the Gulf War. Finally, the participants change back into their original clothes and leave the venue; only to find in their pockets, eventually, a small bag of sand containing an estimated 100,000 grains, the estimated number of casualties in the Gulf War. The description of the game is taken from (Koleva et al. 2001).

Analysis

Thematically, *Desert Rain* dealt with the question of the boundaries between virtual and real in the specific case of the Gulf War. The starting point was the question of whether the representation provided by TV and the media was truthful or fake. The performance was inspired in particular by Baudrillard's statement that the Gulf War was highly virtual, "a pure simulacrum, a conquest by spectacle, nothing but a 'show off of technological superiority' with predictable results"

(Lushetich 2007, p. 20). Through this interactive performance, participants were able to question the boundaries between what they perceived as real or fictional. The work was not based on a special computer system for interactive storytelling, but used different immersive technologies to build a dramaturgy in which events took place thanks to audience participation. The players' experience was not aimed at provoking an engagement with the technology, but rather with the story that could be told with this technology. Therefore, most of the interaction was controlled with the help of the actors, who suggested the actions that needed to be performed in order to achieve the goal of the performance. The whole event was reminiscent of a gaming experience, so the dramaturgy as a whole made people question the war and its representation. The players had to go through different sessions, from the initial briefing to the final video reports, as if they were going through different levels in a game whose reward was escape from the labyrinth. Almost every one of the sessions contained some kind of puzzle to be solved (e.g., finding the exit) and required some kind of physical action. These actions made up the meaning of the whole experience and the dramatic tension built up to the climax, the passing of the rain curtain. When the players were released from the booths, they were also rewarded with the unusual experience of walking through the rain curtain (Koleva et al. 2001). The work was not based on the possibility of changing the narrative sequence, but rather on the possibility for the player to choose his/her own position before the happenings. The more the player was committed to the given goal, the more emotionally engaging the whole system was. The whole dramaturgy of the performance was designed to include certain activities, and it could only continue if these activities were carried out correctly. To this end, several adjustments in the interaction design were necessary. For example, it proved inappropriate for all the players to leave the booths at the same time, as this was interpreted as the end of the performance and interrupted the emotional involvement of the participants. Therefore, this passage was made individual and the players were not allowed to take off their anoraks (ibid., pp. 43–44).

- *Story world*: the Gulf War provides the general context for the participants' actions. Since it is a live performance, the physical space in which the actions are performed (even if it is a virtual world) provides some implicit rules: the cubicle, the ramp, the motel room. In other words, the dramaturgy defines a story world using the space setting and the (verbal or physical) instructions given by the performers of the ensemble.
- *Dynamic elements*: in this case, the event contains a series of narrative environments in which only a specific set of actions is allowed. In the virtual reality section of the show, the dynamic elements processed by the system are multimedia content and the table in which the possible actions are described and linked. However, in this live performance, there are also actors and technicians who intervene and therefore have a set of predetermined actions that are planned by the director (a kind of non-automatic drama manager) and activated at specific moments. In other words, there is a script (almost like rules

of the game) that dictates the collaboration between the computer elements and the human activities.
- *Engine*: the dramaturgy is the core element of this performance and functions as the engine that implements both the sequence of macroscenes and the actions within these scenes. The performance resorts to a kind of game rules and involves the computational implementation of some passages (the navigation in the virtual world) that determine the possible actions at a given moment.
- *Display*: the story is presented by various means and modes. First of all, the space in which the event is inscribed and all the multimedia devices that allow the participants to interact with the whole set of the dynamic elements. It should be noted that this complex form of display allows natural interaction with the space (exploring a room, walking through the rain curtain), but also includes some specific interfaces such as the footpad or the swipe card.

Further details

Reviews of the project, as well as videos and other resources, may be found at: https://www.blasttheory.co.uk/projects/desert-rain.

6.10 2001: *Can You See Me Now?*

Description

This was a location-based performance/game by Blast Theory in which 15 players were connected online and moved around a virtual model of a city, with the goal of not being seen by four runners chasing the players on the real city streets. It was first performed in Sheffield and later in various cities around the world. To start, players had to sign up on a website and were told some basic rules for the event. They had to give their name and the name of a person they had not seen for a long time and would like to meet. Immediately afterwards, they were placed at their starting position in the virtual model of the city. The model showed the city map and also the 3D sketches of some relevant buildings, but there were no details of the surfaces of the rendering or of the moving elements (such as cars). Apart from the players and the runners, no one was visible in this virtual model. The area covered by the performance was generally between 500 and 1000 metres, and participants were not allowed to enter the buildings. Each player was represented in the virtual world by a running avatar. If a runner got close enough (5 metres) to a player, it meant "to see". At that point, the player in question had reached the end of the game and a score was given depending on how long the player could hide from the runners. In the virtual world, the avatar was labelled with the player's name, while the runner appeared as a bright red dot and was very visible even when far away from the player. In the real city, the runners were equipped with a portable microcomputer, a Wi-Fi connection and a GPS and walkie-talkie to communicate with each other and plan their pursuit strategy. They also had a digital camera to take photos of the place where they had "seen" the player on the run. The players could also exchange information in the form of texts through the game system. Each could see the other's location and access the entire flow of information (audio and text). When the player was on the move, the virtual model of the city was usually displayed as an aerial view of the map from a virtual bird's-eye view. When the player stopped and stood still, the visualisation changed and the camera view lowered, zoomed in and rotated to show the space around the player. Parts of the map could be selected at will to zoom in or visualise images of the real city connected to the corresponding points on the virtual map. A player could participate in the performance from anywhere in the world via an internet connection, but for each performance there was a room in the city with dedicated computers that could be accessed. Each session of the performance game could count on a technical team of three people in a control room. From there they controlled the flow of information, the local network on which the whole organisation was based, and the GPS system. This description is taken from Benford et al. (2006).

Analysis

This interactive and location-based performance is a famous example of what is known as pervasive gaming. It was created just as the first smartphones appeared and the new network technologies became available on mobile phones. The theme of the performance emphasised uninterrupted connectivity and the narrative structure borrowed from the well-known game of hide and seek. The content of the story was very limited, but the performance made the most of both the action-based nature of the game and the interactivity that the GPS system enabled (Gibbs 2004). In this particular case, interactivity was synonymous with immersion: two groups of participants (the runners, who were specially instructed performers, and the players, who connected to the game) carried out their activities on two different levels of presence (the real city and the virtual city), but they worked on the same action thanks to a common map. The actions of each individual changed the course of events and possibly made them more exciting, creating a kind of emergent dramaturgy, as is the case with group games. The dramaturgy of this performance aimed to create the feeling of being immersed in a shared space and participating in the events together, even if you are in different spaces:

> The audio channel, the real-time walkie-talkie stream from the runners, was an essential part of the experience. Players reacted strongly to hearing their names mentioned, realising that they had become the target of a chase, and hearing the runners discuss their tactics ... Beyond this, the audio channel also provided a way for players to tune into the runners' actual experience of the city streets, for example, hearing them discuss crossing a road through busy traffic or sounding out of breath when talking about running up a hill"
>
> (ibid., p. 108)

It should be noted that the dramaturgy of this interactive performance included the imponderables due to the sudden loss of the communication signal or other technical unsteadiness. In other words, the designers had included the possible failures in the system (here mainly related to the connections between the participants) as part of the interaction. This involved the ability to foresee the errors and reduce the damage: for example, by including only those areas of the city where there was good connectivity (Benford et al. 2003). In other cases, it was important to design a dramaturgy that incorporated the potential difficulties into the players' experience, that is, to use the available channels of communication with participants to mask the effects of uncertainty. For example, the authors recall that they deliberately "used the term 'seen' rather than 'caught' to introduce a degree of fuzziness as to how close a runner had to get to a player" (Benford et al. 2006, p. 124). The designer of the performance placed great emphasis on the continuity of the event and therefore devised a solution that ensured that communication could be seamless even with less technologically sophisticated means. For example, if the localising system stalled, it was still possible for the participants to manually mark their position (ibid.). More importantly, however, this performance made explicit the technical system behind the game and incorporated it into the audience's experience: in other words, the technical part was included in the dramaturgy of the performance. For example, the participant could use the accidental stall of the GPS system as an element of dramatic tension in the conflict between runners and players.

- *Story world*: the game of hide and seek provides an immediate and clear narrative context for the participants, both runners and players. The real location and its virtual map define the site of the performance and the boundaries of the game area.
- *Dynamic elements*: the participants in the performance and their avatar in the virtual world. The system does not contain narrative units, only a table with ID (for each participant) linked to the GPS coordinates in real time.
- *Engine*: this implements the table with the coordinates in the map and provides real-time information on the display. The dramaturgy of the performance is the actual engine that implements the sequence of scenes and the associated actions. The performance applies the rules of the game and contains the computational component for some of the passages (the navigation in the virtual world), so that the available action is authorised at a given time.
- *Display*: the visualisation of the map, with the tracking of the participants and the exchanged text message; there is also a digital radio channel transmitted to the headphones or speakers.

Further details

Reviews of the project, as well as videos and other resources, may be found at: https://www.blasttheory.co.uk/projects/can-you-see-me-now.

6.11 2003: *Façade*

Description

The concept of Expressive Artificial Intelligence can be traced back to the OZ group at Carnegie Mellon University, largely thanks to the work of Michael Mateas (with his PhD thesis), who later developed the first and ground-breaking interactive theatre experiment, *Façade*, with artist Andrew Stern. The game, which you can still download at https://www.playablstudios.com/facade, is an improvisation in which one player shares a scenario with two artificial agents. The scenario looks like this: the player is a person invited for drinks at the home of friends Grace and Trip, an apparently happily married, sociable and well-off couple. At the beginning of the game, the player chooses a name to use for his or her character. A short time later, the couple's invitation is played as a recorded message on the answering machine. Then the screen shows the corridor of the building and a door that is still closed, while the voices of the hosts can be heard from inside the flat. After the player knocks, the couple welcomes the friend. The game uses a graphic interface that simulates a sketched 3D room (the interiors with furniture) with the two hosts. The game is always in first-person perspective and the player can move freely and operate some of the objects with the mouse or arrow keys. The two hosts communicate in English with recorded voices. The guest can communicate by typing short sentences on the keyboard (they appear at the bottom of the screen). Soon after the first greetings and pleasantries, the player realises that there are some quarrels, frustrations and disagreements in the marriage of the two friends. What the player says or does affects the development of the scenario and its ending. The game lasts more or less 15 minutes and can end in different ways, all of which can be traced back to two main endings: one in which the couple gets back together and overcomes their crisis; one in which they (or even one of them) decide to separate. Then there is a third ending where the player behaves rudely or unkindly and is thrown out of the flat. The system consists of three basic elements. The first is the module that takes care of the character's behaviour, i.e., it sequences the agents' actions to ensure a smooth and consistent flow of events (the authors have developed a special programming language called ABL, A Behaviour Language). The second component is a module that interprets the player's actions (behaviours and dialogues) and assigns meaning to them (in particular, a positive or negative attitude towards each of the hosts) to generate consistent and reasoned responses. The third component is the so-called Drama Manager, that composes the different scenes of the whole game session. The whole structure is based on the concepts of behaviour and beat (dramatic unit). The first are atomic actions (opening the door, taking a glass, pouring the drink); the second are short scenes (consisting of behaviours) that achieve more articulated task (offering the guest a drink) and that can be executed in different ways (the friend asks for a Martini or a wine) and can even be aborted in the process (the friend refuses the drink and prefers to talk about the holiday).

Analysis

The aim of this game is to show how the functions of Artificial Intelligence can be used for expressive purposes in creating dramatic situations. In particular, this improvisation aims at the emotional engagement of the player. On the gaming side, this is the transposition of an improvisation onto a given dramatic scenario. On the narrative side, the work experiments with creating an interactive drama based on the ability to design rules rather than writing a sequence of lines to be delivered. The key element is the system's ability to sequence the action so that the whole act is dramatic, engaging and exciting. In this case, the system has a formal description of the dramatic arc, which is managed by the Drama Manager. This acts as a behind-the-scenes author, directing the development of the plot and sequencing events, themes and character behaviour to both incorporate player improvisation and ensure the build-up of tension to the climax that ends the story. Although not commercialised, it has been downloaded more than five million times (https://www.playablstudios.com/) and widely discussed in the literature on interactive storytelling or video games. It belongs to a stream that has great relevance, albeit in a different form: it concerns games in which Artificial Intelligence plays a key role, especially when the game experience is linked to planning (such as *The Sims* by Maxis or *Black & White* by Lionhead Studios). In the case of *Façade*, the focus is on the ability to engage the player in an emotionally charged relationship with the agents of the drama and their stories (a similar approach underpinned the design of *Milo and Kate* by Lionhead Studios; Pizzo 2011). Unlike other artificial agent interaction experiments, the architecture of this system does not include an explicit computational model for the agent. The properties of the character (e.g., personality, attitude) are implicit in the texts of the individual scenes and are not described by beliefs, desires and intentions, as in the development of autonomous agents. The Drama Manager draws on an archive of pre-defined scenes (each consisting of actions and dialogue) and controls the plot in real time, according to a specific narrative direction and taking into account the player's actions. In other words, in this case, the focus is on the plot and not on the characters. Therefore, *Façade* relies on a clear definition of dramatic action, where the player's possibilities of deviating from the course of the plot are few and are explicitly controlled by the Drama Manager that, in turn, tends to play sequences that steer the action in the desired direction (Mateas and Stern 2007).

- *Story world*: the game presents a very everyday situation and contains some social habits that intuitively lead the player to a usual dialogue action. At the same time, the virtual space in which the action takes place is clearly defined and thus contains a number of implicit rules of behaviour. In particular, the message left on the answering machine acts as an introduction and establishes the social framework of the event.
- *Dynamic elements*: the individual behaviours of the artificial agents and the player (both actions and verbal utterances) are the set of dynamic elements processed by the system. These are also arranged in macro-narrative units (the

beat), which together form the overall development of the dramatic situation. All these elements are organised in an archive that is updated in real time with the information about the behaviours already performed, the player's actions and the evaluation of what is happening (the actions are interpreted as affinity with one of the two artificial agents).
- *Engine*: the Drama Manager is the main sequencer for all units. Thus, the system implements the table of behaviour described in the archive and updates it with the player's actions, following an ordering logic that makes the sequence of events (including atomic ones) believable and reasoned. The game is inspired by artificial intelligence methods. Therefore, the engine plays a key role, because it generates meaningful behaviours by processing the available dynamic elements in real time.
- *Display*: the screen and the speaker present the action to the player through a visualisation of the space from the point of view of a single person. The display provides an intuitive interface that allows the player to type a few short lines of text and move around the flat.

Further details

There are several game play demonstrations of the project that can be reached via the official website at: https://www.playablstudios.com/facade

6.12 2005: *FearNot!*

Description

FearNot! is an example of the use of Interactive Drama techniques in education and training. Prior to *FearNot!*, the group CARTE (Center for Advanced Research in Technology for Education) at the University of Southern California had developed a number of automated systems for pedagogical interactive drama aimed at adult education, but these early systems focused more on the agent model than on the quality of dramatic situations. *FearNot!* (Fun with Empathic Agents Reaching Novel Outcomes in Teaching) has advanced the pedagogical use of interactive drama by combining autonomous agency and authorial control in a complex software architecture. *FearNot!* emerged from the EU project VITEC (Virtual ICT with Empathic Characters, 2002–2005) and puts the player in the role of an observer of bullying episodes and eventually lets them step directly into the role of the victim's counsellor. During the game, which is intended for children and younger teenagers, the player is supposed to develop empathy for the victim and learn from the victim's experience how to deal with bullying. Indeed, after a few episodes it should become clear that the right way to deal with bullies is to seek help and support and to overcome the fear of provoking new aggressions that will inevitably come if they are not stopped by adult intervention. The project used artificial agents in 3D animations to bring to life the dramatic situation in which 8–12-year-old children learn to deal with this kind of crisis. From 2006 to

2009, the EU project Ecircus (Education through Characters with Emotional-Intelligence and Role-Playing Capabilities that Understand Social Interaction) experimented with this approach in several schools across Europe and demonstrated its effectiveness in teaching suitable responses to bullying situations on a large scale. At the heart of *FearNot!* is an agent architecture specifically designed for dramatic role-playing and equipped with emotional intelligence (Aylett et al. 2005). In *FearNot!* the drama manager places the agents (i.e., the characters) in an initial situation whose development is limited to a set of outcomes that intrinsically depend on the agent's goals, abilities and, not least, emotions. The main character – a boy being bullied – who is initially driven by fear, develops through interaction with the player, changes his deliberation and eventually escapes the bullying situation. The whole paradigm was inspired by the Theatre of the Oppressed developed by Augusto Boal (1931–2009). In practice, the game consisted of a series of episodes in which the player witnessed a series of bullying events from a third-person perspective. After witnessing the situation in the third person, the player entered the game in the first person and was able to discuss and suggest possible solutions with the victim until the situation developed into more effective strategies to counter the aggression of the bully. In *FearNot!* each character relied on a BDI agent architecture called FAtiMa (Dias, Mascarenhas and Paiva 2014), which is characterised by the integration of emotions into the agent's planning. In this architecture, the agent's emotions were managed by two specialised modules, the emotion appraisal module, inspired by the OCC model of emotions, and the coping model (for appraisal and coping, see Chapter 4, Section 4.3). The emotion appraisal module determines how the agent reacts emotionally to an event by feeling fear, hope or other emotions in response to an event in the story. The coping module, which aims to rebalance the agent's emotional state that has been disturbed by emotions, takes care of the agent's behavioural response to its own emotional states and determines different actions (flight, avoidance, etc.) in response to different emotions. The planning module then had the task of translating the input from the coping module into a sequence of practical actions, thus implementing the strategy known in psychology as problem-oriented emotional coping. The architecture of FAtiMa also integrated simpler stimulus-response strategies that corresponded to an impulsive and immediate reaction to stressful events.

Analysis

The whole project is based on the idea that the process of cognitive appraisal determines an agent's emotional response to situations, as described in Chapter 4, Section 4.3. Thus, in *FearNot!* the way characters react to events in the story is determined by the emotions they feel in these situations. In the end, the main character manages to escape the fear-avoidance-failure loop triggered by bullying by opening up to new options through interaction with the player. From a pedagogical point of view, the aim of the game is for the player to empathise with the main character, weigh up his options, consider the consequences of his choices from the victim's perspective and finally develop an effective strategy. In *FearNot!*

the player could observe the changes in the character, whose behaviour developed from an immediate, impulsive reaction to the deployment of rational strategies, and verify the effectiveness of these strategies. In *FearNot!* two levels of development can be discerned. At the scene level, narrativity is the logical consequence of the interaction between the characters as established by the premise: given the premise contained in the initial situation (the characters, bully and victim, in the same place, each with their own goals), the scene indeed develops according to the available options of the characters (attack, flee, fight back, seek help). At the story level, the interaction with the player leads to a change in the main character, or more precisely to a change in their options, which are expanded as a result of the player's input. After each bullying episode, the main character asks the player for help in devising an action plan: the player's advice (make new friends, react with violence, ask an adult for help, etc.) changes his/her available options, so that in the next round, when the premise is realised, again with slight variations (different room, different type of aggression, etc.), the main character will behave differently until the final resolution (Vannini et al. 2011).

- *Story world*: the story takes place in a 3D environment representing a school with its typical facilities (rooms, libraries, hallways). Each agent has a library of actions describing their possible actions (knocking the victim down in the hallway, throwing the victim's books on the floor, going to another room, crying). These actions affect not only the material aspects of the story's world (e.g., the position of the characters and props), but also the agents' states of mind and especially their emotions (e.g., gratification for the bully, fear and hope for the victim). The story world does not develop by itself, but is a simple stage on which the dynamic elements are set and on which the action unfolds as a consequence of the clash of these elements.
- *Dynamic elements*: the system is based on a complex, modular BDI agent architecture that is replicated for each of the characters, who interact with each other only in the framework of a predefined series of bullying situations. Each dramatic situation corresponds to a bullying type: for example, the bully is in the same room as the victim and, upon seeing the victim's books, decides to seek self-gratification by throwing them on the floor. These situations – the story units – only encode the initial setting of each bullying situation, but not its development, which depends on the structure of the characters, and are therefore defined as unscripted by the creators of *FearNot!* (Aylett, Dias and Paiva 2006). At the story level, the player takes on the role of the counsellor and becomes a dynamic element that can change the victim's behaviour.
- *Engine*: the Stage Manager follows a cope–discuss–cope scheme, in which random bullying situations involving the bully and the victim are interwoven with the victim's interaction with the player, who suggests new coping strategies to the victim. The cycle repeats until the victim's behaviour changes to effectively cope with the bullying, leading the story to its final resolution. The system also includes a View Manager that generates the correct 3D rendering for each situation.

- *Display*: this is the graphic interface that shows the animation and allows the user to communicate with the agent via a text box on one side of the screen. The user's input is limited to the discussion sessions of the cope–discuss–cope scheme described above, where the user can interact with the victim and enter advice in a text box.

Further details

FearNot! has been developed as part of a larger effort to create an open-source emotional agent for virtual characters and robots, called FAtiMa (Fearnot AffecTIve Mind Architecture). This website (https://fatima-toolkit.eu/showcase) describes the project and collects samples and data from the applications of FAtiMa, including *FearNot!*

6.13 2006: *DramaTour*

Description

The CIRMA (Interdepartmental Centre for Research on Multimedia and Audio-video) at the University of Turin has created an interactive virtual guide to the Royal Apartments in Chiablese Palace in Turin. The driving idea of the project was to create an automatically animated character that would act as a virtual guide through the historical site on a mobile device, allowing visitors to move freely through the rooms. When the project started, smartphones were not yet widely available. Therefore, the production team resorted to a personal digital assistant (PDA) (an ASUS A636 – PocketPC series). These devices were handed out to visitors at the entrance of the Apartments. The system was able to locate the visitor in each room, thanks to a network of wireless access points set up specifically for this purpose, by measuring the signal strength in relation to the individual PDA. The display showed a 3D animated character: Carletto (Charlie), a cute little teenage spider whose family has inhabited the palace for centuries. The character was proud of his ancestors and enjoyed telling visitors the history of the palace in detail, as well as many funny anecdotes about the people who have lived there over the centuries. From time to time, Carletto would resort to his web, which was presented as a kind of technological tool and served as an archive for his memories. The character was portrayed as very outgoing and fond of history, but also as someone who liked to use modern technology; the story went that he had to hide in the corners of different rooms, but was also able to hack the internet and thus appear on the screens of PDAs. The visit began with a kind of narrative introduction that laid the foundation for the relationship with the visitor. The system was able to draw on about a hundred audio and video clips (i.e., units) that were sequenced in real time, depending on the location of the visitor (the room) and the duration of the visit. The project was based on tagging the units according to different criteria. The primary tagging criteria described the function of the unit in relation to the goal: introductory (explaining how the visit works); social (introducing the character, welcoming the visitor); directional (getting the visitor to move through the rooms); phatic (attesting to Carletto's presence while the visitor takes time to observe the room). The most important criterion was the informational one, which characterised the majority of the units. For this reason, the team divided this criterion into different semantic dimensions: topological (describing the location); historical (describing the historical facts related to the location); objects (describing the different pieces of furniture and other items located in the Apartments); chronological (providing a temporal framework for locating the historical events); symbolic (focusing on concepts such as reigns, battles, marriages). All these dimensions were described in ontologies that created a domain-specific formal representation of the information knowledge about the Apartments. The whole tagging system enabled the sequencing algorithm to deploy the unit in a precise and narrative way. The PDA displayed the clip (the audio was played back through headphones), creating the effect of a flowing sequence of information, all linked by narrative logic. The visit lasted about 25 minutes and guided the visitor through the entire extension of the Royal Apartments (Damiano et al. 2007).

Analysis

The virtual guide is about visiting a historical site. In contrast to a museum exhibition, the contents (works, objects, spaces) in such cases cannot be changed or rearranged according to a curatorial narrative, but must be presented as they are. In other words, the paintings cannot be rearranged and displayed in a certain order (e.g., by painter). Therefore, the guide had to build the narrative based on the existing arrangement, making the possible connections between topics (historical, artistic) even when moving from one room to another. The team developed a script based on a general model for visiting a historical site (e.g., where to start, what is the most important information, when to invite people to move on). The system was able to use the units' tagging to adapt the sequence to the behaviour of individual visitors. In *DramaTour*, interaction was limited to the movement of the visitor through the different rooms of the Royal Apartments. Following the script, the engine had to assemble the narrative sequence in real time. The script was developed under the assumption that visitors who stay longer in a room want more information. Therefore, the guide kept adding details and anecdotes or retreating and remaining silent to give the visitor time to reflect. In contrast, in the case of a visitor who was moving quickly, the guide only gave general information about the space. Overall, visitors had the feeling of being guided by a tour guide who did not just name and describe objects or provide information on command, but told a story that related to the particular place and followed a well-formed narrative. This was also the effect of detailed character design. Carletto the spider had a cheerful personality, was proud of his ancestors and became friendlier over time: these characteristics transformed the visit into a storytelling experience where the visitor not only received factual information but could also feel a sense of connection with the character.

Examples of interactive storytelling: description and analysis 161

- *Story world*: this is about the special qualities of the character, such as his personality, and the historical information about the palace and the historical figures associated with it. It is also about the map of the Royal Apartments and all the implicit conventions associated with visiting a historical site. These are the elements that place the visitor in a given and implicit cultural framework.
- *Dynamic elements*: these are the list of units produced (the audio and video clips), the information about the location, the interaction history during the visit and the rules that allow the possible editing between the different units.
- *Engine*: this implements the script to sequence the units consistently with the location of the visitor.
- *Display*: the PDA with headphones shows the clips and allows interaction with the system thanks to the deliberate built-in wi-fi-based localisation.

Further details

The whole project is described on the CIRMA website, available at: https://www.cirma.unito.it/portfolio_page/dramatour/; there is also a web implementation of the visit, available at: https://dramatour.unito.it.

6.14 2012: *The Walking Dead*

Description

This adventure video game series (for single player) comes from the comic book series of the same name (2003–2019) by Robert Kirkman, which is also based on the success of the television series (2010–). The game is loosely based on the comic book but shares the same fictional world and introduces new characters. The years in which the game series was released overlap with the year of the comic book and the TV series, but the stories being told are not identical, creating a complex system of storytelling across different platforms and media. The plot in the game is complex and divided into four seasons and 19 episodes in total (plus additional releases with further content), spanning from 2012 to 2019. A zombie apocalypse has left the state of Georgia in the USA at the mercy of the undead, who move extremely slowly (they are called "walkers") but attack humans. Their numbers are constantly increasing, not only because people are infected by their bite, but also because it seems that sooner or later everyone will turn into zombies. The survivors have no choice but to crush the brains of the corpses to prevent this. The game features numerous characters, but begins with Lee Everett (the player-controlled character), a former university professor sentenced to prison for the murder of a senator who had an affair with Lee's wife. On one of Atlanta's highways, just as a police officer is taking him to the prison, the car hits a zombie, the car goes off the road and Lee wakes up in the midst of the catastrophe. Soon the scene of the accident is overrun by zombies, but Lee manages to escape and meets Clementine, an 8-year-old girl left by her parents with a babysitter for the weekend. Her mother and father have left for Savannah, leaving no messages other than a final dramatic message on the answering machine. Lee decides to look after the girl and with the help of two other boys they manage to leave town. So the two begin their new life on the farm of the father of one of the boys. Although their adventures begin in the city of Atlanta, Lee and Clementine meet several other characters with whom they eventually form a group and travel north to Michigan in search of a survivor camp. As the story progresses, the characters are confronted with very difficult situations, including with each other, and they will discover that the problems stem not only from the zombie threat, but also from the choices they make. After various ups and downs, at the end of the last season it looks like Clementine might be reunited with her parents, but events also suggest that Lee is doomed to turn into one of the walking dead.

Analysis

The game has been critically acclaimed for revitalising the adventure genre with a new design that does not rely on the ability to solve puzzles, fight or explore. The graphic style is reminiscent of the comic book, while the actions that make up the story play out like a movie. Most of the time the player has to decide what to do, but often it feels like the story has an autonomous course and follows its own direction to which the player has to adapt. A key element is the need for the player to make difficult and morally ambiguous decisions. These decisions must be made as the story progresses (i.e., the narrative does not pause to wait for the player to make a decision) and must be made within a certain time (i.e., time is a variable used by the system to determine continuation). In addition to actions that have an explicit goal and immediate consequences (e.g., kill a zombie, open a door), the player (through the character Lee) is asked to perform actions that have no immediate consequences but will influence the attitude that the other characters will develop towards him. To this end, there is a feedback system (on-screen cues) that warns the player. The design aims to give players the impression that they are participating in a story that has its own autonomy and direction, with the unfolding of events depending on the mutual influences between the characters. In this adventure game, the ludic experience remains that of intervening in the world, but it is a narrative world, which means that the actions mainly affect the value system that links the behaviours of the different characters involved. So it is not about quick reflexes or solving puzzles in a given environment, but about emotionally engaging with the world of the characters and navigating it accordingly (Koenitz et al. 2015).

- *Story world*: there is a broad narrative context (the comic books and the TV series) that makes it a saga. There are also the conventions of the genre (the zombie stories). This reference context offers the player a particular orientation. Also noteworthy is the particular way in which the conventions of the adventure video game are only partially adopted. This creates a meta-narrative in which the player reviews the similarities and differences to previous video game experiences.

- *Dynamic elements*: the story is divided into scenes, which are finite narrative units. These include the behaviour of the characters (both the player and the non-playable characters). Although these behaviours are important to the progression of events, the emphasis is on the sequence of narrative units. The agents are mainly described as a network of attitudes and values that influence the course of the scenes and are inscribed in a system of rules that define possible events and their consequences.
- *Engine*: as in any modern video game, the engine is a very complex element that encompasses different modules (for the flow of the story, for graphic rendering, etc.). It is important that the engine implements the rules for coordinating the different behaviours and for sequencing the different scenes.
- *Display*: the screen highlights the cinematography of the story, but occasionally also provides additional information and other feedback while the player uses the appropriate device (keyboard, gamepad) to interact.

Further details

An extensive and detailed description of the game, with links to the comic book and the TV series is available on Wikipedia at: https://en.wikipedia.org/wiki/The_Walking_Dead_(video_game_series).

6.15 2013: *Nothing for Dinner*

Description

This is an interactive drama created at the University of Geneva as part of a project coordinated by Nicolas Szilas with the collaboration of Jean Dumas, Urs Richie, Thomas Boggini and Nicolas Habonneau. The story takes place in the flat where young Frank lives with his family (father, mother, sister, grandmother). His father Paul suffers from memory loss and other behavioural problems due to the effects of a stroke. The action begins when the mother is still at work and has asked Frank to cook dinner. So the boy has to complete the task by trying to involve his father and at the same time react to the actions of the other members present in the house. It is not a video game, because it is not about solving puzzles or scoring points. Rather, it is a system that allows the user to experience a stressful situation: the dramatic improvisation is meant to help the user (in the role of Frank) test his/her decisions and behaviour in dealing with the complicated situation. As Frank, the player can navigate through the large living/kitchen area of the flat using the arrow keys on the keyboard or pointing with the mouse. While Frank is trying to achieve the main goal (preparing dinner), other characters trigger different events: for example, the sister wants to fix the DVD player, the neighbour comes to return a book, the grandmother offers her help, the father has to take his medicine. The graphical interface uses a 3D rendering engine (Unity) and visualises the actions of all characters on the screen. When Frank addresses another character, the portrait of the current addressee appears in the top centre of the screen. When the user clicks on the picture, a list appears on the screen with the different behaviours of Frank that are possible at that moment in relation to that specific character: when one is selected, the corresponding action is performed. Note that the action can be physical ("go to the fridge and check the food") or verbal. In this case, a dialogue is displayed at the bottom of the screen (there was also an implementation where the lines of dialogue were spoken by a synthetic voice). Things do not always go as planned, because Paul constantly has mood swings, or he forgets things, or other incidents happen in the meantime, so Frank's goals always have to do with the intentions of the other characters (Habonneau et al. 2012).

Analysis

Nothing for Dinner is based on *IDtension*, a generative system for interactive drama conceived and developed by Nicolas Szilas. The system starts from the formalisation of a general structure of drama (consisting of elements and functions) that can support virtually any dramatic story, but also pays attention to the process of authoring specific stories. The system architecture is divided into the following five modules:

1. The story world: this contains the basic entities of the story (e.g., characters, goals, tasks, subtasks or segments, obstacles).
2. The facts concerning the world or the characters (e.g., the door is closed).
3. The narrative logic contains about 40 rules, defines the logical conditions that make events possible, and calculates the set of possible actions for each phase of the narrative. The narrative sequencer orders the actions and calculates their effects for the purpose of dramatic effect.
4. The user model, which stores the status of the information provided at a given point in the story and provides an estimate of the impact of each action on the user.
5. The theatre, which provides visualisation and interaction between the computer and the user.

This is, therefore, an interactive story that does not use a hypertext graph to organise the narrative units, but generates actions based on the situation, the user's choices and the autonomous characters, and attempts to drive the story forward based on a model of dramatic tension inscribed in the system. In this case, the design team has not determined the possible connections (edges) between established and prescribed events (nodes), nor has it decided in advance what direction the plot should take. The team behaved more like a therapist who invites the user to participate in a situation with some defined boundaries (the home environment) together with other characters who have been assigned a certain personality (attitudes and goals). This means that the rules of the story world are fixed, while what happens in it is left to the collaborative process between the user and the intelligent system. Every decision Frank makes is taken by a system that takes care of producing and managing the events that follow, giving the user an essential sense of control and agency in the story (Szilas 2003).

- *Story world*: the specific environment in which the story is set and the situation in which the protagonist finds himself/herself define the narrative context. The game conventions allow the user to navigate quite easily to achieve a goal that is clearly defined from the beginning (the preparation of dinner). The introductory information places the experience in the realm of education and allows the project to avoid all the traditional elements characteristic of video games (e.g., scoring points).
- *Dynamic elements*: there are basic elements such as agents, environment and objects. These are associated with certain activities and mental states. For the sequence of events, there are rules that link these elements to prescribed logical situations. The elements and rules are in turn linked to a user model whose status is constantly updated.
- *Engine*: the narrative sequencer is the module that implements the rules, orders the actions, creates the dramatic tension and controls the visualisation and interaction. For this purpose, there is also a special module for the graphics engine that generates the rendering in real time.
- *Display*: the screen offers an over-the-shoulder protagonist's point of view and allows the user to see all the information and commands necessary for interaction.

Further details

The project can be tested at: http://nothingfordinner.org/portal/.

6.16 2018: *Black Mirror: Bandersnatch*

Description

This is an interactive film distributed by Netflix in 2018 as part of the *Black Mirror* series. It was written by Charlie Brooker, the creator of the series, and directed by David Slade. Set in 1984 London, the film is about a young programmer, Stefan Butler, who wants to turn the gamebook *Bandersnatch* into a video game. Stefan pitches his work to the video game company Tuckersoft, for which the famous game designer Colin Ritman also works. The story goes off the rails due to the psychological problems of the protagonist, who feels partly responsible for the early death of his mother. His relationship with his father is not easy either and the sessions with the psychoanalyst do not seem to improve his torment. Moreover, Colin's involvement brings more turmoil as the famous game designer is troubled by suspicions that there is a secret government mind control programme. Meanwhile, the deadline for the video game approaches and Stefan's condition does not improve. He is even more distraught because he feels that his own life has too much in common with that of Jerome F. Davis (the tormented author of the game book by which he was inspired), who deliriously beheaded his own wife. Like Davis, Stefan is haunted by the image of a "branching pathway", a symbol that keeps coming to his mind and which had led Davis to murder. In his panic, Stefan feels that his decisions are being controlled by someone else and tries desperately to find out who that someone is. The story can have several intermediate endings: some offer a more complete sense of the story, others appear as dead ends from which one must go back and start again. In one of the storylines, Stefan confronts his analyst, but then it turns out to be a film set where his father is just an actor. In another, Stefan goes through a mirror and finds himself as a child just before his mother is killed in a train crash. Other endings are more violent, and we see Stefan murder his father and end up in prison. Or the story suddenly switches to the present, where Colin's daughter, now grown up, is working for Netflix and trying to turn *Bandersnatch* into an interactive film. If the TV is equipped with smart technology, the viewer can choose between two options with the remote control at several points in the film. The action never stops, and if no choice is made within 10 seconds, the system makes an automatic decision. If the choices lead to a dead end where there is no continuation, the system again suggests the last choice to continue. However, if one of the production-defined closures is reached, the system either shows the credits or allows the user to start again and explore other options.

Analysis

Although Netflix had already tackled interactive storytelling with some products for children (*Puss in the Book: Trapped in an Epic Tale*, 2017). *Bandersnatch* is the most successful and, above all, the most popular interactive film. By giving the audience the power to change the course of the story, this film provides one of the clearest examples of how the role of the viewer is called into question. For while the experience of watching an episode of a television series remains almost unchanged (you watch it on TV, you do not have to buy a special device, there are no special rules to learn, you use the remote control), the viewer becomes the user. On the other hand, this very feature has led to some critical remarks about the interactivity of the work. The production had to maintain a strong authorial control over the development of the story, and so the spectator had access to a narrative that, although multilinear, seemed to be subject to very precise developmental control. Indeed, as we have seen, there are choices that are right for the development of the story towards a closure while others lead to undeveloped branches where the system only offers the possibility of going back and starting again (Elnahla 2019). But it is the question of control over the course of events that creates an interesting metanarrative in this dystopian film, thanks to this limited interactivity. The viewer is in the same position as the protagonist, wondering who is really in control of events. At a certain point, one of the options available to the viewer is to reply to the protagonist: "You are being controlled by someone on Netflix." The sentence is certainly directed at Stefan, but it could also concern the viewer, who is being watched by the platform (even for commercial purposes) as she/he makes her/his choices (Conley and Burroughs 2020).

- *Story world*: the TV series, in which this episode is set, defines the dystopian context. The conventions of television remain virtually unchanged, apart from the possibility of very simple interaction via the remote control. The characters, the setting, the development follow a traditional and well-established dramatic model.
- *Dynamic elements*: the work is organised starting from narrative units associated with a list of choices and links that create possible continuations.
- *Engine*: this implements the choices by activating the next unit on the basis of the given connections
- *Display*: the television screen proposes sequences of units as defined by the engine and shows the choices with which the audience can interact.

Further details

The movie can be seen on Netflix; its detailed description can be found on Wikipedia, including a large list of references, available at: https://en.wikipedia.org/wiki/Black_Mirror:_Bandersnatch

6.17 2019: *The Invisible Guardian*

Description

This is an interactive film (隐形守护者) developed by China's New One Studio and released online on Steam in 2019 after nearly two years of production. The work was adapted from an earlier text-based spy game *Latent Red Road* by Orange Light Game Platform. The interactive film is shot in live action, but uses the form of static shots as in photo novels: the view pans and zooms across a static image, or sequences of images are cut together to render an action. The player plays the role of the protagonist Xiao Tu, an underground member of the Chinese Communist Party. The story is set in Shanghai in 1939, during the Second Sino-Japanese War, when the Japanese army invades the city. This was a very chaotic time, marked by conflict between the regime of Wang Ching-wei (installed by the Japanese army), the National Government of China, the Chinese Communist Party and various gangs in the city. In these turbulent times, spies and counter-intelligence were everywhere. The protagonist is an undercover agent of the Communist Party. Two years before the events depicted in the film, he is said to have been a patriotic student in Shanghai who rallied the streets against the Japanese invasion, was arrested and put in prison. After his release, he goes to Japan to study. At the beginning of the game he is officially pro-Japanese and deputy director of a press agency, but in reality he is a member of the secret Chinese Communist Party. The aim of the game is to infiltrate the Japanese, provide the Communist Party with information and stay alive. There are many co-protagonists and supporting roles in the story (34 in total) and some of them are also undercover agents, such as Zhuang Xiaoman, officially an intelligence officer of Wang Jingwei's regime, but in reality an agent of the National Government of China.

The Invisible Guardian consists of six main chapters in which the player is faced with various decisions that appear as clickable links on the screen during the game: if the player makes the right decision, the game continues; otherwise, the story ends either with the protagonist's dismissal and transfer to a rural area, or with his death. If one of these "bad ends" happens to the player, the game can start over at the last choice and move on to another branch. If the player manages to complete the first six chapters, the game gives access to four more chapters leading to four endings with a deeper sense of closure. Each of these final chapters can lead to an ending or to the next chapter. The endings are summarised as follows: "Fusang Requiem", in which Xiao Tu becomes a Japanese soldier but does not live long and eventually dies in a foreign land; "Brave New World" and "For Whom the Bell Tolls", in which Xiao Tu joins the National Government of China and either realises he has lost his way or is killed by a National Government official. The clearly more fulfilling ending of the game is the fourth, "Red Youth", in which Xiao Tu has achieved his goals and finally marries, his wife gives birth to a child and they live on a farm. Because of their alleged association with the Japanese, they are considered traitors and are discriminated against for 30 years until Xiao Tu finally receives Communist Party approval in the 1980s and his efforts are recognised as a secret agent.

The game uses the track-switching structure to tell the story and consists of 699 video clips for a total of ten hours of gameplay. It contains 192 switching points where the player must make a decision. Apart from the four full closure endings that mark the accomplishment of the game, there are 112 bad endings. At any point in the game, the player can access the flow chart of the chapter being played and see which chapter has already been completed or still needs to be played.

Analysis

With this interactive film game, New One Studio wanted to enter the European and American markets. The company was founded in 2015 and has since produced interactive films using various technologies. This is one of their biggest productions. Filming began in 2017 and was motivated by the success of a text-based interactive narrative (*Hidden Red Way*) developed by a student under the nickname of Fantasia. Of course, the game followed on from previous foreign successes such as *Japan's 428: Shibuya Scramble* (2008) or North America's *Bandersnatch* (2018) (see Section 6.16); nevertheless, it opened a new page for the spread of interactive film in China, where interactive fiction has shown great potential for development. Interactive text-based narratives on the internet have become increasingly popular among young Chinese audiences in recent years, thanks mainly to two platforms such as Punch and Qiaobooks. The former (http://www.puncheers.com/) was launched in 2017 and combines text with multimedia elements (images, voices and short videos). The latter was founded in 2016 with the aim of developing Chinese interactive novels in a more literary direction and competing on an international level. *The Invisible Guardian* wanted to merge the standard of commercial films with interactive fiction and therefore put a lot of resources into the production (set design, costumes, casting). Although the tree structure of the narrative is fairly standard, the player's engagement is ensured by the emotional bond with the protagonist and by a series of choices that challenge moral and political values rather than relying on puzzles. The protagonist's relationships with the other characters are handled in the form of alliances or antagonisms, they are determined by the player's choices and play a key role in the selection of the various endings. The game was a great success when it was first released, even though it received bad reviews when the Steam platform had technical problems and could not update the last chapter of the story. An important merit of this work is that it focuses mainly on the immersive power of the narrative, motivating the player through the protagonist's choices rather than the actions to be performed. In addition, the company has decided to sell the game at a price roughly equivalent to the price of a cinema ticket in China. The impact of this video game is unprecedented for other interactive works and represents a turning point in interactive storytelling in China. Chinese audiences are showing increasing interest, and there are also more artists producing and developing interactive narratives.

- *Story world*: the historical setting is one of the main elements guiding the player through the narrative. The espionage story is also a familiar genre that provides guidance to the player, while the cultural and political values conveyed in the narrative guide the story towards the desired ending, where the hero fulfils his mission and remains loyal to the original goal of the Communist Party, even if this involves many sacrifices.
- *Dynamic elements*: the narrative is based on a graph of narrative units and edges, with the former presented as film clips of varying length and the latter as player alternatives.
- *Engine*: this implements the sequence according to the player's selection of available choices.
- *Display*: the screen renders the audio video clip and provides the alternative choices in the form of superimposed texts to click on.

Further details

The game is distributed only in Chinese on Steam, available at: https://store.steampowered.com/app/998940/_The_Invisible_Guardian/?l=tchinese&cc=cn. Many of the reviews and other commentary are in Chinese but there are various gameplay videos with English commentary on YouTube, such as https://www.youtube.com/watch?v=U9Zu-fowE7I.

6.18 2020: *Down the Rabbit Hole*

Description

Acclaimed by the critics and nominated by the Venice Film Festival (Venice VR Expanded, in association with La Biennale di Venezia), *Down the Rabbit Hole* is a production of the Sweden-based company Cortopia that brings the magic of Lewis Carroll's well-known narrative universe, Wonderland, to a playable Virtual Reality experience. Praised by gamers and experts for the naturalness of its movements and the accuracy of its creation of the story world, *Down the Rabbit Hole* immerses the player in a "minuscule miracle" where Carroll's imagination comes alive and extends 360° around the player with the vividness of a children's comic book. *Down the Rabbit Hole* is a prime example of remediation in Bolter's terms (Bolter and Grusin 1999; Bolter 2007). It brings Carroll's iconic characters (the enigmatic Cheshire Cat, the wise and cryptic Caterpillar, the desperate White Rabbit, etc.) to the stage through a sequence of encounters that capitalises on the popularity of the original tale across all ages and latitudes. The visual design of the game is a mixture of the illustrations from the original book and quotes from the Disney film (1951). It goes a long way towards giving the player a sense of familiarity with the environment, interrupted only by the opening and closing scenes. The first scene of the game sets the story within the framework of a tale of adventure and mystery told by a grandfather (the narrative voice of the whole game) to his grandchild at bedtime. Consequently, in the final scene, the grandfather says goodnight to the almost sleeping child and the player with some final comments on the ending (whether it is just, acceptable, etc.), which almost places the story in the style of a moral narrative. From this first incident onwards, the rest of the story corresponds exactly to the player's knowledge of the narrative universe of Wonderland: the protagonist, a girl, accidentally falls down the rabbit hole while searching for her lost pet, Patches; after landing in Wonderland, she immediately encounters the White Rabbit, which triggers the game's second main quest, as she accidentally scatters the invitations to the Queen's party, that the White Rabbit was in charge of, everywhere. Getting the pet (Patches) back and finding the lost invitations then become the character's main goal in the game. To complete her quest, the girl must solve puzzles to progress in the exploration and collect as many invitations as possible. *Down the Rabbit Hole* is designed to take about two hours to play and has been released for Oculos Quest, Oculus Rift, PlayStation VR, Steam VR and Viveport.

Analysis

If we stick to Belisle and Roquet's definition of virtual reality as "always on the verge of arrival" (2020, p. 3), *Down the Rabbit Hole* can be considered a success in its own way, having met both audience expectations in terms of immersivity and pleasure – as evidenced by user ratings – and critics' expectations in terms of the game's strong narrative imprint. However, a closer look at the game reveals that the narrativity ultimately revolves mainly around the conversations with the characters and that, while the vividness of the story world undoubtedly invites exploration, the agency is mainly focused on the intellectual sphere challenged by the successive puzzles, ultimately making the player's actual effort to collect the lost invitations secondary. In fact, the player's final reward depends on the number of invitations collected. The number of invitations (some, most, all) unlocks a maximum of three different endings following a largely fixed sequence of scenes. From the point of view of the player's role, *Down the Rabbit Hole*, with its duality, can be seen as paradigmatic of the possibilities and limitations of virtual reality. The player's relationship to the protagonist – an avatar of Alice (Ryan 2006) – is twofold: on the one hand, the player is Alice, the character through whom he/she acts in the world in the first person; on the other hand, the player is a kind of genius who is separated from the story world, who controls the protagonist like a puppeteer who lingers in the air and literally sees Alice from a third-person perspective. The protagonist repeatedly meets other characters, but apart from their ironic, slightly formulaic conversations with the player, they play no clear role in the progress of the story. Instead, the player's real antagonist is the story world itself, Wonderland, which sets up obstacles and reveals the locations of collectibles depending on how well the player is able to solve the puzzles. Finally, the game's soundtrack also plays a significant role in building immersion: following the mood-cue model presented by Smith (2003), the finely crafted music creates a mysterious and promising atmosphere that prepares the ground for the incidents, creates the necessary tension and invites the player to act when the environment allows it, which is also underlined by the sound design that accompanies the exploration of the objects.

- *Story world*: this leverages on the famous fairy tale by Carroll and consists of a series of famous locations (the Caterpillar's Forest, the White Rabbit's House, the Queen's Castle) where the player has to solve puzzles by interacting with NPCs and objects in order to get from one location to another – similar to a game level.
- *Dynamic elements*: the entire story takes the form of a list of units, each set in a particular environment within the story world and further divided internally into smaller units whose exact duration and even presence depend on the player's commitment to the game (a strongly committed player may take up to half an hour longer than a casual player if they want to explore all the possibilities in each scene). Each unit involves the character's behaviour (collecting an object, choosing a path) and the incidents occurring in the story world (the girl falling down the rabbit hole getting bigger); these two elements together ensure that the story progresses according to a constrained set of storylines (list of units). The character's behaviour can be roughly divided into three main categories: solving puzzles, collecting objects, and making decisions. In some cases, they take the form of dialogue acts (directing, committing, etc.) in the conversational interactions with the NPCs.
- *Engine*: the engine combines the challenges and the interactions with the characters by following a predetermined scheme for the sequences of the units, where the characters and incident types depend on the current locations.
- *Display*: the environment described as an "immersive diorama" is a 3D environment rich in colourful props and other objects arranged in accurately designed layouts that recreate indoor spaces (rooms, corridors, staircases, holes) and outdoor areas (gardens, forests, etc.) in which the player follows the main character by freely directing his or her gaze in a 360° area. An important element of the display is the auditory channel through which the

narrator's voice describes, comments on and connects the story incidents. In conversations, the player communicates with the NPCs by pointing and clicking on signposts.

Further details

More information about the game is available at: https://downtherabbitholegame.com/, where there is also an interview with the director Michael Gordon Shapiro.

References

Arfman, J. M. and P. Roden. 1992. "Project Athena: Supporting Distributed Computing at MIT". *IBM Systems Journal* 31 (3): 550–563. doi:10.1147/sj.313.0550.

Aylett, Ruth, João Dias, and Ana Paiva. 2006. "An Affectively Driven Planner for Synthetic Characters". In Derek Long, Stephen F. Smith, Daniel Borrajo, and Lee McCluskey (eds), *ICAPS 2006 – Proceedings, Sixteenth International Conference on Automated Planning and Scheduling, ICAPS'06*. Cumbria: AAAI Press, pp. 2–10. doi:10.5555/3037104.3037106.

Aylett, Ruth S., S. Louchart, João Dias, Ana Paiva, and M. Vala. 2005. "FearNot! – An Experiment in Emergent Narrative". In Themis Panayiotopoulos, Jonathan Gratch, Ruth Aylett, Daniel Ballin, Patrick Olivier, and Thomas Rist (eds), *Intelligent Virtual Agents*. Berlin: Springer, pp. 305–316. doi:10.1007/11550617_26.

Bainbridge, Jason. 2014. "'It Is a Pokémon World': The Pokémon Franchise and the Environment". *International Journal of Cultural Studies* 17 (4): 399–414. doi:10.1177/1367877913501240.

Belisle, Brooke, and Paul Roquet. 2020. "Guest Editors' Introduction: Virtual Reality: Immersion and Empathy". *Journal of Visual Culture* 19 (1): 3–10. doi:10.1177/1470412920906258.

Benford, Steve, Rob Anastasi, Martin Flintham, Adam Drozd, Andy Crabtree, Chris Greenhalgh, Nick Tandavanitj, Matt Adams, and Ju Row-Farr. 2003. "Coping with Uncertainty in a Location-Based Game". *IEEE Pervasive Computing* 2 (3): 34–41. doi:10.1109/MPRV.2003.1228525.

Benford, Steve, Andy Crabtree, Martin Flintham, Adam Drozd, Rob Anastasi, Mark Paxton, Nick Tandavanitj, Matt Adams, and Ju Row-Farr. 2006. "Can You See Me Now?" *ACM Transactions on Computer-Human Interaction* 13 (1): 100–133. doi:10.1145/1143518.1143522.

Bolter, Jay David. 2007. "Remediation and the Language of New Media". *Northern Lights: Film and Media Studies Yearbook* 5 (1): 25–37. doi:10.1386/nl.5.1.25_1.

Bolter, Jay David, and Richard Grusin. 1999. *Remediation: Understanding New Media*. Cambridge, MA: MIT Press.

Buckingham, David, and Julian Sefton-Green. 2003. "Gotta Catch 'em All: Structure, Agency and Pedagogy in Children's Media Culture". *Media, Culture and Society* 25 (3): 379–399. doi:10.1177/0163443703025003477.

Conley, Donovan, and Benjamin Burroughs. 2020. "Bandersnatched: Infrastructure and Acquiescence in *Black Mirror*". *Critical Studies in Media Communication* 37 (2): 120–132. doi:10.1080/15295036.2020.1718173.

Damiano, Rossana, Cristina Gena, Vincenzo Lombardo, Fabrizio Nunnari, and Antonio Pizzo. 2007. "A Stroll with Carletto: Adaptation in Drama-Based Tours with Virtual

Characters". *User Modeling and User-Adapted Interaction* 18 (5): 417–453. doi:10.1007/s11257-008-9053-1.

Davenport, Glorianna. 1988. "*Interactive Multimedia on a Single Screen Display*". Paper presented at NCGA 88. National Computer Graphics Association Conference: Current Applications of Videotechnology in Computer Graphics Systems.

Dias, João, Samuel Mascarenhas, and Ana Paiva. 2014. "FAtiMA Modular: Towards an Agent Architecture with a Generic Appraisal Framework". In Tibor Bosse, Joost Broekens, João Dias, and Janneke van der Zwaan (eds), *Emotion Modeling: Towards Pragmatic Computational Models of Affective Processes*. Cham: Springer International Publishing, pp. 44–56. doi:10.1007/978-3-319-12973-0_3.

Douglas, Yellowlees Jane. 1993. "Where the Senses Become a Stage and Reading Is Direction: Performing the Texts of Virtual Reality and Interactive Fiction". *TDR (1988–)* 37 (4): 18. doi:10.2307/1146290.

Egenfeldt-Nielsen, Simon, Jonas Heide Smith, and Susana Pajares Tosca. 2008. *Understanding Video Games: The Essential Introduction*. New York: Routledge. doi:10.1017/CBO9781107415324.004.

Elnahla, Nada. 2019. "*Black Mirror: Bandersnatch* and How Netflix Manipulates Us, the New Gods". *Consumption Markets and Culture* 23 (5) : 506–511. doi:10.1080/10253866.2019.1653288.

Ensslin, Astrid. 2007. *Canonizing Hypertext. Explorations and Constructions*. London: Continuum. doi:10.1017/CBO9781107415324.004.

Gibbs, Michael. 2004. "Locative Media". *Art Monthly* October (280): 1–26. doi:10.4324/9781315887036.

Habonneau, Nicolas, Urs Richle, Nicolas Szilas, and Jean E. Dumas. 2012. "3D Simulated Interactive Drama for Teenagers Coping with a Traumatic Brain Injury in a Parent". In D. Oyarzun, F. Peinado, R. M. Young, A. Elizalde, and G. Méndez (eds), *Interactive Storytelling. ICIDS 2012*. Berlin: Springer, pp. 174–182. doi:10.1007/978-3-642-34851-8_17.

Jenkins, Henry. 2009a. "Revenge of the Origami Unicorn: The Remaining Four Principles of Transmedia Storytelling". Blog. Available at: http://henryjenkins.org/blog/2009/12/revenge_of_the_origami_unicorn.html.

Jenkins, Henry. 2009b. "The Revenge of the Origami Unicorn: Seven Principles of Transmedia Storytelling (Well, Two Actually. Five More on Friday)". Blog. Available at: http://henryjenkins.org/blog/2009/12/the_revenge_of_the_origami_uni.html.

Jerz, Dennis G. 2007. "Somewhere Nearby Is Colossal Cave: Examining Will Crowther's Original 'Adventure' in Code and in Kentucky". *DHQ: Digital Humanities Quarterly* 1 (2): 1–33.

Jordan, Tim. 2004. "The Pleasures and Pains of Pikachu". *European Journal of Cultural Studies* 7 (4): 461–480. doi:10.1177/1367549404047146.

Koenitz, Hartmut, Gabriele Ferri, Mads Haahr, Digdem Sezen, and Tonguç İbrahim Sezen 2015. "A Concise History of Interactive Digital Narrative". In Hartmut Koenitz, Gabriele Ferri, Mads Haahr, Digdem Sezen, and Tonguç İbrahim Sezen (eds), *Interactive Digital Narrative*. New York: Routledge, pp. 11–21.

Koleva, Boriana, Ian Taylor, Steve Benford, Mike Fraser, Chris Greenhalgh, Holger Schnädelbach, Dirk vom Lehn, Christian Heath, Ju Row-Farr, and Matt Adams. 2001. "Orchestrating a Mixed Reality Performance". In *Proceedings of the SIGCHI Conference on Human Factors in Computing Systems*. New York: ACM Press, pp. 38–45. doi:10.1145/365024.365033.

Lippman, Andrew. 1980. "*Movie-Maps: An Application of the Optical Videodisc to Computer Graphics*". Paper presented at 7th Annual Conference on Computer Graphics and Interactive Techniques, SIGGRAPH 1980, pp. 32–42. doi:10.1145/800250.807465.

Lushetich, Natasha. 2007. "Blast Theory: The Politics and Aesthetic of Interactivity". Master of Arts thesis, University of Exeter. doi:10.4324/9780429283956-9.

Mackay, Wendy E., and Glorianna Davenport. 1989. "Virtual Video Editing in Interactive Multimedia Applications". *Communications of the ACM* 32 (7): 802–810. doi:10.1145/65445.65447.

Mateas, Michael, and Andrew Stern. 2007. "Writing *Façade*: A Case Study in Procedural Authorship". In Pat Harrigan and Noah Wardrip-Fruin (eds), *Second Person: Role-Playing and Story in Games and Playable Media*. Cambridge, MA: MIT Press, pp. 183–212.

Montfort, Nick. 2003. *Twisty Little Passages: An Approach to Interactive Fiction*. Cambridge, MA: MIT Press.

Morie, Jacquelyn Ford. 2012. "Female Artists and the VR Crucible: Expanding the Aesthetic Vocabulary". In Ian E. McDowall and Margaret Dolinsky (eds), *The Engineering Reality of Virtual Reality 2012*, Society of Photo-Optical Instrumentation Engineers (SPIE), Conference Series. doi:10.1117/12.910974.

Murray, Janet H. 2001. *Hamlet on the Holodeck: The Future of Narrative in Cyberspace*. Cambridge, MA: MIT Press.

Naimark, Michael. 2006. "Aspen the Verb: Musings on Heritage and Virtuality". *Presence: Teleoperators and Virtual Environments* 15 (3): 330–335. doi:10.1162/pres.15.3.330.

O'Donoghue, Caroline. 2020. "What the Weird World of Pokémon Can Teach Us about Storytelling". *The Guardian*, 27 January. Available at: https://www.theguardian.com/games/2020/jan/27/what-pokemon-can-teach-us-about-storytelling-nintendo-games.

Pizzo, Antonio. 2011. "Attori e Personaggi Virtuali". *Acting Archives Review* 1 (1): 83–118. Available at: https://www.actingarchives.it/review/archivio-numeri.html.

Ryan, Marie-Laure. 2006. *Avatars of Story*. Minneapolis, MN: University of Minnesota Press.

Smith, Greg M. 2003. *Film Structure and the Emotion System*. Cambridge: Cambridge University Press. https://doi.org/10.1017/CBO9780511497759.

Stenger, Nicole. 1991. "Mind Is a Leaking Rainbow". In Michael Benedikt (ed.), *Cyberspace: First Steps*. Cambridge, MA: MIT Press, pp. 48–57.

Szilas, Nicolas. 2003. "*IDtension*: A Narrative Engine for Interactive Drama". In Stefan Göbel, Norbert Braun, Ulrike Spierling, Johanna Dechau, and Holger Diener (eds), *Technologies for Interactive Digital Storytelling and Entertainment. TIDSE 2003 Proceedings*. Darmstadt, Germany: Fraunhofer IRB Verlag, pp. 187–203.

Thome, Diane. 1995. "Reflections on Collaborative Process and Compositional Revolution". *Leonardo Music Journal* 5: 29–32. doi:10.2307/1513158.

Vannini, Natalie, Sibylle Enz, Maria Sapouna, Dieter Wolke, Scott Watson, Sarah Woods, Kerstin Dautenhahn, *et al.* 2011. "'*FearNot!*': A Computer-Based Anti-Bullying-Programme Designed to Foster Peer Intervention". *European Journal of Psychology of Education* 26 (1): 21–44. doi:10.1007/s10212-010-0035-4.

Weizenbaum, Joseph. 1966. "ELIZA: A Computer Program for the Study of Natural Language Communication Between Man and Machine". *Communications of the ACM* 9 (1): 36–45. doi:10.5100/jje.2.3_1.

Wolf, Mark J. P. 2011. *Myst and Riven: The World of the D'ni*. Ann Arbor, MI: digitalculturebooks. doi:10.3998/lvg.9835611.0001.001.

Wolf, Mark J. P. 2012. *Encyclopedia of Video Games: The Culture, Technology, and Art of Gaming*. Santa Barbara, CA: Greenwood Press.

Index

Aarseth, Espen 59
Abbott, H. Porter 108
ABL ("A Behaviour Language") 102
Accidental Lovers 20
action library **16**, 48, 49, 57
acts x, 31, 85, *101*
Adventure (game) 2, 25, 33, 64, 102, 133, 134
Afternoon, a Story 26, 27, 28, 60, 102, 137, 138
agency 30, 40, 6, 62, 80, 147, 156, 165, 170; local agency 61, 67; global agency 61, 63, 73
agent model 46, 53, 72, 156
algorithm xiv, xv, 13, *14*, 16, 18, 35, 76, 98, 112, 115, 160; sorting algorithm 36; algorithm metadata 76; algorithmic execution 82, 83; generation algorithm 92; algorithm plot 94 genetic algorithm 107; initialisation algorithm 109; storytelling algorithm 113; simulation algorithm 118; Eliza's algorithm 130, 131
Angels 33, 140, 141,142,
Anna Karenina, 27
Antúnez Roca, Marcel·lí 65
appraisal 52, 53, 54, 115, 157
appraisal rules 53
Aristotle 17, 26, 50
artificial agent 2, 7, 18, 43, 50, 53, 69, 73, 130, 131, 154, 155, 156
Aspen Movie Map 135, 136
Assassin's Creed: Odyssey 62
Asteroids xii
Augmented Reality (AR) 5, 86, 146
autonomous agent 6, 43, 72, 155
avatars 7, 77, 119, 149, 151, 153, 171

bad ending 28, 168
Bad News 117, 118, 119

Bainbridge, Jason 47
Balzola, Andrea 4
Bandersnatch (*Black Mirror*) 6,20, 25, 84, 165, 166
Barros, Leandro Motta 106
Bates, Joseph 47
beat 102, 103, 104, 105, 106, 124, 154
Belief Desire Intention (BDI) 45, 46, 47, 50, 52, 53, 54, 65, 157, 158
Belisle, Brooke 170
Benford, Steve 152
Bolter, Jay David 170
Borges, Jorge Luis 138
Boston: Renewed Vistas 19
bounded rationality 45, 49
Bradbury, Ray 1
Bratman, Michael 45, 46, 49
Braun, Norbert 91
Brave New World 1, 23
Brutus 94
Buckingham, David 147

Campbell, Joseph 26, 91
Can You See Me Now? 70, 151
Carnegie Mellon University 6, 47, 154
Carroll, Lewis 170, 171
Carroll, Noël 45
Cavazza, Marc 51, 95
character-centred **17,** 50, 81
chronicle 10
činčera, Radúz 1
City in Transition: New Orleans, 1983–86 139
climax 26, 69, 100, 103, 104, *105*, 106, 120, 150, 155
Clore, Gerald L. 53
closure/s 11, 28, 30, 38, 45, 59, 61, 119, 137, 166, 168
Cohen, Philip R. 46

Colby, Benjamin N. 91, 92
Collins, Allan 53
complication 9, 18, 26, 69, 88, 89, 121
compufiction xii, 2
computation xii, 3, 13, 18, 53, 60, 63, 70, 91, 151, 153, 155
computational (see computation)
conflict 6, 38, 50, 51, 95, 102, 106, 108, 109, 112, 124, 125, 147, 153, 167
constraint/s 15,19, 34, 35, 51, 60, 82, 84, 86, , 91, 95, 98, 109,110, 113, 116, 171; cause-and-effect constraints 138; constraint-based approach 148; event constraints 100; general constraints, 115; knowledge constraints, 115; plot constraints 94, 108, 102; precondition/ effects constraints 123, 122; set of constraints 17 22, 88, 92, 93 94, 108; story world constraints 99, 114; tighter/ wider constraints 106
Corneille 17
Crawford, Chris 4, 63
crisis 26, 103, 104, 154, 156

D-Dag 20
database narrative 19, 20, 139
Davenport, Glorianna 19, 139
Dennet, Daniel C. 45
Desert Rain 68, 148
Dickens, Charles 64
Digital Storytelling 2, 3, 47
DoPPioGioco 35 , 74
Down the Rabbit Hole 25, 168, 171
Dragon's Lair 62
drama manager 91, 102, 104, 106, 150, 154, 155, 156, 157
Drama xii, 8, 10, 22, 25, 39, 50, 68, 95, 105
dramatic arc 100
dramatic character 6
dramatic conflict 100, 101, 116
dramatic goal 13
dramatic media 6, 100
dramatic narration 119
dramatic tension xv, 6, 9, 59, 63, 100, 105, 106, 124, 150, 153, 164, 165; creation of dramatic tension 9, 101, 120; dramatic tension and conflict 102
dramatic writing 6, 8
dramatis persona 87, 88
DramaTour 25, 36, 92, 102, 159, 160
Dramatron 116
Dumas, Jean E. 163
Dwarf Fortress 116, 117

edge 14, 35, 40
effects (as precondition and effetcs) 43, 49, 57, 69, **97**, 98, 104, 123, 124, 137, 164; effect of the actions 115, 120, 55; effect of the events 107, 114; effects of the unit 27, 28, 43, 44, 56, 122, 125
Egri, Lajos 68
Electronic Arts (EA) 16
Eliza 2, 130, 131, 132
emergent narrative 81, 108, 117, 119,
Emotion Model (EM) 73
emotional appraisal 53, 72
emotional coping 53, 73, 157
emotions: model of emotions 35, 52, 71, 73, 74, 75, 100, 101, 120, 124; mental state xv, 52, 71, 165; moral emotions 53; emotional frame 54; audience's emotions 1, 5, 23, 42, 60, 70, 71, 72, 73, 119, 131, 150, 155; character's emotions 10, 16, 72, 86,100, 102, 104; artificial agent's emotions 17, 28, 51, 52, 117, 157, 158
Esslin, Martin 6
exploration 118, 139, 143, 145, 148, 170, 171; exploration as narrative structure 33, 102, 136; exploration of environment 119, 120, 134, 142, exploratory 28, 119, *exploratory narration* 119
Extended Reality (XR) 5,

Fabulator 106
Fahrenheit 451 1
FaTiMa 54, 157
Feagin, Susan L. 45
FearNot! 54, 72, 73, 156, 157, 158, 159
Field, Syd 26
Finnegans Wake 138
Flaubert, Gustave 16
folk psychology 45, 52
Forster, E.M. 10
fractal pattern 26
Freytag, Gustav 26, 100
Friends 51, 100

Galyean, Tinsley Azariah 15
Gameforge 107
GEMEP 75
generative model 14, 15, 75
generative system 13, 164
Gervás, Pablo 87
GESTER 94
Giovannelli, Alessandro 72
goal state 54, 55, 57
Gordon, Andrew S. 112

GPT-3 115
Grasbon, Dieter 91

Habonneau, Nicolas 163
hierarchy 14, 37, 89, 90, 91, 94, 108, 148
Hirshbiegel, Oliver 20
Holland, Norman N. xii, 6
Horace 25
Huxley, Aldous 1
hypertext 19, 30, 37, 83, 84, 137, 138; hypertext Fiction 26; hypertext graph 35, 164; hypertext model 28, 75; hypertext narrative 39, 123

IDtension 106
improvisation 13, 32, 109, 117, 155, 163
inciting incident 26
initial state 39, 48, 54, 55, 56, 83, 84, 85, 107, 108, 109
intelligent agent xv, 44, 45, 50, 52, 100
intentional stance 45
intentions 8, 17, 32, 45, 51, 69, 82, 155, 164
interactive drama 2, 106, 155, 156, 163, 164,
interactive fiction xii, xiii, 2, 6, 20, 27, 84, 91, 116, 119, 168
Internet 3, 16, 20, 67, 112, 144, 152, 159, 168

James, Henry 64
Jenkins, Henry 146
Jordan, Tim 147
Joyce, James 138

K-film 38
Kinoautomat 1
Korsakow 19, 38
Krag-Jacobsen, 20
Kulešov (effect) 34

Lakoff, George P. 89, 91, 121
Large Language Model (LLM) 115
Laurel, Brenda 6
Lebowitz, Michael 113
Levesque, Hector J. 46
Levring 20
Lexia 26, 137, 138
Louchart, Sandy 60
Loyal, Bryan Aaron 47
Lubart, Todd 85, 112

Mad Dog McCree 62
Madame Bovary 16, 50
Manovich, Lev 19

Mateas, Michael 6, 60, 154
McKee, Robert 26, 72
Metadata 33, 34, 36, 37, 38, 76
Mexica 114
Mimesis 110
Minecraft 116
mood cue model 171
moral emotions 53
moral values 40, 53, 106
Mörderische Entscheidung (Murderous Decision) 20
multilinear 11, *12*, **16**, 28, 30, 35, 121, 166
Murray, Janet H. 15, 59, 61, 114
Myst 25, 28 33, 102, 120, 143, 144

Niesz, Anthony J. xii,
nodes 14, 15, 35, 39, 68, 69, 84, 89, 134, 143, 164
Non-Player Character (NPC) 117
Nothing for Dinner 163, 164

O'Donoghue, Caroline 147
One Man and His House 1
Ortony, Andrew 53
OZ group 6, 47, 154

Pac-Man xii
Pajares Tosca, Susana
Pérez Y Pérez, Rafael
Pixar 16
planning 15, 17, 31, 56, 62, 98, 100, 102, 108, 139, 155, 157; automated planning 46; hierarchical planning 47; Hierarchical Task Network (HTN) 47, 49; Partial Order Planning (POP) 47, 48, 55, 98; planner 47, 48, 51, 54, 56, 72, 94, 106, 110; planning formalism 91; planning-based plot 95, 96, 109; STRIPS 94
plot generation 51, 80, 81, 87, 92, 95, 97, 98, 100, 102, 110, 112, 113
plot-centred **17**
plot grammar 87
Poetics 17
Pokémon 76, 145, 146, 147, 148
Porteous, Julie 51
preconditions 27, 28, 56,57, 69, 92, 94, 95, 98, 102, 111,122: precondition examples 43, 49, 55, 56, **97**, 104, 123, 124; precondition of actions 54, 55
premise 38,46, 68,158
procedural author xiv,15, 16, 45, 47, 48, 57
Procedural Reasoning System (PRS) 47
Propp, Vladimir 87, 89, 91, 92, 108, 121, 122

Racine 17
Radiant A.I. 107
Radiant Story 107
reaction rules 54, 73
remediation 170
retelling 117
Reynolds, Jeremy R. 32
Roquet, Paul 170
Rosa, Paolo 4
Ryan, James 117
Ryan, Marie-Laure 107

Saarinen, Leena 20
Scheherazade 112
Sefton-Green, Julian 147
segmentation x, 26, 27; segmentation into units, xv 13, 25, 26, 39 69; segmentation of event 32, 33
Smith, Greg. M. 71, 171
Smith, Jonas Heide
Soft Cinema 19
Speer, Nicole K. 32
Spindle 116
states of the world 43, 45, 48, 52, 53, 54, 55, 72, 98
Stenger, Nicole 140, 141, 142
Stern, Andrew 154
Story Director 109
Storygraphia 40, 55, 56, 57, 77, 85, 122, 124, 125, 128
Storyspace 84, 137
Storytron 86
STRIPS 94
Super Mario 7
suspense 31, 91, 98
Swanson, Reid 112
Szilas, Nicolas xiii, xiv, 106, 163, 164

tagging xv, 35 74 140 159 160; examples of tagging *29, 36,* 38; tagging system 76, 122; tagging vocabulary 69; units' tagging 33, 74, 159, tag 35, 36, 55, 121.
TALE-SPIN 110
Talk of the Town 118
template-based model 92
Thalhofer, Florian 19
The Elder Scrolls IV: Oblivion 107
The Elder Scrolls V: Skyrim 107
The Garden of Forking Paths 138
The Invisible Guardian 28, 30, 33, 167, 168
The Walking Dead 6, 62, 161,
Thome, Diane 141
Tokyo Chronos 9
Tolstoy 17
Tuomola, Mika 20
Twine 84

Unity 86
UNIVERSE 100

Vinterberg 20
virtual environment xiii, 135, 149
Virtual Reality (VR) 5, 70, 140, 141, 142, 150, 170, 171
Virtual Storyteller 109
Virtual Storytelling 3
Vogler, Christopher 26
von Trier 20

Wanderer 9
Wechsler, Robert 66
Weizenbaum, Joseph 2, 130, 131
WordsEye 107

Zacks, Jeffrey M. 32